Managing Knowledge

Building Blocks for Success

Gilbert Probst, Steffen Raub and Kai Romhardt

JOHN WILEY & SONS, LTD
Chichester · New York · Weinheim · Brisbane · Singapore · Toronto

All rights excluding German and French editions
Copyright © 2000 by John Wiley & Sons Ltd,
Baffins Lane, Chichester,
West Sussex PO19 1UD, England
National 01243 779777
International (+44) 1243 779777
e-mail (for orders and customer service enquiries):
cs-books@wiley.co.uk
Visit our Home Page on http://www.wiley.co.uk
or http://www.wiley.com

English edition adapted from the German original *Wissen Managen*.
© Frankfurter Allgemeine Zeitung GmbH, Frankfurt am Main 1998
© Betriebswirtschaftlicher Verlag Dr. Th. Gabler GmbH, Wiesbaden 1998

Other Wiley Editorial Offices

John Wiley & Sons, Inc., 605 Third Avenue,
New York, NY 10158-0012, USA

WILEY-VCH GmbH, Pappelallee 3,
D-69469 Weinheim, Germany

Jacaranda Wiley Ltd, 33 Park Road, Milton,
Queensland 4064, Australia

John Wiley & Sons (Asia) Pte Ltd, 2 Clementi Loop #02-01,
Jin Xing Distripark, Singapore 129809

John Wiley & Sons (Canada) Ltd, 22 Worcester Road,
Rexdale, Ontario M9W 1L1, Canada

Library of Congress Cataloging-in-Publication Data

Probst, Gilbert.
    [Wissen managen.   English]
    Managing knowledge : building blocks for success / Gilbert Probst, Steffen Raub, and
Kai Romhardt.
      p.   cm.
    ''English edition adapted from the German original, Wissen managen''—T.p. verso.
    Includes bibliographical references and index.
    ISBN 0-471-99768-4 (hardback : alk. paper)
    1. Knowledge management.   I. Raub, Steffen.   II. Romhardt, Kai.   III. Title.
    HD30.2.P75613   1999
    658.4'038–dc21   99-37215
                                                                            CIP

British Library Cataloguing in Publication Data

A catalogue record for this book is available from the British Library

ISBN 0-471-99768-4

Typeset in Times by Wyvern 21 Ltd, Bristol
Printed and bound in Great Britain by Biddles Ltd, Guildford and King's Lynn
This book is printed on acid-free paper responsibly manufactured from sustainable forestry, in
which at least two trees are planted for each one used for paper production.

Contents

Preface

The words 'knowledge management' are on everyone's lips; but what is their practical significance? What useful advice can we give to managers and knowledge workers who are confronted every day by the latest developments in the knowledge society? This book summarizes our many years of experience as researchers and consultants in the field of knowledge management. We have founded a think-tank for exchanging best practices and managing knowledge-based projects. Its members include DAIMLERCHRYSLER, DEUTSCHE BANK, HOLDERBANK, HP, INSEL, MOTOROLA, NOVARTIS, ROCHE DIAGNOSTICS, SIEMENS, SWISSCOM, UBS, WINTERTHUR INSURANCES and XEROX.

Two features distinguish this book from other publications on knowledge management; they are its user-friendly structure and its clear practical orientation. We introduce a wide range of knowledge management techniques and assess their possible effects. Our own understanding of the issues derives from a series of consulting and research projects that have brought us into close contact in recent years with many different aspects of knowledge management.

Our aim is not to string together pieces of anecdotal evidence about knowledge, but rather to create a practical language for talking about knowledge management. This language will help managers to distinguish the most important issues in the knowledge society, and to talk about them in terms that others will understand. Unfortunately, there has been little attempt in the past to clarify terminology in the fields of knowledge management and organizational learning. The subject area is a broad one, and discussions easily become mired in terminological confusion. Many hours may be lost in discussing nuances of meaning. Worse still, different people may leave the discussion with different interpretations of the terms used, and begin to organize activities accordingly. In companies where knowledge management is taken seriously, every effort should be made to achieve the clearest possible use of basic terms. Plain definitions of different kinds of knowledge (implicit/explicit, individual/collective, etc.), and a clear distinction between knowledge and information are essential preconditions for fruitful discussions. This book offers a set of terms that have proved their value.

If you are not clear at the outset about the goals of your knowledge management activities, you will start with an unfocused programme and run the risk of failure. Your energies will be dissipated in broad agendas that are not directed towards solving your problems. We have often encountered knowledge management 'missionaries' who were good at philosophizing about the learning organization, but not, unfortunately, at translating their visions into concrete activities producing measurable benefits.

We also see evidence of a further trend that may cause difficulties. The revolution in information technology and the triumph of the Internet have caused many decision-makers to forget the need to allow for the human factor when structuring data and information systems. If basic rules of psychology are disregarded, attempts at knowledge management will fail. Much of the material that is sold today under the title 'knowledge management' relates only to the informational base of the organization. *Knowledge*, however, is the whole body of learning and skills that *individuals* (not machines) use for solving problems. Knowledge is always tied to people, and is therefore not reproducible in information systems. Companies that content themselves with adjusting the structure of their intranets and data banks do not deal adequately with most of the knowledge problems that arise in organizations.

Just as dangerous is a premature fixation on particular techniques. We have observed organizations that have built their entire knowledge management strategy around a single technique, or have employed a consultant to introduce a particular 'knowledge instrument'. Stop and think: there are hundreds of techniques for managing knowledge; and any management technique can be extended to include knowledge aspects. Concentrating on a single dimension can close the door to a wide variety of potential solutions. In this book, we hope to give you some insight into the range of possibilities, and encourage you to make your own choice. There are no standard solutions for dealing with knowledge. One company may find it expedient to make its knowledge base accessible to competitors, while another may need to keep its competencies secret. In some companies, the sharing of knowledge needs to be increased; in others, employees spend so much time sharing and distributing their knowledge that they have no time left for work. Beware of consultants who promise solutions without making a careful analysis of the company's problems. Such promises are not credible.

Explore the potential and the limits of individual techniques for managing knowledge. Every technique has its own characteristics, and therefore its own limitations. Choosing a suitable instrument for changing the knowledge base of a company requires an understanding of knowledge problems, and of the spectrum of effects of the various available techniques. This book will point you in new directions.

Knowledge management can also be understood from a personal viewpoint. The easiest way to approach the subject is to make yourself aware of how you deal with your own knowledge. Ask yourself the following questions: What knowledge do I possess? What skills do I have? Why do I not pass them on to others? What would have to happen for me to change my behaviour? How can I change my own portfolio of competencies? These questions show us that we are not talking about an inanimate resource, but about a part of ourselves – a part that allows us to do certain things. It is a precious possession that determines what level of esteem we enjoy in social groups. We do not surrender it gladly, or allow others to manage it for us.

Giving others access to our knowledge requires trust. Trust is a fertile ground for many knowledge-related processes, for example making knowledge transparent; sharing and distributing knowledge; utilizing knowledge. An employee who fears for his job is not likely to share his expertise; he is more likely to try to make himself indispensable. In the absence of trust, all talk of an open knowledge culture is hollow. Employees will consign it to the limbo of passing trends. Consider how serious you are about knowledge management, and whether you can be a credible advocate of it.

So much for the content of the book. Now to its structure, which makes it easy to use in practical contexts. You can, of course, simply read it from start to finish, and work through all the material – if you have the time and the interest. However, it is more likely that you will consult it because you need to find out about particular issues. In the latter case, it is helpful to decide on the basic questions and then refer to the relevant chapters (or, in our terminology, the appropriate 'building blocks'). The modular structure of the book makes it easy to locate the topics that interest you. A selective approach has suited most of the companies with which we have worked on knowledge management in recent years, because they all have different problems. One company may be trying to avoid losing its employees; another may be wondering why they do not use the intranet that cost so much to install.

Each chapter focuses on a single building block of knowledge management, but without neglecting its links with others. You can use the book in the same way. Once you have a general idea of the subject and the main issues, you can select the specific topics that affect you directly. Each chapter poses basic questions, provides a wealth of examples from industry, and offers a framework for solving the problems.

All the chapters contain accounts of our experiences; they also treat conceptual issues and existing techniques. Research in a practical setting cannot help but generate valuable knowledge. We have been working for many years with a group of major companies; we develop new approaches in collaboration with them, in projects and workshops set within the framework of our 'building block' concept. At the end of each chapter, we have provided a short summary and some useful rules. Add to them from your own experience, and share the knowledge with us.

The chapters can be read individually and in any order. However, it is worth remembering that people need a framework to help them find their bearings, position their activities within the larger picture, and judge interactions and dependencies among different elements.

An earlier version of this book, published in German, became the best selling work in Knowledge Management in the German-speaking world and is a benchmark in its field.

We are grateful to our translator, Anne Thomas, for her excellent adaption of this book into English. She has shown an enormous amount of patience and we look forward to working with her again.

1
Managing Knowledge: The Challenge

INTRODUCTION

To survive and compete in the 'knowledge society', companies must learn to manage their intellectual assets. There is probably little that is new to be said about the management of classical production factors; the management of knowledge, on the other hand, is in its infancy.

Knowledge is the only resource that increases with use. This chapter will show you why companies increasingly accept the challenge of knowledge management, and what rewards they can expect for doing so. Professional knowledge managers face enormous demands because of the explosive growth in knowledge, its short lifespan, and the increasingly knowledge-intensive nature of all management processes. You should act promptly: if you wait until your competitors' efforts at knowledge management start to show results, it may be too late for you to catch up.

MANAGING KNOWLEDGE: THE CHALLENGE

A hot topic

Knowledge as a competitive factor has hit the business headlines with a bang. Companies are urged to make more use of the 'hidden treasure' in the minds of their employees. Innovative firms set up work groups on knowledge management, while chairmen emphasize the special part which knowledge will play in shaping the future of their companies. Professional organizers advertise workshops and conferences on knowledge management, and business consultants offer their services. Does all this mean that companies are condemned to fail unless they take deliberate steps to manage their knowledge?

Success of knowledge-intensive companies

Many knowledge-intensive companies have achieved spectacular success in recent years – success which is reflected in their stock market performance. SAP, the software producer, now outstrips VOLKSWAGEN in stock market capitalization. The Internet company NETSCAPE has overtaken APPLE, and MICROSOFT – the ultimate 'thinking factory' – puts industrial giants like BOEING and KODAK in the shade. The size of a company's industrial premises and administrative buildings is no longer a reliable measure of its importance or industrial capability.

MANAGERS DISCOVER KNOWLEDGE

Moving towards the 'knowledge society'

The long-predicted 'information society' and 'knowledge economy' are now emerging as tangible realities. Leading management theoreticians argue that it is much more profitable for a company to invest a given sum in its knowledge assets than to spend the same amount on material assets. James Brian Quinn, the well-known American professor of management, states that in many companies, three-quarters of added value is attributable to the possession of specific knowledge (cf. Quinn 1992, 1993 and *The Economist* (11.11.95);* Charles Handy, a leading management theorist, believes that we are already at a stage where the value of a company's intellectual capital is often several times that of its material assets (cf. Handy 1990).

Trends in industry

The revolution in communications technology has brought economic changes which enhance the importance of knowledge. In modern industrial nations, knowledge-intensive industries are responsible for a steadily increasing proportion of the national net product. This trend naturally affects the financial success of individual companies, prompting more of them to recognize the fundamental importance of knowledge as a resource. In the number-conscious management world, few will be surprised to learn that the initial impetus came from a stock-taking exercise.

Taking stock of knowledge

Balance sheets are a familiar tool in accounting and financial management. Most executives would react with bewilderment, however, if they were asked to produce the figures for their company's intellectual assets. One of the first companies to take stock of its knowledge was the Swedish SKANDIA ASSURANCE AND FINANCIAL SERVICES (AFS). In 1993, the company published the first accounts of its intellectual assets, as a supplement to the traditional business results. This was a novel departure (see Figure 1.1).

Indices of knowledge

The main reason why SKANDIA AFS publishes accounts of its intellectual capital is to provide a more systematic breakdown of non-material

---

* See also Sveiby 1997; Davenport & Prusak 1998; Edvinsson & Malone 1997; Stewart 1997).

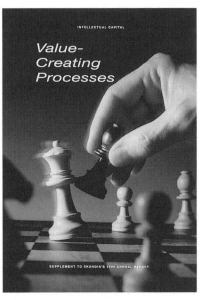

Figure 1.1 SKANDIA's yearly report on intellectual capital

assets previously known collectively as 'goodwill'. An ingenious system of indices is used to enter the knowledge and skills of highly trained employees, together with other factors such as customer relations, the company's market reputation, and its information technology. A diagram known as the 'navigator' is then constructed to show the relationships between the company's strategic trends and the variables chosen to define its intellectual capital.[1]

Absence of management tools

SKANDIA's revolutionary attempt to make its intellectual capital more transparent highlights a management problem which has become increasingly apparent in recent years. Techniques and tools for managing the classical production factors (labour, capital and land) have been progressively refined; but virtually no progress has been made in creating professional tools for managing knowledge assets. As a result, organizations often make too little use of their intellectual resources. They may not use their patents sufficiently; they may not exploit and develop specific employee skills; or they may fail to derive competitive advantage from particular strengths, such as mastery of highly developed technologies.

The first knowledge managers

The widespread inability of management to deal with knowledge as a resource has prompted a range of recent initiatives. New positions have been created, often with imaginative titles: many companies now have a director of intellectual capital, or a director of knowledge, or a knowledge or intellectual assets manager. The people who hold these positions have markedly different functions, even though they are all officially concerned with intellectual assets. Some work on strategic analyses of competencies, while others develop ways of indexing knowledge, or create better communications infrastructures, or look for more efficient ways of managing patent portfolios. The common factor in their work is that all of them are responding to the challenge of an increasingly competitive environment in which improved management of intellectual assets can bring critical advantages.

Managers need to consider how the growing importance of knowledge might affect their own company's competitive position. They must therefore understand the basic dynamics of our knowledge-oriented society.

THE KNOWLEDGE ENVIRONMENT: TRANSPARENT – OR TURBULENT?

Environmental trends

The knowledge environment in which companies must function today is structurally much more complex than that which existed several centuries ago. This is largely due to three closely related trends: the explosive rate at which knowledge grows, the extent to which it has become fragmented, and its increasing globalization.

From a quantitative point of view, human knowledge has grown exponentially. Following Gutenberg's invention of the printing press, it took more than 300 years for the worldwide volume of information to double for the first time. Since then, it has doubled virtually every five years. Between 1950 and 1975, for example, as many books were produced as in the 500 years following the invention of the printing press (cf. Badaracco 1991, p. 17 and Arthur Anderson 1996, p. 7). In the last 30 years, the proportion of research and development workers in the total workforce of Western industrial companies has doubled. The use of applied technologies shows a similar and related growth curve.

Specialization

The increase in the overall volume of knowledge has led to specialization within scientific disciplines. A century ago, an all-round scholar could acquire a general understanding of the state of research in almost every area of science; today, even within one subject, people of different specialities may have trouble understanding each other. The first two editions of the *Encyclopaedia Britannica* were produced by just two scientists; today, it takes tens of thousands of experts to work on each new edition (cf. Badaracco 1991, pp. 17ff.) (see Figure 1.2).

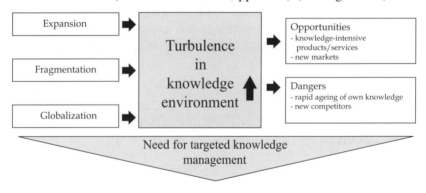

Figure 1.2 Trends in the knowledge society

Globalization

The continuing trend towards a global economy has led to globalization of knowledge. The success stories of CNN and MICROSOFT illustrate the move towards a 'global village', in which differences in time and place lose their significance. All these changes mean that it is now impossible to know about all existing products, product variants, production technologies, or patterns of competitive advantage among countries, even at a general level. At the beginning of the 1970s, the USA still produced more than 70% of the world's new technologies; now, centres of scientific and technical excellence are spread around the world (see Badaracco 1991, p. 28). The area around Bangalore, India, is now a world centre of software production; this is a prime illustration of the fact that the globalization of knowledge is little affected by boundaries between developed and less developed countries (cf. *The Economist* 23.3.96).

MORE KNOWLEDGE: THREAT OR OPPORTUNITY?

'Intelligent' products

Many companies perceive the increasing complexity of the knowledge environment as a threat; yet there are many ways in which dynamic developments in knowledge can bring new opportunities to compete. Innovative companies are finding that they can increase the value of products which have relatively simple basic functions by making them more knowledge-intensive. This may mean enabling a product to adapt itself to changing conditions, or to collect and store information and apply it for the benefit of the user.[2] In a country like Switzerland, which has several languages, a credit card may automatically 'choose' the mother tongue of the user when inserted into a cash dispenser or petrol pump. The credit card supplier has taken information about the customer and integrated it into the product, thus creating an 'intelligent' application.

Sensitivity to environmental conditions

Other relatively simple examples of intelligent products are textiles which change their characteristics according to the prevailing temperature and humidity, or window glass which reflects or absorbs sunlight according to the weather, thus keeping room temperature constant. In these cases, the 'intelligence' of the product is based not on stored information, but on built-in sensitivity to the environmental conditions. Many companies are trying to develop more sophisticated applications: GOODYEAR, for example, is working on an 'intelligent tyre', which registers sinking air pressure via a computer chip and triggers a warning signal.

Functions of knowledge in service provision

There are many ways in which the value of a service can be increased by adding a knowledge component. CITIBANK has a system which recognizes atypical spending patterns in the use of credit cards, thus alerting customers to the possibility of loss or misuse. Many hotel chains and travel companies have also recognized the value of intelligent customer data banks. They record individual preferences, so that in future, the client will automatically be given a first-class non-smoking window-seat on the plane, or the refrigerator in his five-star hotel room will be stocked with his favourite champagne.

Strategic relevance of knowledge

If a company with a well-developed knowledge base operates in a knowledge-intensive environment, it is probable that its specific competencies will develop a dynamic of their own, thus creating new strategic opportunities. MASSEY-FERGUSON, the American tractor manufacturer, developed a satellite-supported system to help optimize harvests. The harvesting machine is equipped with a satellite positioning system which records the yield of each square metre. Farmers can then target their yield-increasing measures more precisely, thus reducing costs. This device was originally regarded as an incidental component of the tractor, but its spectacular success prompted MASSEY-FERGUSON to continue to develop instruments for yield management (compare this example with Davis & Botkin 1994).

Transfer of competencies

Companies in other industries have also developed new areas of business on the basis of existing competencies. Airlines, for example, have highly productive booking systems; the more innovative companies – most notably AMERICAN AIRLINES – have been able to transfer this competence to the hotel trade and the entertainment industry. In some cases, the secondary business proved so profitable that it eclipsed the original airline business.

Most car manufacturers now offer individual finance packages as a way of advertising a new model. This is yet another instance of a knowledge-intensive component being added to the basic product.

CASE STUDY: KUONI (Swiss travel agency)

Knowledge-intensive services in the business travel sector: cost analysis using 'Knows'

'KUONI makes your holiday better.' In the past, this slogan reflected the company's main activity, and determined its image. The picture has now changed.

In the 1990s, providers of business travel services specialized rapidly, and the technology that they use became more complex. Many business trips are international, and there are many ways of making bookings and arrangements. This has increased the pressure on those employees who are responsible for arranging a company's business travel; they often feel overwhelmed at the prospect of organizing it all themselves.

When companies seek support from travel agencies, they expect high levels of organizational ability and technical competence. In addition, transparency of costs may be a critical factor, because of the growth in company expenditure on business trips: after salaries and IT, travel is often the third major expense category.

In view of the vigorous growth of the business travel sector, KUONI decided to transform itself from a simple travel agency into a 'Business Travel Information Management Company'. It planned to offer its customers the kinds of information they need in order to improve their management of business travel. The provision of a knowledge-enriched service was a strategic success.

KUONI now consistently publicizes the knowledge-intensive components in its business travel service. In its efforts to become the 'trustee of the travel budget', it offers customers a comprehensive range of services, including special offers and special trips to trade fairs, as well as ordinary business trips. KUONI's computerized customer files contain all data relevant to business travel in the companies it serves. For each employee, it can store class of travel, car rental category, and personal preferences regarding seating or food.

At the heart of KUONI's knowledge-oriented approach to customer support lies a recently developed software system for analysing the costs of journeys. This unique system – called 'Knows', which stands for Kuoni Nationally Offered Worldwide Statistics – enables the company to assemble and process all data on the travel which a customer has previously arranged through KUONI. The data package can be evaluated and presented according to customer requirements, and affords maximum transparency of travel costs. Spending on flights, hotels and car rental can be broken down according to destination, class of travel, provider and period. Since the second annual report, comparison figures for the previous year have also been given. Management information flows direct to the customer from all important business destinations through the network of KUONI associates in the Business Travel International (BTI) Association.

The information is presented in a convenient format which makes it easy to answer questions like which airline has attracted the greatest share of bookings, or which destination is the most expensive. 'Knows' helps the customer to monitor business travel more efficiently, and also to locate opportunities for bulk bookings which carry discounts. This additional service helps KUONI to retain all of a customer's business in the long term (see Figure 1.3).

Knowledge management

KUONI's success with Knows shows how knowledge-based products can open new market opportunities and strengthen a company's long-term competitive position. However, these products also present fresh challenges. KUONI only succeeded with Knows because it created the right conditions by organizing systematic management of its knowl-

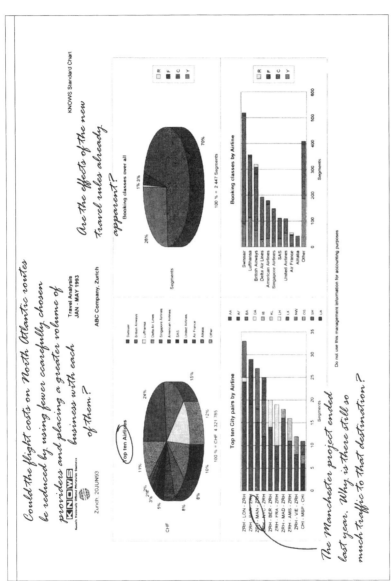

Figure 1.3 Meaningful customer information provided by Knows

edge assets. Any company which accepts the challenge of knowledge management must first create a clear picture of what it knows and what it does not know. It will then be in a position to develop strategies based on its competencies.

SUMMARY

- Most companies now operate in an increasingly dynamic knowledge environment. Products and processes are more knowledge-intensive. Forward-looking managers will take appropriate action.
- A company's intellectual assets can be analysed, balanced and managed, but we need other approaches and instruments than managing the traditional production factors.
- The present study of knowledge management includes an overview of the necessary concepts and methods.

KEY QUESTIONS

- As a manager, you know your products, markets and competitors. But how much do you know about the knowledge which is critical to your company's success, and which determines the dynamics of your competitive environment?
- Is the current competitive position of your company more affected by its intellectual capital, or by its other resources?
- Which companies in your industry think ahead, and which simply think things over? To which group does your company belong?
- Where do the 'boundaries of knowledge' in your industry currently lie? Where are new technologies being developed, and where do innovative management ideas come from? Which industries are developing knowledge that could pose a threat to you? Conversely, in which other industries might you be able to apply your own knowledge?

2

The Company's Knowledge Base

INTRODUCTION

Do you know how management decisions may affect company's knowledge base – i.e. individual and collective skills – in the long term? Can you explain to a workshop supervisor what core competencies are, and how he personally contributes to them? Decision-makers may express a desire to turn the company into a learning organization, and they may declare that in future they will make better use of the ideas of their colleagues; but this is not enough. We need a clearer language in which to put our visions of learning on a factual basis. It is easy enough to explain the difference between expenses and costs, or cash flow and profit; but we are often at a loss to explain the differences between data, information and knowledge, or implicit and explicit knowledge. This chapter offers practical definitions of the main terms used in knowledge management, to help you to build and extend your personal knowledge vocabulary.

THE COMPANY'S KNOWLEDGE BASE

In response to the challenges described in the last chapter, executives are increasing their efforts to treat knowledge as a manageable resource. However, they often seem to lack even a basic understanding of the elements of company knowledge. Our aim in writing this book is to provide a systematic guide to managing knowledge as a resource. We shall therefore start by outlining the basic concepts (see Figure 2.1).

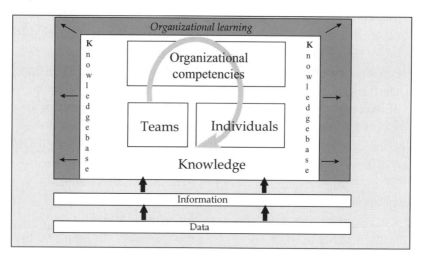

Figure 2.1 Structure of organizational knowledge base

Points of view

First we shall examine the differences between data, information and knowledge. A tendency to confuse these terms is responsible for many misunderstandings about knowledge management. We shall then consider the differences between the knowledge of individuals and that of groups. Finally, we shall introduce the concepts which are central to knowledge management.

BASIC COMPONENTS OF THE KNOWLEDGE BASE

Basic distinctions

Different people have different ideas about the nature of knowledge. In the academic world and in business practice, individuals define their own terminologies to suit a particular approach or problem.[1] Here, we shall start by drawing distinctions between symbols, data, information and knowledge (see Figure 2.2).

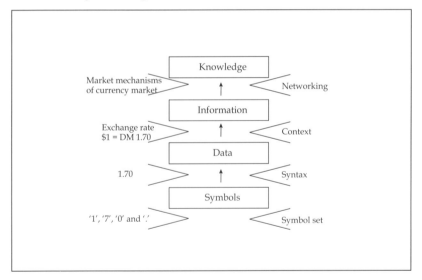

Figure 2.2 Relationships between levels in conceptual hierarchy (from Rehäuser & Kremar 1996, p. 6)

Relationships between levels

Moves between these levels are often described as an enrichment process. When rules of syntax are applied to symbols, they become data. Data are capable of interpretation within a particular context, thus providing the receiver with information.[2] When information is net-worked, it can be used in a particular field of activity, and this we may call knowledge.[3] Sometimes additional levels are described, such as wisdom, intelligence, or ability to reflect.

Practical relevance

The practical interest of dividing the knowledge base into different levels is clear if we consider the case of the travel company KUONI, described in Chapter 1. 'Knows' has a comprehensive database, which can be accessed by means of powerful hardware and software. This forms an essential part of KUONI's knowledge base; but in itself, it is far from sufficient. It can only be turned to competitive advantage by adding the skills of competent employees. KUONI's travel advisers make a vital contribution by transforming data into information and knowledge.

Interpretation and recommendations

The essential task of the travel advisers is to interpret, i.e. to organize quantities of data within the context of the customer's business travel requirements. An experienced adviser can assemble a mass of data on flight dates, destinations and prices, and prepare and present it meaningfully. The data now have an informational value. The KUONI adviser can apply his or her knowledge and experience to the informa-tion and make recommendations for the future management of the customer's travel budget.

Linking the levels

Knowledge managers can only develop an integrated approach if they can (a) distinguish between data, information and knowledge, and (b) recognize the relationships among them. Failure to do so has probably contributed to the present situation in which bodies of data, informa-tion and knowledge may be completely dissociated from each other within a company. The information technology department is often responsible only for structuring and maintaining the 'data and informa-tion side'. The staff training section is there to teach individual skills, while the research and development department is responsible for product innovation. This separation of functions results in lack of co-ordination between different areas. Even where data and information are perfectly managed, this is of little value if employees lack the skills to use the information which is made available to them, or to exploit new discoveries and allow them to influence their decisions and daily activities.

An integrated view

To ensure that the company's knowledge base is well used, and that it continues to develop, managers must take an integrated view of data, information, and the knowledge of individuals and groups. Knowledge management must be able to deal with the raw materials of knowledge as well as with knowledge itself (see Figure 2.3).

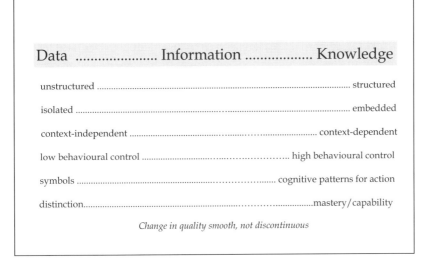

Data .... Information .... Knowledge

unstructured .... structured

isolated .... embedded

context-independent .... context-dependent

low behavioural control .... high behavioural control

symbols .... cognitive patterns for action

distinction..mastery/capability

Change in quality smooth, not discontinuous

Figure 2.3 The data/knowledge continuum

Condensing data into knowledge

Rather than drawing sharp distinctions between data, information and knowledge, it may be more helpful to place them along a continuum with data at one end and knowledge at the other. We seldom see a problem in clearly defined stages; we are more likely to approach its solution by taking a great many small steps. Scattered signs come together to form cognitive patterns on which actions can be based. Skills and knowledge are acquired slowly; they develop over time, by means of a process in which quantities of information are assembled and interpreted. This process may be conceptualized as a progression along the continuum from data, via information, to knowledge.

THE KNOWLEDGE BASE: INDIVIDUALS AND GROUPS

Individual competencies

When 'Knows' was introduced, KUONI invested heavily in training. This shows management recognition of the fact that the skills of individuals are vital to the organization's knowledge base. The ability to transform data into knowledge and to use it for the benefit of the company makes the individual employee the primary agent of company knowledge. However, the expertise of individuals is not the only kind. Many of the processes which are basic to successful organizational action depend even more on collective elements in knowledge.

Organizational competencies

Successful training can rarely be attributed entirely to the outstanding skills of an individual trainer or training organizer. A successful basketball team needs not only gifted members, but also good mutual understanding among all the players. Similarly, organizational processes which function well depend on successful interactions among many participants. The planning and implementation of a training programme may involve a wide range of employees from finance, senior management, personnel training, buildings management and line management. All these people will contribute to the outcome of the programme. If they succeed in working together productively, then the company gains an organizational competence which forms a collective element in its knowledge base.

Knowledge Workers as the Main Creators of Value

Reassessment of the labour factor

A significant proportion of a company's knowledge is stored in the minds of its employees. The greater the role of knowledge in value creation, the more important are the intellectual activities of highly skilled workers. Their work is no longer regarded merely as the 'labour factor' in production; managers are increasingly willing to recognize that employees are producers and owners of non-material assets (cf. Harrigan & Dalmia 1991).

Trends in intellectual work

For knowledge-intensive companies, careful maintenance of intellectual assets is a vital management task. This is reflected in changes in staffing figures for modern industrial countries. According to recent estimates from the USA, 60% of all employees are already knowledge workers, and four out of five jobs are in the so-called knowledge-intensive industries (see Tapscott 1996). The trend for employees to work with their heads rather than their hands continues.

Key workers

Organizational knowledge may be concentrated in individuals. An extreme case occurs where particular key workers become central and virtually irreplaceable bearers of knowledge. If they leave the company, whether by choice or not, they leave gaps which are extremely difficult to fill. This is illustrated by events which took place in the advertising agency SAATCHI & SAATCHI.

SAATCHI & SAATCHI

In December 1994, as a result of sustained pressure from the principal shareholders, Maurice Saatchi was dismissed from his post as chairman of the company. Saatchi, a controversial figure, had founded and managed the firm. His dismissal was intended to prevent a further sharp fall in the company's share prices, and it was greeted with initial enthusiasm. However, the consequences were fatal. Maurice Saatchi quickly formed a new company, continued to trade under the name of Saatchi, and recruited many of the most creative employees from the old company. Owing to this enormous loss of intellectual capital, CORDIANT, the company which succeeded SAATCHI & SAATCHI, lost customer accounts worth over £50m. in a matter of weeks. The share price collapsed by a further third in the following six months.[4]

VOLKSWAGEN VS GENERAL MOTORS

The danger of losing knowledge when key workers depart is by no means restricted to traditionally creative industries such as advertising, design or entertainment. A case in point is the dramatic move of José Ignacio López, chief of purchasing at GENERAL MOTORS, to VOLKS-WAGEN.

This move was the subject of a lengthy debate. GENERAL MOTORS initially made massive demands for damages, alleging that documents or computer files had been transferred illegally. However, this dispute was eclipsed by the fact that here too, the loss of a key employee was followed by the exodus of a whole group of highly skilled managers. Uncoded intellectual assets of incalculable value were carried off in the heads of the renegades, and were irrevocably lost for GENERAL MOTORS.

Losing knowledge through downsizing

There are many less dramatic instances of companies losing knowledge when they lose knowledge workers. Restructuring sometimes involves mass redundancies, which are made without regard for their effects on the company's knowledge base. The results can be calamitous. DAF, the Dutch manufacturer of goods vehicles, lost a considerable proportion of its essential know-how during a large-scale downsizing operation. According to estimates, up to 70% of DAF's knowledge base was damaged by the redundancies. Similar mistakes have been made by IBM and the chemical giants DOW CHEMICAL and ICI (see Lester 1996, p. 13).

Taking stock of knowledge assets

Mishaps of this kind emphasize the need for vital competencies to be carefully identified and evaluated. Very few companies currently have a clear understanding of which knowledge assets are important to their success, and how these assets are distributed over different parts of the company and among different functions and workers; yet without such an understanding, rational management of knowledge workers as a vital organizational resource is impossible.

Working conditions for knowledge workers

Companies need to retain the expertise of their knowledge workers, and help them to work efficiently. These workers will clearly require better than average working conditions (cf. Drucker 1992 and Harrigan & Dalmia 1991). Important experts can probably only be retained in the long term by companies which introduce innovative personnel management policies, providing opportunities for personal development and a meaningful career within the company. This calls for a new approach to personnel management.

Collective Competencies: More Than the Sum of the Experts

Collective knowledge

The individual abilities of knowledge workers form the basis of successful company activity. However, the success of many projects and strategies also depends on whether different knowledge workers and different components in the knowledge base can be combined efficiently. The concept of organizational learning proceeds from the fact that the ability of an organization to solve problems and to act as a whole cannot be explained solely in terms of the individual skills of its members.[5] An organization's problem-solving potential often depends largely on the collective components of its knowledge base. Collective knowledge, which is more than the sum of the knowledge of individuals, is particularly important to the long-term survival of organizations.

Competitive strength through organizational competencies

According to the Harvard professor Leonard-Barton, the exceptional success of such widely different companies as CHAPARRAL STEEL, HEWLETT PACKARD, JOHNSON & JOHNSON and 3M is due to the exceptional skill with which these companies manage collective knowledge. They are particularly efficient at combining isolated resources and individual employees into a network of organizational competencies (cf. Leonard-Barton 1995).

Group processes

Constant problem-solving by groups improves the efficiency of current activities, and combines organizational processes and the skills of individuals to form new organizational knowledge. Internal implementation and integration of this new knowledge make it less likely that the fresh solutions will become isolated 'islands of knowledge', and more likely that best practices will spread within the company. Importation of knowledge and constant experimentation in groups can keep an organization's competencies flexible and directed towards the challenges presented by competitors.

Internal accumulation of skills

Collective knowledge is a vital element in competitive strategy. Organizational competencies generally consist of many different resources and individual knowledge elements, woven together to form a whole which is sometimes difficult to define. Unlike raw materials or manufactured components, which competitors can obtain on the open market, competencies cannot be bought.[6] They are the outcome of a frequently lengthy process of internal accumulation, and are therefore especially valuable as competitive assets (cf. for example Dierickx & Cool 1989).

The time factor

Once a company has established a lead in collective knowledge, it is difficult for competitors to catch up. They cannot do so simply by increasing investment. It takes time to acquire skills: a student will probably learn less in a one-week crash course than by working at a slower pace over a longer period. This is the reason why companies cannot usually halve the time taken to develop a product by doubling the budget and the number of people working on it.

Interactions between resources

The development of organizational competencies may also depend on the existence of a certain critical mass, in this case the positive effects of certain combinations of resources. It is often easier for an 'early mover', i.e. a company which has entered the market promptly, to achieve the sales figures needed to make a product viable. Existing resources and competencies may also facilitate the development of new competencies; for example, a company which has a dense sales network may achieve shorter innovation cycles thanks to its quicker perception of customer requirements.

Indefinable competencies

It is difficult for competitors to analyse collective knowledge.[7] Who can say exactly how BMW manages to convey the impression of 'the ultimate driving machine', why flying with THAI AIRWAYS is 'smooth as silk', or why some household appliances are 'good – from experience'? The perceived excellence of these products is due in part to clever marketing, which underpins the advertising message. It is also the result of a whole series of special competencies which competitors cannot define clearly, and thus cannot easily imitate.

ESSENTIAL TERMINOLOGY

A few basic terms will recur throughout this book; we shall now define them as clearly as possible. Current terminology is chaotic; we hope to bring a little order to it, while at the same helping the reader to find his or her bearings.

Our definition of knowledge

- Knowledge is the whole body of cognitions and skills which individuals use to solve problems. It includes both theories and practical, everyday rules and instructions for action. Knowledge is based on data and information, but unlike these, it is always bound to persons. It is constructed by individuals, and represents their beliefs about causal relationships.

This definition helps us to specify more precisely the knowledge assets of an organization. We then need a definition of the organizational knowledge base.

The organizational knowledge base

- The organizational knowledge base consists of individual and collective knowledge assets that the organization can use to perform its tasks. The knowledge base also includes the data and information upon which individual and organizational knowledge are built.

The knowledge base undergoes regular changes. Collectively, these changes constitute organizational learning.

Organizational learning

- Organizational learning consists in changes in the organization's knowledge base, the creation of collective frames of reference, and growth in the organization's competence to act and to solve problems.

Managers are interested primarily in learning processes which they can control. The main difference between knowledge management and organizational learning is that the former is an active and directive process. Organizational learning is the name given to changes in the organization's knowledge base, whereas knowledge management involves deliberate intervention.

Knowledge management consists of an integrated set of interventions which take advantage of opportunities to shape the knowledge base.

Companies must develop their knowledge in a targeted fashion, and not leave it to develop haphazardly. It is useless for managers to amass knowledge aimlessly; they should aim to ensure the use and development of skills and knowledge which are relevant to the organization's objectives. Knowledge is not the same as cognition: it must show its usefulness in practical applications.

SUMMARY

- Knowledge is the whole body of cognitions and skills that individuals use in order to solve problems. Knowledge is based on data and information, but unlike them, it is always bound to persons. The management of data, information and knowledge must therefore always be co-ordinated.
- The knowledge base of an organization consists of individual and collective knowledge assets which the organization can use to perform its activities.
- The problem-solving potential of a company depends on its highly skilled 'knowledge workers' and on collective 'organizational competencies'.
- The scope and structure of the organization's knowledge base change as a result of organizational learning.

KEY QUESTIONS

- Is your company or department able to transform data into meaningful information, or are you drowning in floods of data?
- Do your company's employees have the skills they need to use the information successfully?
- What role does the knowledge which is present within your business area or function play in creating the company's 'organizational competencies'?

- Who is responsible for data management in your company? How well do they understand your field of work? How could their activities be used as a basis for the management of information and knowledge?

3
Building Blocks of Knowledge Management

INTRODUCTION

'Everything that I have read about organizational learning and knowledge management has been too abstract to be of any use. I want to know how to make a start. How can I organize my learning needs?'

If you are new to knowledge management, a proven frame of reference can save you a lot of effort. We have worked with a number of well-known companies to map out the core processes in knowledge management and the main problem areas. This has enabled us to break knowledge management down into modules, or 'building blocks'. These building blocks will help you to analyse your own situation and to structure your knowledge management activities. They will also direct your attention to neglected areas where problems can arise. This chapter contains a brief description of each building block, and thus provides an overview of the whole book. Our building blocks of knowledge management do not conflict with classic strategic planning; on the contrary, they enrich it by defining ✓ unambiguous knowledge goals and providing a clear assessment ✓ of existing knowledge.

BUILDING BLOCKS OF KNOWLEDGE MANAGEMENT

Concept development

Until recently, the question of how companies might keep up with the dynamics of their knowledge environment was of interest mainly from the viewpoint of organizational learning. However, analyses of learning infrastructures and the organizational learning climate are often too abstract to serve as a basis for practical interventions, and are frequently dismissed as intellectual gymnastics. The real need among managers is for methods of influencing the organization's intellectual assets and guiding their development. We therefore offer an integrated framework for knowledge management which will serve as a guideline for all interventions aimed at structuring knowledge resources.

THE FRAMEWORK: PRAGMATIC, SIMPLE AND USABLE

Action research approach

We believe that a pragmatic framework for knowledge management must:

- Translate the company's problems into knowledge problems, and assess the effects of decisions on the organization's intellectual assets
- Avoid generalized solutions, and help us to understand problems which are specifically about knowledge
- Direct our attention to existing problems, and help us to keep our hold on reality
- Provide an action-oriented analysis matrix and proven tools
- Develop criteria for measuring success

- Be compatible with existing systems and integrate existing approaches to finding solutions
- Be formulated in comprehensible language that can be used in everyday company activities

Knowledge management should help managers in general to treat knowledge as a resource, and should stimulate practical ideas that can be implemented. We have worked with many companies to identify the questions which they regarded as having the greatest practical importance. The content and structure of this book are the outcome of a process based on the ideas and principles of action research.[1] We shall now proceed to introduce and describe the main building blocks of knowledge management.[2]

KNOWLEDGE MANAGEMENT DEFINED THROUGH ACTION RESEARCH

Research in a practical setting

Our concept of knowledge management is based partly on theoretical considerations and partly on real problems. Working with senior managers from widely different branches of industry, we identified practical problems which had a clear knowledge dimension. We held many interviews and workshops, and made a number of detailed case studies. Our investigations took place mainly during a two-year period of intensive collaboration with companies of significant size within the framework of the Forum for Organizational Learning and Knowledge Management.[3] The results are currently being used in a wide variety of knowledge projects in companies which are members of the forum.

Identifying the Most Important Entry Points

Core processes

We started by grouping and broadly categorizing the problems we encountered in the various companies. This enabled us to identify a number of activities which we regard as the core processes of knowledge management, and which are all fairly closely related. Interventions can of course be made in single core processes, but this will inevitably affect others. Managers should therefore avoid trying to optimize knowledge activities in individual areas without considering the wider effects (see Figure 3.1).

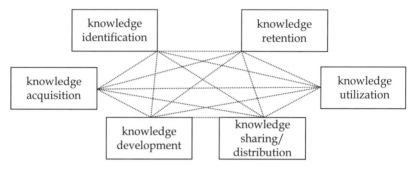

Figure 3.1   Core processes of knowledge management

Identifying knowledge: how can I achieve internal and external transparency of existing knowledge?

Knowledge identification

Identifying external knowledge means analysing and describing the company's knowledge environment. A surprisingly large number of companies now find it difficult to maintain a general picture of internal and external data, information and skills. This lack of transparency leads to inefficiency, uninformed decisions and duplication. Effective knowledge management must therefore ensure sufficient internal and external transparency, and help individual employees to locate what they need.

Acquiring knowledge: what forms of expertise should we buy from outside?

Knowledge acquisition

Companies import a substantial part of their knowledge from outside sources. Relationships with customers, suppliers, competitors and partners in co-operative ventures have considerable potential to provide knowledge – a potential that is seldom fully utilized. Firms can also buy knowledge which they could not develop for themselves by recruiting experts or acquiring other particularly innovative companies. Systematic knowledge management must take these possibilities into account.

Developing knowledge: how can we build new expertise?

 Knowledge development *why*

Knowledge development is a building block which complements knowledge acquisition. Its focus is on generating new skills, new products, better ideas and more efficient processes. Knowledge develop- ○ ment includes all management efforts consciously aimed at producing capabilities which are not yet present within the organization, or which do not yet exist either inside or outside it. Traditionally, knowledge development is anchored in the company's market research and in its research and development department; however, important knowledge can also spring from any other part of the organization. In this building block, we examine the company's general ways of dealing with new ideas and utilizing the creativity of its employees. When considered from the point of view of knowledge management, even activities which were previously regarded simply as production processes can be analysed and optimized so as to yield knowledge.

Sharing and distributing knowledge: how can we get the knowledge to the right place?

Knowledge sharing and distribution *why*

The sharing and distribution of knowledge within an organization are a vital precondition for turning isolated information or experiences into something which the whole organization can use. The key questions are:

- Who should know how much about what, or be able to do what, and to what level?
- How can we facilitate the sharing and distribution of knowledge?

It is not necessary for everybody to know everything: on the contrary, the principle of division of labour calls for a meaningful description and management of the scope of knowledge distribution. The most important step is to analyse the transition of knowledge from the individual to the group or organization. Knowledge distribution is the process of sharing and spreading knowledge which is already present within the organization.

Using knowledge: how can we ensure that knowledge is applied?

 ### Knowledge utilization

The whole point of knowledge management is to make sure that the knowledge present in an organization is applied productively for the benefit of that organization. Unfortunately, successful identification and distribution of important knowledge do not guarantee that it will be utilized in the company's everyday activities. There are a number of barriers which hinder the use of 'outside' knowledge. Steps must therefore be taken to ensure that valuable skills and knowledge assets – such as patents or licences – are fully utilized.

Retaining knowledge: how can we make sure that we do not lose it?

 ### Knowledge retention

Competencies once acquired are not automatically available for all time. The selective retention of information, documents and experience requires management. Organizations commonly complain that a reorganization has cost them part of their memory. The processes for selecting, storing and regularly updating knowledge of potential future value must therefore be carefully structured. If this is not done, valuable expertise may be simply thrown away. Knowledge retention depends on the efficient use of a wide range of organizational storage media.

Practical Building Blocks of Knowledge Management

Completing the concept

The core processes of knowledge management as we have described them yield a broad picture of the operational problems that may arise in dealing with knowledge as a resource. There may also be difficulties if a company fails to embed its handling of knowledge within an overall strategy. Operational interventions should be made within a framework that will co-ordinate them and give them direction. It is for management to create such a framework. We have therefore added two further building blocks, namely, knowledge objectives and knowledge assessment. This extends our concept of knowledge management and turns it into a management system. Knowledge goals clarify the strategic direction of knowledge management and the concrete objectives of specific interventions. The process of knowledge assessment completes the system. It provides the data essential for strategic control of knowledge management projects.

Knowledge objectives: how can we give direction to learning?

Knowledge goals

Knowledge goals give direction to knowledge management. They establish what skills are to be developed, and at what levels. Normative knowledge goals are aimed at creating a knowledge-aware company culture in which the skills of individuals are shared and developed. This sets the scene for effective knowledge management. Strategic knowledge goals define the core knowledge of the organization and specify the skills that it will need in the future. Operational knowledge goals are concerned with implementation of knowledge management; they convert normative and strategic goals into concrete objectives. This should prevent knowledge management from drying up at staff or strategy levels, and should also avert a situation in which knowledge is sacrificed to business operations.

Knowledge assessment: how can we measure the success of learning processes?

Knowledge assessment

We need methods for measuring normative, strategic and operational knowledge. The way in which knowledge goals are formulated determines the ways in which they can be assessed. The quality of the goals therefore becomes apparent at the assessment stage, if not before. Unlike finance managers, knowledge managers cannot fall back on an established set of indices and measurement procedures. They must strike new paths. Knowledge management makes demands on resources, so it must be shown to be effective. The monitoring process is essential for effective adjustment of long-term knowledge management procedures (see Figure 3.2).

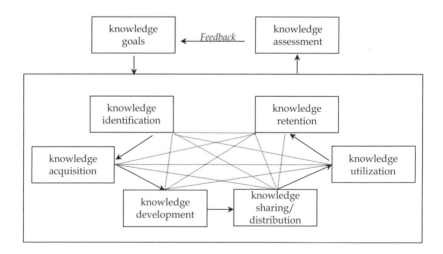

Figure 3.2   Building blocks of knowledge management

Building blocks of knowledge management

We regard these eight elements as the building blocks of knowledge management. They provide an outline of the areas where active knowledge management is possible. Figure 3.2 shows the building blocks and their logical interrelationships. The greater part of this book is devoted to a closer examination of the field covered by each block, and the tools which can be used within it. This examination begins in the next chapter (Chapter 4).

KNOWLEDGE MANAGEMENT AS AN INTEGRATION TASK

Knowledge as a structuring principle

Our suggested building blocks of knowledge management constitute an integrated approach. Most of the existing ways of classifying knowledge management activities are structured according to general management principles. Some, for example, follow McKINSEY's '7-S Model',[4] while others base themselves on general categories such as leadership, culture, technology and measurement.[5] A unique advantage of the approach developed here is that it puts knowledge in the centre, as the sole structuring principle. The building blocks of knowledge management contain activities which without exception are directly knowledge-related. Their relationships with each other do not depend on any form of external logic. We believe that this is the only kind of approach that will enable us to translate existing management problems into knowledge problems, and thus to anchor knowledge securely as a basic variable.

Levels in the organization

This integrated concept of knowledge is complemented by an integrated approach at other levels. Knowledge management includes measures which mainly affect individuals and groups, e.g. interventions in personnel management, and others which affect the organizational level, e.g. company development, strategic planning or information technology. It thus performs a bridging function among individuals, groups and organizational structures. Knowledge management also unites dissimilar functional areas under a common interventional strategy.

Strategic and operational aspects

Knowledge management is linked to strategic management in that both are aimed at protecting long-term competitive advantages by developing organizational competencies. However, the building blocks of knowledge management also define all the operational management phases which may be worked through in order to meet this objective. The overall structure of the approach, which follows the classical management system of goal-setting, implementation and monitoring, makes it compatible with different management approaches and emphasizes the search for goal-directed methods of control.

Openness to different approaches

Our concept of knowledge management is also compatible with existing projects. A knowledge management project based on our ideas can be readily integrated with existing projects, even if these follow other approaches to management or intervention. This compatibility is mainly due to the fact that the building blocks of knowledge management can be used as a guideline for interventions at different levels.

SUMMARY

- The term 'organizational learning' denotes the change processes which take place in an organization's knowledge base. 'Knowledge management' is the structuring and moulding of these processes.
- The six core processes of knowledge management are: knowledge identification, knowledge acquisition, knowledge development, knowledge sharing and distribution, knowledge utilization, and knowledge retention. Once knowledge objectives are set and

existing knowledge assessed, a management system can be constructed which will give a helpful start to all knowledge managers.
- Knowledge management can be applied to individuals, groups, or ✓ organizational structures. It has strategic and normative aspects as well as the operational one.

KEY QUESTIONS

- Is your company satisfied with a general description of the nature and requirements of a 'learning organization', or are learning objectives described in more specific terms?
- Have you already made your own analysis of the existing knowledge and knowledge processes in your company?
- In which building blocks of knowledge management do you see your main problems?
- In which areas of knowledge management are you particularly strong, and why?

4
Defining Knowledge Goals

INTRODUCTION

What areas of knowledge are vital to your commercial success today? Will they be the same tomorrow? Knowledge loses its value rapidly in the global race to develop expertise, so it must be fostered and maintained systematically. Companies struggle to gain the lead in particular areas of knowledge; once they have an advantage over their competitors, they must develop definite strategies to exploit it. Do you know which kinds of knowledge give your company competitive leverage? Are you applying this knowledge to new business areas, or are you concentrating on areas where your competitors are stronger?

Many companies have a culture in which knowledge is withheld for political reasons. How can you motivate individuals to develop their knowledge purposefully, to improve their skills, and to feed the new knowledge back into the organization? We shall show you how to translate the general goals of your company into normative, strategic and operational knowledge goals. We shall also describe successful companies where leadership through the pursuit of knowledge goals is now the norm.

DEFINING KNOWLEDGE GOALS

The front line

When we started the joint venture, we thought that the two companies would be developing a product together. It turned out later that we had completely misunderstood our partners' motives. All they wanted was access to our knowledge of the market. They already had a product up their sleeve, so they put little effort into the joint development activities. We had not thought about what knowledge we might gain from them. (*Senior manager of a high-tech joint venture*)

There has been a lot of talk in our company recently about organizational learning and intelligent organizations. However, when I look at our strategy documents, they are full of costs, quality and customer value. How can we know what it is that we should be learning, when our strategic planning contains no knowledge goals? (*Manager of a multinational producer of branded goods*).

For two years we have been running a project called 'Core Competency Management'. We have adjusted our strategy as a result of the project, but it is proving incredibly difficult to implement. It is almost impossible to harmonise all the functional programmes with the new strategic goals. . . . (*Employee in central planning of a large concern*).

Significance of goals in management

One of the core tasks of management is to define goals so as to give direction to the company's essential processes.[1] Agreement on strategic goals is the core element in strategic planning, which in turn provides the basis for implementation and monitoring. The company's goals determine the general direction in which its activities develop. They do this mainly by influencing the behaviour of employees.[2]

Goals and organizational learning

The processes involved in defining goals are the starting point of knowledge management. As the comments at the beginning of this chapter show, the idea of organizational learning is positively regarded and can be helpful in stimulating change. However, unless learning processes and knowledge assets are specified, learning is little better than a vague metaphor for change and continuous improvement. Organizational learning only becomes efficient when specific goals are formulated. We shall now consider what knowledge goals are; why they are needed; what functions they perform; and at what levels they can be formulated. We shall also examine the special challenges that confront us when we try to define them.

WHY KNOWLEDGE MANAGEMENT?

Knowledge goals are seldom formulated

In most companies, the organizational knowledge aspect is still disregarded when goals are formulated, whether at the normative, strategic or operational level. Vision and mission statements, which should contain the essentials of the normative goals, are mostly filled with information about market performance, financial and organizational features, employment and management principles, and the strategic direction of business activities.

Absence of strategic knowledge goals

Goals at the levels of corporate strategy and business strategy are usually concerned with markets and competition. They often specify which markets are to be given priority, and what the desired positions are in those markets. They may also list the products or services needed to win customers. They do not, however, specify what areas of knowledge should be developed. Operational goals are usually derived from normative and strategic goals, so their knowledge content is generally no higher.

DAIMLER-BENZ

At the beginning of the 1990s, DAIMLER-BENZ had a vision of itself as an 'integrated technology company'. In setting its goals, the company largely ignored the knowledge aspect. Its strategic goals at that time were to extend the production of cars and utility vehicles to include all kinds of vehicle and all forms of transport technology. However, there was no specification of the skills and know-how that would be needed to integrate rail, air and space technology successfully into the company's existing activities, nor of the necessary financial and technical services. It would be an exaggeration to say that this omission was entirely responsible for the failure of the plan for an 'integrated technology company'. Nevertheless, the strategy would have seemed more cautious and realistic had it been accompanied by a more detailed analysis of the company's knowledge portfolios at that time, and of the levels of investment needed to acquire the appropriate expertise for the new business areas.

3M

We turn now to a company which deliberately places the development and care of its knowledge base in the forefront of its planning activities. We shall see how knowledge issues can be integrated into goals at many levels.

CASE STUDY: MINNESOTA MINING AND MANUFACTURING (3M)

Knowledge goals in research and development
3M manufactures over 60 000 different products, and has a worldwide turnover of $US15.1 billion (1994). Its brand names, such as Post-its ™ and Scotch tape ™, are now in common use as the everyday names for whole categories of articles; this contributes substantially to the company's image and profitability. 3M is also active in many different markets. Its businesses fall into two major sectors: industrial and consumer articles, and health. They include car care products, electronics, industrial materials, dental and skin care preparations, office supplies, telecommunications and transport technology. Since July 1996, the business in image systems and data technology has been operating as an autonomous company called IMATION.[3]

3M is generally regarded as an exceptionally creative company. In the business year 1994 alone, it registered 543 patents. More than 6% of its turnover came from products developed during the same year, while products that were four years old or less contributed an astonishing 30%. The company spent 7% of its turnover on research and development; this was twice the US average.

It is difficult for outsiders to understand how 3M deals with such an enormous range of products so successfully. On closer examination, however, we see that the product portfolio is not just a random mixture. It depends on about 100 basic technologies, mastery of which accounts for the success of most of the products. Selective development of these technologies, combined with product innovations based on technologies already mastered, is ultimately responsible for the internal cohesion of the company's activities.

The strategic organization of 3M's research and development also supports coherent company development. Divisional laboratories in the different business areas work on the actual products, while two higher levels of research are devoted to pure research and to converting the findings into procedures and basic technologies. The rule for co-operation between the levels is that products are the property of the divisions, but new or improved technologies belong to the whole company. Knowledge goals can thus be defined in a way which transcends the different business areas, and gives direction to research and development.

The strategic knowledge goals ensure that competencies develop coherently and consistently. In the business areas, there are various mechanisms for converting the competencies into new products. Basic technologies are often combined in novel ways to yield innovative applications, for example, expertise in adhesives was combined with coating technology to develop Post-its ™. Similarly, knowledge of abrasives was combined with adhesive strip technology to develop Safety Walk ™, a particularly effective non-slip floor covering.

New products sometimes develop from analogies

between different situations. 3M used its experience of making repair products for damaged cable coverings to develop Scotchcast ™ support bandages.

3M's research and development goals thus have two functions. First, they ensure that core competencies are developed and retained in the form of comprehensively mastered basic technologies. Second, they support a generally coherent development of the company because access to the technologies is guaranteed to all divisions. The company's unique competencies are embodied in a variety of end products, and this provides the connecting thread which runs through 3M's many and diverse activities.

Knowledge goals complement traditional planning

As 3M's activities illustrate, the introduction of knowledge goals need not entail a complete revolution in planning. Strategic and financial planning goals, such as desired return on capital, or growth of turnover or market share, will continue to be significant. However, the increasing importance of knowledge as the critical dimension in company success means that knowledge goals should now be included alongside the traditional ones.

KNOWLEDGE GOALS AT DIFFERENT LEVELS

Combined effects of goals at different levels

Our examination of how 3M sets its knowledge goals emphasizes the strategic aspect of knowledge. Decisions about which competencies should be retained and which extended have been a strategic constant in 3M's development. However, strategic goals can only be fully effective if they are (a) embedded in a suitable company context, and (b) consistently put into operation.

Goals at three levels

Figure 4.1 shows how goals can exist at different levels.[4] Normative knowledge goals pertain to the general vision of company policy and all aspects of company culture. Strategic knowledge goals are then set for long-term programmes aimed at realizing the vision. Finally, operational knowledge goals help to ensure that strategic programmes are implemented in daily company activity. Ideally, knowledge goals at all three levels should complement each other and should contribute jointly to the realization of company goals.

	Structures	Activities	Behaviour
Normative Management	Company charter – legal structures effects on KM (secrecy rules, etc.)	Company policy – knowledge vision and mission statement – identification of critical areas of knowledge	Company culture – knowledge sharing desirable – innovative spirit – intense communication
Strategic Management	Organization structures – conferences, reporting structure, R&D organi- zation, experience groups Management systems – EIS, Lotus Notes	Programmes – co-operation – building core competencies – information provision	Approach to problems – orientation to knowledge goals – problem oriented knowledge identification
Operational Management	Organizational processes – control of knowledge flows Deployment processes – knowledge infrastructure – supply of knowledge	Tasks – knowledge projects – build expert databanks – introduce CBT	Performance and co-operation – knowledge sharing – knowledge in action

Figure 4.1   Knowledge issues at different goal levels

We shall now examine ways of formulating knowledge goals and their potential benefits at each of the three levels described above.

WHY IS OUR KNOWLEDGE VALUABLE?

Properties of normative knowledge goals

Normative knowledge goals offer managers opportunities to create a knowledge-friendly company culture and to devise appropriate pol-

icies. The normative aspect relates to a company's general preparedness to take knowledge into account. The first and most important step
towards knowledge-oriented management consists in accepting the
fact that knowledge is vital to company success.[5] In other words, the
primary normative knowledge goal is to create a knowledge-aware or
knowledge-friendly company culture.

Normative knowledge goals:

- Create the conditions for knowledge-oriented strategic and operational goals
- Are aimed at creating a knowledge-aware company culture
- Require commitment and conviction on the part of top management

Normative knowledge goals as a management task

As in most areas of company culture, it falls to management to persuade others to accept normative knowledge goals. It is most important
that top management should show a convincing level of engagement.
Two conditions must be met if managers are to present the link
between company knowledge and company success in a credible light.
First, the terms 'knowledge', 'information' and 'learning' must be part
of management vocabulary. Second, knowledge management must be
effectively presented as a source of growth and profit, and not just as
trimming, or as a 'nice-to-have'. Admittedly, pronouncements such as
'We want to be a learning organization!' or 'We believe that knowledge is central to value creation and success!' will not in themselves
solve any problems. Nevertheless, as general aims, they provide a
normative direction. Without a direction of this kind, knowledge management is less likely to be implemented successfully at strategic and
operational levels.

Normative knowledge goals in 3M

3M realized that efficient innovation is primarily a question of company culture. The company therefore chose to base its management of
innovation on a policy of trust, openness and tolerance of errors, with
the aim of encouraging workers to feel free to try out new ideas. This

is reflected in the time budgeting system: all employees have the right to spend 15% of their time on projects other than their own current placement. 3M managers are given a set of 10 rules which are intended to encourage an innovative atmosphere (cf. Uhl 1993):

Innovation management in 3M

MINNESOTA MINING AND MANUFACTURING (3M)
The 10 rules of innovation management are:
1. Give your people space to think.
2. Remove any taboos on thinking.
3. Permit mistakes.
4. Praise innovation.
5. Promote intensive communication.
6. Act as a coach for innovations.
7. Involve important customers.
8. Innovations can come from many sources.
9. Products belong to the sales department, but technologies belong to the whole company.
10. Expect obstacles to innovation.

The influence of normative measures on knowledge processes

The role of normative measures in knowledge development is to promote a culture of trust in which mistakes are tolerated, thus encouraging a spirit of innovation among employees. Normative goals can also be formulated for other building blocks of knowledge management. If a company suffers from the 'not invented here' syndrome, it needs normative goals to promote greater openness to the world outside and a readiness to experiment and imitate.[6]

The knowledge vision and mission statement

Attempts to make targeted changes in the company culture are beset by many imponderables. Usually, one can only change the company's internal environment; one cannot force people to change their behaviour simply by issuing orders. One way of affecting the internal environment is to formulate a vision and mission statement for knowledge. Traditionally, a vision and mission statement contains statements about the ideals to which a company believes itself to be committed. A vision and mission statement for knowledge contains analogous statements about the significance of knowledge and how it should be treated in general.

Practical relevance of the knowledge vision and mission statement

The effectiveness of an instrument of this kind is critically dependent on how far the principles in the vision and mission statement can be shown to be feasible in practice. The statement must be presented not as a document for press and shareholders, but as a guide for employees. It may be helpful to present it as a method for thinking.[7] Its function is then to encourage people to think about knowledge aspects whenever they make strategic or operational decisions.

The knowledge vision and mission statement of PHONAK LTD

PHONAK is a highly innovative company which produces hearing aids. It has a knowledge vision and mission statement of the kind just described, and it has developed a 'knowledge quadrant', to give direction to its innovative efforts. The company positions its own activities in relation to two knowledge dimensions: first, whether the activity is based on existing knowledge or on knowledge to be developed; and second, whether the knowledge is internal or external. Co-operative ventures with leading innovative institutions help PHONAK to develop new expertise and to combine it with knowledge which exists outside the company. Minimum amounts of management time and capital are invested in the development of new expertise. At the heart of the knowledge quadrant is the company's own knowledge vision and mission statement, which emphasizes cultural values such as openness and trust, and strategic aims such as technological leadership (cf. Schmitz & Zucker 1996) (see Figure 4.2).

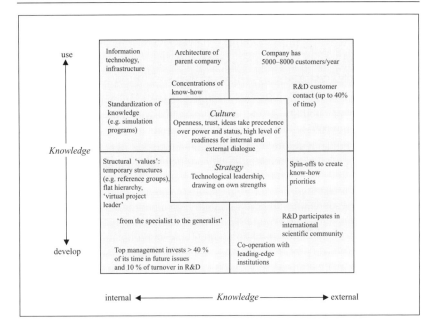

Figure 4.2 Phonak's knowledge quadrant

The role of incentives

For normative measures to succeed, employee incentives must be attuned to the knowledge goals in the vision and mission statement. Behaviours that promote the development and acquisition of knowledge, and – more importantly – its sharing and distribution, must be taken into account in employee assessments, and in calculating salaries and non-financial rewards.

Introducing knowledge management positions

The creation of positions specifically to deal with knowledge can have considerable symbolic influence on a company's knowledge culture. Examples might include appointing a director for knowledge, or setting up a knowledge project team. McKinsey, for example, has a director of knowledge management, who is responsible for internal knowledge creation processes and is known as the 'Mr Inside' of the knowledge business. However, simply creating the posts is not in itself a complete solution: the knowledge manager or knowledge team must also be perceived as a catalyst in the long-term process of introducing knowledge perspectives and a knowledge vocabulary into all areas of management. The knowledge manager tries to supplement the existing goal systems by adding knowledge goals. He or she is also a kind of professional translator who transforms existing goals into knowledge objectives, thus constantly challenging employees to be aware of knowledge issues.

WHAT KNOWLEDGE DO YOU WANT TO EXTEND?

Knowledge angles on production

Itami, the well-known Japanese management researcher, was among the first to advocate adding a knowledge dimension to strategic goals. In his study of the interactions between an organization's activities and the development of its knowledge base, he describes a direct route for knowledge growth, through research and development, and an indirect route, through operational activities. The existence of the second route means that what a company does partially determines what it knows. Itami therefore believes that production processes should always be considered in the light of their potential for increasing knowledge (compare the account in Itami 1987). In practice, this might mean that a company should itself manufacture the essential components of a product, regardless of cost, in order to retain critical know-how.

Strategic consequences

Itami's arguments lead him to suggest that companies should structure their many relationships with the environment so as to achieve not only financial success, but also growth of knowledge assets. Successful implementation of a strategy depends on the expertise present in the company; conversely, however, strategic decisions also determine what new expertise will be acquired. If strategic decisions are made without regard for their effects on knowledge, this may hinder the development of new expertise, and even contribute to the erosion of existing skills and knowledge.[8]

Functions of strategic knowledge goals

Essentially, strategic knowledge goals have two different functions. If they are based on an existing strategy, they make it easier to evaluate the feasibility of the strategy from the point of view of knowledge requirements. If they are formulated as independent goals, they can help to generate new strategic options.

Diversification: likelihood of success

The first function is relevant when assessing diversification strategies. It has been shown empirically that diversifications into related products or industries have very much better prospects of success than ventures into unrelated areas. It is easier for companies to transfer existing skills than to build up new ones.[9] This means that if a company wishes to enter new product or market areas, defining knowledge goals can help it to judge the chances of success, and to calculate what resources it would have to invest.

New strategic options

Analysing existing portfolios of competencies is a strategic method for finding new fields of activity. If this method is used to identify possible diversifications, new markets or additions to the product range, the new activities should be feasible on the basis of existing knowledge resources. 3M is an example of how an expressly knowledge-oriented strategy can be implemented through consistent investment in basic technologies, combining different technologies and making use of product analogies. 3M's enormous range of apparently unrelated end products is in fact surprisingly coherent when we consider the underlying competencies. MICROAGE is another company that has used existing knowledge to find a new strategic option.

CASE STUDY: MICROAGE

From computer wholesaler to configuration adviser
MICROAGE, a computer wholesale company in Tempe,
Arizona, has grown rapidly since its foundation in 1976.
In the business year 1994, it had a turnover of $US2.2
billion, which represented an increase of 47% on the
previous year. This achievement was due in part to a
radical change in direction which the company had made
some years previously. It decided to stop operating
simply as a wholesaler of hardware and accessories
produced by APPLE, COMPAQ, HEWLETT PACKARD and IBM,
and to become a configuration adviser to large
companies.[10]
    The CEO, Jeffrey McKeever, justified this strategy – which
later proved to have been a far-sighted one – in terms of
changes in MICROAGE's knowledge environment. Networks
were becoming steadily more complicated, and were often
assembled by using components from many different
manufacturers. Customers therefore expected more
information about possible network configurations and the
compatibility and performance features of widely different
products. McKeever saw the chance of using the company's
knowledge of customer needs, amassed over many years of
selling, to provide a service. MICROAGE therefore
transformed one of its warehouses into a factory, where
today, up to 125 tonnes of hardware per day are assembled
into unique configurations to suit customer requirements.
By exploiting knowledge that had so far lain unused,
MICROAGE succeeded in completely redefining its position in
the value creation chain.
    This new activity brought changes to the way in which
knowledge was managed in MICROAGE. Previously,
knowledge acquisition had been a by-product of the main
activity, which was selling. Now, knowledge about specific
customer requirements had to be assembled much more
carefully. The new company strategy was an outcome of
knowledge acquired incidentally, but the adoption of the
strategy influenced the measures taken to preserve that
knowledge.

Complementary function of knowledge goals

Strategic knowledge goals can complement traditional strategic planning by providing a description of expertise that will be needed in the future, and thus safeguarding the organization's knowledge assets. They show which competencies should be developed or preserved, and which have become obsolete. They may also contain plans for strategic moulding of the organizational structures and management systems which will be needed to support this. Their functions may be summarized as follows.
Strategic knowledge goals:

● Define the kinds of expertise to be acquired for the future
● Often reveal in doing so the content of the organization's core knowledge
● Permit strategic alignment of organizational structures and management systems

Knowledge strategy

For some time now, research into strategic management has been much occupied with ways of implementing strategic knowledge goals. Prahalad and Hamel, for example, point to the existence of a deliberate knowledge strategy in NEC as the reason for that company's remarkable commercial success. Their longitudinal comparison of the development of NEC with that of GTE shows the difference that carefully considered knowledge goals can make to the long-term development of a company.

Selective development of core knowledge

At the beginning of the 1980s, GTE had an excellent prospect of becoming a leading supplier of information technology. Ten years later, however, the Japanese concern NEC, which had initially occupied a clearly inferior position, became the market leader. For short-term financial reasons, GTE pulled out of a number of business areas, thus speeding the erosion of its knowledge base; NEC on the other hand deliberately invested in technologies relevant to market segments that held promise for the future. By managing its core knowledge carefully and concentrating on the development of semiconductors,

NEC was able to move into new business areas. It outstripped most
of its competitors in the process. Today, NEC is the only company
which can claim to be a leader both in semiconductors and in computers and communications equipment.[11]

Core competencies

Prahalad and Hamel's core competence approach, which is partly based
on the investigation just mentioned, has evoked a strong response in
management circles.[12] It postulates that a company will be better able
to maintain its growth and profitability in an ever-changing competitive
environment if it regards itself as a portfolio of competencies. Prahalad
and Hamel are mainly concerned with technological skills, which are the
'core competencies', and are therefore at the root of competitive survival. On the basis of these competencies, the company develops a series
of core products; these underlie the competitive strength of end products
in the individual business areas (see Figure 4.3).

Non-technological competencies

Non-technological competencies can also yield competitive advantages.[13] UNILEVER, for instance, is careful to set up multicultural management teams. This increases the company's cultural sensitivity, and
helps it to succeed in a wide range of countries and markets. JOHN-
SON & JOHNSON describes its strong company culture and its emphasis
on ethical principles as core competencies which enable it to react
quickly and to manage effectively in sensitive areas such as the production of medicines (cf. *The Economist* 11.11.95).

Knowledge as a basic success factor

Treating knowledge as a basic organizational resource brings significant
opportunities. Strategy becomes a tool for steering the company towards
systematic accumulation of individual and collective expertise and
deliberate management of knowledge. In practice, this means concentrating on a limited number of activities and carefully fostering a few
knowledge assets that are essential to the company's success. In the face

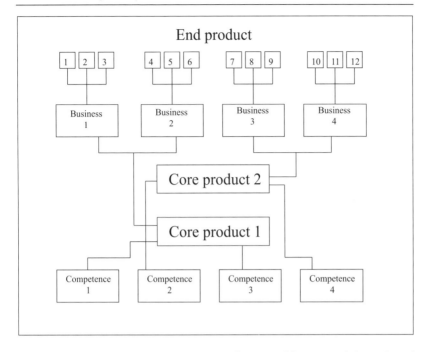

Figure 4.3 Competencies: the roots of competitiveness. Adapted and reprinted by permission of *Harvard Business Review*. From 'The Core Competence of the Corporation', by C. K. Prahalad & G. Hamel, May/June 1990. Copyright © 1990 by the President and Fellows of Harvard College; all rights reserved

of increasing global competition, a company can only be sure of succeeding if it occupies a 'best in the world' position, and it can only reach that standard in a limited number of areas. Japanese companies like SONY and NEC are good examples: they are highly competent, but only in clearly defined areas. Treating knowledge as a basic success factor also means that strategic decisions – for example about outsourcing, diversification or joint ventures – can be made consistently according to a single principle, i.e. the knowledge that company wishes to retain or develop.

The time factor

Knowledge-based strategies must allow for the time factor in competitive situations. Knowledge now loses its value at an increasing rate, and any company that stops developing new knowledge is on the road to nowhere.[14] Concentrating on expertise that is important today can bring failure tomorrow. Companies must therefore preserve a balance between concentrating their efforts on present needs and being ready to change. Firms like HEWLETT PACKARD, which continue to be successful in dynamic, high-tech industries, often replace their products by better ones long before the end of their life cycle. They keep time on their side by proactive adjustment of knowledge goals.

Competence matrix

Instruments for defining strategic knowledge objectives are still in their infancy. An examination of the early attempts shows that there is still plenty of room for creative adaptation of existing instruments for strategy development.[15] One possibility is to describe the company's knowledge base with the aid of a matrix. Two axes – size of knowledge lead over competitors and current internal utilization of knowledge – are used to create four quadrants. Organizational competencies are then positioned in the matrix, which yields standard knowledge strategies for each[16] (see Figure 4.4).

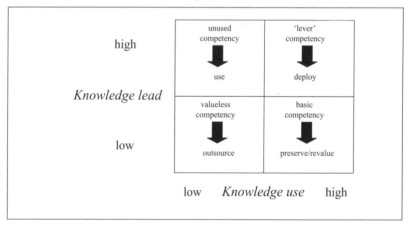

Figure 4.4 Matrix of knowledge strategies

Maintaining competencies

An activity which falls in the lower left-hand quadrant – narrow lead, low level of utilization – could be outsourced. It cannot be used to gain a competitive advantage, and it is not needed to support higher-level competencies.

Basic competencies

Competencies that fall in the lower right-hand quadrant – narrow lead, high level of utilization – may be basic to the company's activities. The company's strategic knowledge objectives must allow it to retain the essentials of a certain number of basic competencies. If the competency is not needed for internal application, outsourcing should be considered. Alternatively, the competency might be improved to a level where it yields competitive leverage.

Unused competencies

The upper left-hand quadrant – strong lead, low utilization – represents unexploited potential. In many companies, there are areas of expertise which lie fallow, even though they contain know-how that is superior to that of competitors. There is often little awareness that this valuable knowledge exists. The suggested strategy here is to put these assets to work, since they represent a potential competitive advantage.

'Leverage' competencies

The upper right-hand quadrant – strong lead, high utilization – contains the competencies that provide the company with its competitive leverage. However, expertise which is superior to that of competitors and is already being capitalized on the market can often be used on other markets too. In this situation, strategic knowledge goals should work in harmony with strategic planning to find innovative options for entering new business areas.

MAKING VISIONS COME TRUE

Implementing knowledge management

New management ideas often wither at the stage of strategic reflection, and the results are never actually implemented. Many companies have analysed and described their core competencies, but only a few have been able to draw the appropriate conclusions for their business activities. The danger of this happening to knowledge management can be reduced by defining operational knowledge goals. Operational goals lead to systematic control and monitoring of knowledge in the context of projects and implementation processes. Where short-term considerations relating to markets and competition are likely to be influential, it is especially important for companies to remember their underlying knowledge assets. Operational knowledge goals are meant to take knowledge management beyond staff and management levels, and to ensure that it is not sacrificed to operational activities. For these reasons, operational knowledge goals must be clearly formulated, and observed strictly throughout the organization.

Operational knowledge goals:

- Ensure that knowledge management is implemented at the operational level
- Translate normative and strategic knowledge goals into concrete, practicable objectives
- Optimize the infrastructure of knowledge management
- Ensure that interventions are appropriate to the level at which they are made

Translating goals

Consistency among normative, strategic and operational knowledge goals can be guaranteed if operational goals are derived from the other two kinds by a process analogous to translation. Translating strategic goals into operational ones – against the background set by the normative goals – helps companies to see exactly how their knowledge goals can be implemented, and how far they are compatible with goals of other kinds. It is also the first step towards actual implementation. A specific operational knowledge objective might be something like: 'In our research project with X University, three functional prototypes are to be developed by the end of the year. A prototype is functional if . . .' ; or, 'Our internal experts must be more accessible to customers. Acceptable response times are . . .'

Operational context

There are several stages in the process of translating strategic knowledge goals into operational ones. In the first phase, strategic knowledge goals must be assigned to appropriate target groups at the operational level, and time frames must be decided. Several divisions or functional departments may be involved in implementing a strategic knowledge goal. There may also be several target dates, or different groups may be involved at different times.

Co-ordination with existing goals

In the second phase, the knowledge goals must be harmonized with ✓ existing traditional goals. Operational knowledge goals are only a subcategory of the full range of operational goals. A personnel department might have as its knowledge goal: 'All employees serving customers must be trained to take orders on a lap-top computer.' However, the department may have to reconcile this goal with other strategic and operational goals, for example, 'The training budget must be reduced to 0.2% of the volume of orders.' The department must then order its priorities to fit its limited resources, and will probably look for potential synergies with other measures.

Breaking down the goals

In the third phase, the operational knowledge goals for a particular ✓ part of the company must be broken down among departments, projects, groups and individuals. Ideally, this process will result in a personal development plan for each employee, in which individual knowledge objectives for a particular period are defined. These individual targets will in turn contribute to the attainment of knowledge goals at corporate level.

Top-down versus feedback

It should be remembered throughout that a purely top-down approach carries uncertain prospects of success. At all stages, there is likely to be feedback necessitating some adjustment of higher-level knowledge goals. Implementation of knowledge objectives may be hampered or delayed because of restrictions on resources, incompatibilities with other company goals, or unexpected gaps in the portfolio of com-

petencies. Conversely, unexpected areas of expertise may be discovered during the translation process. These may render the knowledge
objective partly superfluous, thus freeing extra resources. It may also
be possible to transfer knowledge objectives which cannot be met in
one department into another.

Appropriate interventions

The translation process results in a hierarchy of knowledge objectives.
One of the essential functions of this hierarchy is to provide a guide
to an appropriate range of interventions. A good rule is that the scale
and importance of the knowledge goal should be compatible with the
chosen level of intervention. A language course for a group of
employees, or a re-engineering project in the research and development department, are not at the same level of significance as
reorienting the direction of a whole business area towards different
technology, or establishing a more innovative company culture. These
measures all call for radically different procedures, and make different
demands on resources.

Adaptation of existing tools

There is as yet no specific set of instruments for defining operational
knowledge goals, and it is probably not necessary to develop any. An
alternative approach is to take well-known mechanisms for defining
goals of other kinds, and adapt them for knowledge purposes. This is
a promising solution, and a much cheaper one. A knowledge element
can be added to a variety of instruments for formulating goals at different levels of intervention. In a business unit, for example, knowledge
goals can be added as a supplement to the yearly targets. The knowledge goals may be described in qualitative or quantitative terms; they
may specify measures, persons responsible and deadlines. Similarly,
knowledge supplements may be added to goals at area or department
level, or to project plans (see Figure 4.5).

Management by knowledge objectives

Objectives for employees can easily be enriched by the addition of
knowledge elements. Under a system of management by objectives,
each employee is expected to perform certain tasks and achieve certain

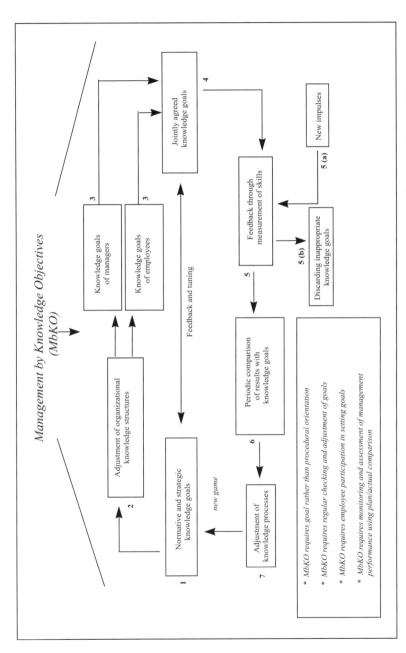

Figure 4.5 Management by knowledge objectives (based on Odiorne 1965, p. 102)

Management by Knowledge Objectives (MbKO)

1 Normative and strategic knowledge goals

2 Adjustment of organizational knowledge structures

3 Knowledge goals of managers

3 Knowledge goals of employees

4 Jointly agreed knowledge goals

Feedback and tuning

5 Periodic comparison of results with knowledge goals

5 Feedback through measurement of skills

5 (a) New impulses

5 (b) Discarding inappropriate knowledge goals

6 Adjustment of knowledge processes

new game

7

* MbKO requires goal rather than procedural orientation
* MbKO requires regular checking and adjustment of goals
* MbKO requires employee participation in setting goals
* MbKO requires monitoring and assessment of management performance using plan/actual comparison

results. To this one might add the acquisition or development of personal skills, thus introducing 'management by knowledge objectives'. The employee and his or her supervisor would agree on a set of training objectives, to be measured and adjusted periodically. To ensure the strategic relevance of the training measures, the objectives would be set within the framework of the company's normative and strategic knowledge goals.

DIFFICULTIES IN FORMULATING KNOWLEDGE GOALS

Finding a common language

There are various difficulties attached to the process of defining knowledge goals within a company. The absence of a common language is a fundamental problem, and one which is often underestimated. Other management disciplines, such as finance, logistics, etc., have a detailed vocabulary at their disposal: the objectives for an investment project, for instance, can be described unambiguously in financial terminology. Knowledge managers, however, have only a few terms in common at present. Any attempt to define knowledge goals must usually start with efforts to reach agreement on such basic terms as data, information, skills, competencies and knowledge. Regular discussion of knowledge-related questions would help, since an accepted language would probably evolve with experience.

Lack of instruments

There are no established instruments for formulating knowledge goals. The more specifically one tries to formulate objectives, the more obvious this becomes. At the normative and strategic levels, it is not too difficult to formulate relatively global goals for expertise; at the lower levels, however, it becomes progressively more problematic. The tools are still in their infancy, and relatively unwieldy in use.[17]

Quantifiability

The absence of a generally agreed vocabulary and suitable instruments results in formulations that are not sufficiently detailed, and therefore difficult to quantify. 'If you can't measure it, you can't manage it' is a common maxim in management, but it does nothing to solve the present problems. There will only be progress in quantifying and implementing knowledge goals if knowledge management is allowed an experimental phase in which to develop its own set of instruments and methods.

Operational sluggishness

A further obstacle to formulating knowledge goals, and thus to implementing knowledge management, is a phenomenon that we call 'operational sluggishness': it is much easier to work with familiar tools that are not affected by the problems described above than it is to introduce new concepts. Knowledge management must therefore clear the usual hurdles which stand in the way of introducing something new. The relatively abstract procedure of formulating goals is particularly difficult in an area which is not yet fully understood.

Power

Power relations can also influence the formulation of knowledge goals. Knowledge objectives for individuals always have some bearing on the balance of power between the employee and the organization, since the interests of the two are not always compatible. We shall return to this question when we examine the acquisition, development and distribution of knowledge.

Illusions of control

An intangible resource such as knowledge is usually controllable only to a limited extent. We should therefore avoid illusions of control in our attempts to formulate knowledge goals. All activities aimed at knowledge management should be approached cautiously, one step at a time, and by adjusting the organizational context.

Characteristics of company goals

Despite the many difficulties involved in formulating goals, every approach to management includes them. Goals are still the best way of describing a desired state of affairs.[18]. Research has shown that goals typically consist of a number of elements; ideally, any goal should contain all of them (cf. Hauschildt 1977, pp. 7ff. and Hauschildt 1993, pp. 144ff.) (see Table 4.1).

Table 4.1

Goal components	Content of goal components	Example
• goal object	general subject area of goal	external relations
• goal characteristics	variables for evaluating alternative solutions	language competence
• goal measures	exact measurement instructions for evaluation	language test
• contribution to achieving goal	planned or required levels for goal achievement	600 points
• time frame	time frame for goal achievement	by mid-1998
• target person	persons responsible for achieving goal	external relations leadership

Quantitative and qualitative goals

Another important distinction is that between qualitative and quantitative aspects of goals. The same goal can be described in very different ways depending on whether quantitative measures or qualitative terms are chosen. A goal may be described in financial terms, by specifying viable turnover, profit margins and return on investment. This would be a quantitative description. The improvement of a company's public image, on the other hand, is a goal which is very difficult to specify unambiguously in quantitative terms. In this latter case, qualitative criteria are more likely to be important.

A pioneering venture

Formulating helpful knowledge goals is still in many ways a pioneering venture, and one which requires imagination and courage. Dörner's work on strategic thinking in complex situations may be of use (Dörner 1996). Some goals involve striving towards a particular state of affairs, while others involve avoiding something; goals may also be simple or complex, general or specific, and clear or unclear. Formulating them therefore demands flexibility of thought and a specific understanding of each knowledge context. Figure 4.6 contains examples of knowledge goals of different kinds.

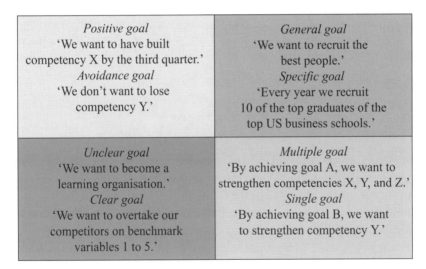

Positive goal 'We want to have built competency X by the third quarter.' *Avoidance goal* 'We don't want to lose competency Y.'	*General goal* 'We want to recruit the best people.' *Specific goal* 'Every year we recruit 10 of the top graduates of the top US business schools.'
Unclear goal 'We want to become a learning organisation.' *Clear goal* 'We want to overtake our competitors on benchmark variables 1 to 5.'	*Multiple goal* 'By achieving goal A, we want to strengthen competencies X, Y, and Z.' *Single goal* 'By achieving goal B, we want to strengthen competency Y.'

Figure 4.6 Goal types and their relationship with knowledge management (based on Dörner 1996, pp. 79ff.)

Functions of company goals

Knowledge goals must perform the same classical functions as traditional goals: they must serve as a basis for decision-making, co-ordination, motivation and monitoring.[19] The decision-making function of knowledge goals means that they must enable management to compare alternative courses of action in terms of their effectiveness and efficiency.[20] The co-ordinating function involves balancing irreconcilable objectives, and adjusting different interests at an early stage so as to avoid frictional losses during implementation.[21] The motivational function is directly related to co-ordination, since the provision of common goals increases the commitment of all employees involved in implementation. Finally, the monitoring function covers measurement and assessment of progress, which is only possible by reference to clearly defined objectives.

Functions of goals at different levels

If we consider the functions of the different kinds of goals described above, we see that normative and strategic goals primarily support decision-making and co-ordination, while operational goals motivate employees during implementation. Operational objectives also support the monitoring function, because their practical import and their relatively limited scope make them suitable as a basis for monitoring.

Links between goals and monitoring

In general, goals should be directly and meaningfully related to measurement and evaluation. This relationship is evident in our approach to knowledge management. For the sake of clarity, the two corresponding building blocks – formulating knowledge goals and evaluating knowledge – will be treated separately in this book. We must therefore emphasize at this point that when goals are being defined, thought must always be given to methods of subsequent evaluation. Chapter 11 contains a more detailed discussion of this approach to systematic monitoring of knowledge.

SUMMARY

• Knowledge goals ensure that processes of organizational learning have a direction, and that the success or failure of knowledge management can be checked. They represent a translation of company goals into knowledge terms.

- Companies make too little use of knowledge goals as a practical planning tool.
- Knowledge goals should be formulated at normative, strategic and operational levels.
- Normative knowledge goals establish the conditions for an innovative and 'knowledge-aware' company culture.
- Strategic knowledge goals define the company's future range of competencies.
- Operational knowledge goals translate normative and strategic ideals into objectives that can be implemented.
- The formulation of knowledge goals is beset by numerous problems. These include the absence of a 'knowledge language' and a lack of instruments. There are also difficulties arising from questions of power and from the need to adopt new methods.
- Knowledge goals supplement traditional company goals at many levels. It is essential in today's conditions to consider the effects of most long-term management decisions on the organizational knowledge base.
- The principles inherent in the company culture can be anchored in a knowledge vision and mission statement. However, they must also be 'lived' by management if they are to exert a real influence on the behaviour of employees.
- An approach in which knowledge is deliberately included can open new strategic options.
- When knowledge goals are formulated, thought must always be given to ways of measuring their implementation.

KEY QUESTIONS

- Where do knowledge issues already make an appearance, direct or indirect, in the goals of your organization?
- How are company goals translated into knowledge goals?
- What kind of knowledge culture do you have? What kind of status does knowledge enjoy in your company, and how can you demonstrate this?
- Is knowledge taken into account in discussions of strategy? Do you have some idea of what constitutes the 'core knowledge' of your organization, and of the direction in which this knowledge needs to develop in the future?

- In your immediate environment, where might you introduce knowledge goals to supplement existing goals?
- What are your personal knowledge objectives? What do you want
  to learn? Are your objectives consistent with the knowledge goals
  of your company?

5

Identifying Knowledge

INTRODUCTION

Nobody can know everything – but we should know where to find whatever it is that we need. It is easy to lose track of developments because the volume of knowledge grows at an explosive rate, and the content becomes increasingly specialized. Knowledge, both internal and external, is not automatically visible, so organizations must create transparency. To succeed competitively, companies must know who are the experts on important topics, both within the organization and outside it. Do you know how many projects are currently in progress in your company, and what their purpose is? Do you have access to a knowledge broker who will assemble vital information for you from the Internet, or from the rapidly expanding global databases? We shall describe many ways of helping you to locate knowledge, both inside and outside your company. Knowledge maps, Yellow Pages of experts, and your own intranet are just a few examples.

IDENTIFYING KNOWLEDGE

The front line

Almost every day I need quick and easy access to knowledge that I am sure must exist somewhere in our global organization. Our internal knowledge assets are not easily visible, so I have to find another solution, and this costs time and money. (*Manager of a multinational bank*)

Until recently, we in the central office did not know what new products were being developed by our subsidiaries and associates around the world. This was a result of our decentralisation policy. We have the largest global research budget for the industry, yet a researcher in Canada does not know whether someone in France is tackling the same problems. (*Manager of an international industrial concern*)

We don't care if other people know what we know. Know-how by itself is not enough. To gain an advantage, a company must be able to answer the question: What can I do with this knowledge? (*Entrepreneur in a high-tech industry*)

Internal invisibility of knowledge assets

In many organizations, poor access to knowledge is part of life. Big international companies in particular often complain that they have lost sight of their internal competencies and knowledge assets in important areas.[1] Market studies on the same theme may be carried out at different points in the organization. Valuable knowledge assets may go unnoticed and unused, and managers may not know that the company has internal experts on a given subject. The company may waste time reinventing the wheel, because it does not know that a solution already exists elsewhere.

The flood of information

Managers today have too much information rather than too little. The flood of specialist literature, memos, technical reports, e-mails and conference invitations obliges them to make a selection. They have computer systems which enable them to access a wide range of databases and accounting systems, and the vast world of the Internet. Despite all this, many still feel that they are badly informed. 'I have all the information except what I need!' is a common complaint. Managers often suspect that the knowledge they want exists somewhere. What they lack is a way of accessing the knowledge environment, and of identifying particular kinds of knowledge, both internally and externally.

Adequate, not absolute, transparency

When building organizational competencies, we must first know enough about the relevant knowledge assets to decide where to start pursuing our knowledge goals (Chapter 2). If we seek absolute transparency, we shall waste our efforts, and ultimately we shall fail. Our knowledge goals will point us towards the areas and sources of knowledge which we need in order to strengthen our existing competencies or create new ones. Our search must cover both internal and external sources of knowledge.

Visibility of employees and structures

Making internal knowledge visible means determining the current status, i.e. making the organization aware of its own abilities. What experts do we have, and how might they help the organization to increase its competencies? Who has information that is vital to our knowledge goals? Questions such as these relate to employee visibility. However, we also need to make collective knowledge transparent. What are rules for sharing knowledge within the company? Which internal networks are most important for the exchange of information?

Understanding the knowledge environment

The first step towards identifying external knowledge is to examine systematically the organization's relevant knowledge environment.

Organizations often see only that which they have previously learned to see. They miss many important details. As a result, they lose opportunities to import knowledge, to co-operate with external experts, or to use important networks outside the boundaries of the organization.

Benchmarking

Many companies assess their own capabilities by comparing their skills and productivity with those of competitors. Best practices are identified, both inside and outside the industry. Companies are found which are superior to all their competitors in some aspect of their functioning, e.g. short-term management of financial resources. Benchmarking[2] is a set of theoretical methods and practical aids which help companies to identify their own weak spots relative to the competition. It provides not only a stimulus to seeking new competencies, but also the means and sources of knowledge for doing so.

In addition to the traditional external benchmarking, the internal variant is also gaining ground. Companies which have followed a consistent policy of internal benchmarking in recent years have usually been surprised by the results. An examination of comparable processes in comparable units revealed in many cases deviations of 200–300% in the main measures of efficiency. Benchmarking experts maintain that a ratio of 1 : 2 is the rule rather than the exception. In extreme cases, a deviation ratio of up to 1 : 10 has been found (for references see Szulanski 1996, p. 27). Internal benchmarking and the identification of internal best practices are essential preconditions for the process of best practice transfer.[3]

Benefits of knowledge transparency

Selective identification of knowledge yields a level of transparency which permits individuals within an organization to find their bearings and gain better access to the external knowledge environment. This helps them to achieve synergies, set up co-operative projects and make valuable contacts. The organization thus makes more efficient use of internal and external resources and increases its own ability to react appropriately.

Implications of admitting ignorance

Identifying the gaps in one's knowledge and skills can be an effective trigger for learning processes. Many organizations are reluctant to admit ignorance, since entertaining new ideas can seriously destabilize their world view.[4] However, organizations which decide to reverse their skills deficits and close their knowledge gaps can make a good start by creating a suitable level of transparency of internal and external knowledge.

IF THE COMPANY ONLY KNEW WHAT IT KNOWS . . .

Nobody is responsible for transparency of knowledge

An important reason why knowledge assets are often not visible is that no one is responsible for making them so; indeed, it may be impossible to assign clear responsibilities in this area. The personnel department knows the skills of appointees, but this information is often not passed on to the rest of the organization. The IT department installs networks and communications software which could support location of information and useful contacts, but IT experts rarely see this as one of their main duties. So who is responsible? Is it up to managers to help employees find their way through the jungle of a large organization, either by setting an example or by providing selected information? Or is each employee responsible for locating relevant information and contacting the right experts? These questions are not easy to answer. Personnel departments, IT departments, managers and many others can certainly make a contribution to raising the visibility of internal knowledge assets. Organizations should also support their employees by providing appropriate infrastructures.

Obstacles to transparency of knowledge

Organization charts and manuals do not normally contain a 'transparency creation centre'. This is a problem because of the increasing movement of employees in many companies: regular restructuring, job rotation and increased fluctuation make it easy to lose sight of who is responsible for what ('the person who was in charge yesterday is somewhere else today, and tomorrow he will be with our competitors'). The vogue for lean management has led to the removal of many 'redundant' positions. As a result, skills and knowledge which used to be present at several points in the organization are no longer duplicated in this way, and may therefore be even more remote from people who need them. Radical decentralisation programmes and re-engineering projects have torn apart central integrating functions and informal networks. In extreme cases, 'autonomous' parts of the company know little more about their sister companies than they do about their competitors. In addition, many staff jobs have been abolished as 'unproductive overheads', or had their activities cut back. In the 1980s, staff functions were hailed as a means of achieving synergies; today, they have been much reduced in many organizations. Their co-ordinating role in ensuring multiple use of knowledge assets has thus been seriously weakened.

Positive influences on transparency of knowledge

The trends we have just described make internal knowledge less visible and more difficult to identify. However, there are other developments which work in the opposite direction. In 1995, 25% of all PCs sold were capable of multimedia use, and 70% of all PCs in companies were networked (source: TELECOM-PTT). This means that in many organizations, the technical means for locating knowledge are already present. The dismantling of hierarchies and the rise of knowledge workers and experts have led to a more open style of communication. Vertical communication through official channels is increasingly being replaced by horizontal contacts. Experts speak directly with each other, and this improves the quality of the contacts. The direct superior is thus losing his or her importance as a major filter of knowledge.

These trends are progressively eroding existing hierarchies, hence the increasing tendency in organizational theory to describe organizations as networks (cf. Drucker 1988). Organizational theory advocates radically new forms of organization in response to these new trends in communication. However, simple measures are often sufficient to raise the visibility of internal knowledge. We shall now describe some of the measures and instruments for achieving this at individual and group levels.

The Unknown Experts

Ignorance of skills of the company's employees

The smallest unit in knowledge management is the individual employee. The individual has skills, intuition and experience. These are partly known to the organization. Personnel departments usually hold information on employees' education and on their linguistic and other skills. However, these 'master data' contain only some of the employees' abilities. Other important items are not recorded, because of data protection requirements for example. This lack of visibility hinders employees' access to the expert knowledge of their colleagues, thus reducing the likelihood that they will make use of it.

Directories of experts and Yellow Pages

Directories of experts and employee handbooks offer an effective and relatively cheap method of locating experts and specialists anywhere in the world. HOFFMAN-LAROCHE, the Swiss chemical company, used this method to raise the worldwide visibility of their researchers' specialist knowledge. The information was listed in a 'Yellow Pages' format (cf. Seemann & Stucky 1996), and the resulting directory was distributed throughout the organization. The directory contained lists of problems which occur frequently in product development, together with the names of potential problem-solvers. This offered developers much easier access to internal expertise. 'Islands of knowledge' were interconnected, and the costs of locating suitable people with whom to discuss special problems were considerably reduced.

Knowledge maps

Knowledge maps of various kinds may also be used to locate expertise. In general terms, knowledge maps are graphic representations of experts, knowledge assets, knowledge sources, knowledge structures or knowledge applications (Eppler 1997). They increase transparency and support identification of experts or sources of knowledge, thus enabling the user to classify new knowledge in relation to existing knowledge, and to link tasks with experts or knowledge assets. Knowledge maps can be classified into a number of groups according to their structure.[5] All the information they contain can be computerized, organized according to various criteria, and presented visually with the aid of computer graphics. This greatly simplifies access to any types of knowledge that can be formalized, and makes them accessible to large numbers of people at any time and in any location.

Knowledge topographies

Knowledge topographies identify people who possess particular skills and knowledge (e.g. marketing knowledge), and indicate the level of their knowledge. A system of this kind offers a relatively quick guide to who knows what, and at what level (see Figure 5.1).

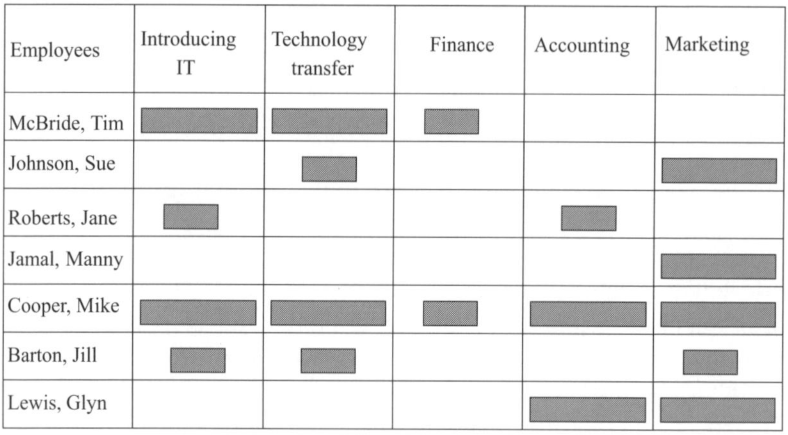

Employees	Introducing IT	Technology transfer	Finance	Accounting	Marketing
McBride, Tim	■	■	■		
Johnson, Sue		■			■
Roberts, Jane	■			■	
Jamal, Manny					■
Cooper, Mike	■	■	■	■	■
Barton, Jill	■	■			■
Lewis, Glyn				■	■

Figure 5.1 Knowledge topography

Maps of knowledge assets

Maps of knowledge assets show where and how particular knowledge assets are stored. It makes a great deal of difference to the user whether the information is in a computer centre, on diskettes, on paper, or in the memory of a retired specialist. Maps of knowledge assets thus take into account the level of aggregation of the knowledge and offer the user valuable information on possible ways of processing it further.

Geographical information systems

Geographical information systems (GIS) show the geographical organization of knowledge assets. A geographical map of sales areas, for example, is useful for planning marketing activities. This method of representation is intuitively meaningful, and can make an enormous difference to the effectiveness of management decisions. The rapid growth in the market for GIS applications, particularly on CD-ROMs, is therefore unsurprising.

Knowledge source maps

Knowledge source maps show which persons in a team, an organization or the external environment can contribute important knowledge to particular tasks. The names of experts in the field of knowledge under examination are emphasized, e.g. by using italics (see Figure 5.2).

Knowledge matrices

Another possibility is to show knowledge assets in the form of a knowledge matrix. For any problem, relevant knowledge and skills can be positioned in a knowledge matrix based on two dimensions. The use of different distinctions (e.g. internal/external, new/existing, implicit/explicit . . .)[6] opens different perspectives on the organization's knowledge assets and reveals trends[7] (see Figure 5.3).

Knowledge maps should be produced in the stages shown in Figure 5.3. It is useful to start with particularly knowledge-intensive processes or sensitive knowledge assets; these should be selected, coded and linked to their own navigation system. The system should be updated on a decentralized basis, because this is the only way to ensure that updating will continue permanently.

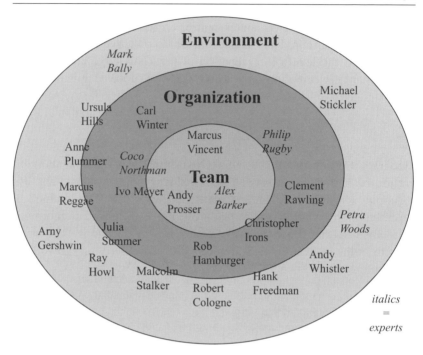

Figure 5.2   Knowledge source maps

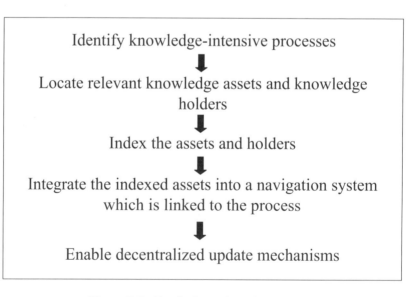

Figure 5.3   Producing a knowledge map

There are a number of problems with knowledge maps:

- They distort internal power relations by popularizing knowledge, since it moves to lower levels in the hierarchy.
- They must not be allowed to remain static, and to degenerate into extra routines or instructions.
- They must not intrude into people's private lives.
- They must be seen as living documents, which are never complete and which undergo a process of constant development. The quality of the data and information in knowledge maps decides their success and usefulness. They should therefore be confined to knowledge components of high value, especially in the start-up phase, and they should be linked to existing systems.
- They are difficult to create at times when the number of jobs is being reduced, because people are reluctant to make their knowledge explicit for fear of becoming less necessary and losing their own jobs.
- They must be supported by a common language which covers the different fields of knowledge. Only a controlled vocabulary can guarantee consistent use of terms and classification of information along different knowledge dimensions.
- They only become fully effective when the company has begun to value knowledge as a resource. Knowledge maps are most productive where there is an efficient internal knowledge market (cf. Preissler, Roehl & Seemann 1997).

Transparency at all costs?

Transparency has its price. Measuring and recording skills cost time and money: interviews must be held, questionnaires distributed and test procedures developed. There must be an adequate return for the effort and expense. Increased visibility should therefore only be sought in relation to skills which are critical to the organization. 'Visibility at any price' is nonsense, and can even be counter-productive.

Respecting private life

Many employees keep their business and private lives strictly separate. They do not automatically offer their employers the information, skills and contacts gained in their own time. This is a natural barrier against being swallowed up entirely by work, and it protects private life. The point of making knowledge more transparent is to reveal hidden talents and potential; but there are limits when privacy is threatened.

Making expert knowledge explicit is not always a good thing

Raising the visibility of knowledge should also facilitate access to the intuition and experience of internal experts, i.e. to their tacit knowledge. Management researchers are now investigating ways of making this unconscious or tacit knowledge communicable.[8] It is said that expert knowledge can only be used for purposes of innovation if unconscious elements are first formalized and then combined with other elements in the organization's intellectual capital. However, the costs of retrieving tacit knowledge can be very high, and disproportionate to the expected benefit. In most cases, prompt identification of the appropriate experts is all that is needed.

Transparency can be damaging

Visibility has its drawbacks. Headhunters can penetrate organizational databases in which experts are identified, and thus quickly locate interesting candidates. Employees may become defensive about excessive freedom of information on their personal strengths and weaknesses. Data protection laws are valuable in this context. Too much openness can lead to thoughtless divulging of sensitive information, and this may be exploited by competitors. Careful thought should be given to the question of where increased visibility would bring benefits, and what the damage would be if the information were leaked. On the other hand, the 'security first' argument can be used to justify concealment of all kinds. It can lead to experts becoming isolated, so that their know-how does not contribute to organizational decisions.

Natural enemies of transparency

Transparency gives many people easier access to previously unknown experts and to information which they did not know existed. Those who are already well informed have nothing to gain; indeed, they lose the advantage of possessing knowledge which others do not have. People who have built their internal reputations on being in the know ('Ask X, he always knows about these things') are rarely interested in a simple and comprehensive method of locating knowledge. For them, the absence of visibility is an effective aid to retaining their own power base. Transparency of information thus has its natural enemies.

Making Collective Knowledge Visible

The significance of collective knowledge

Organizational competencies cannot be explained simply as the sum of the skills of individuals.[9] WAL-MART's retailing competencies are not based entirely on the skills of its employees. The company has developed streamlined structures which also depend partly on efficient computer systems and co-operation with suppliers. It is the combination of all these elements which underlies WAL-MART's almost inimitable organizational competency. Its organizational knowledge resides in networks of relationships, secret rules of play, and widely shared values; it is also incorporated into the company's expert systems and protected rights. The organization is not itself fully aware of the significance and the interaction of these components of the collective knowledge base. WAL-MART's managers would probably find it difficult to explain their collective competencies to outsiders, or even to transfer them to a different setting.[10] A different logic must therefore be applied when dealing with organizational competencies as opposed to individual skills.

Mapping core processes

Companies are increasingly organizing themselves around core processes. At least since the appearance of the best-seller *Re-engineering the Corporation* (cf. Hammer & Champy 1993), there has been much talk of the 'process-oriented organization'. This radical change in the organization of structures and processes calls for a new approach to internal competencies. From the point of view of knowledge, the important thing is to know which experts and knowledge structures are needed to support a given core process. Competency maps can create transparency here, since in addition to locating knowledge and skills they also identify procedures, tasks, methods and responsibilities (cf. Eppler 1995). The following example shows how a competency map of this kind can be produced.

CASE STUDY: HOFFMANN-LAROCHE

Creating a competency map
HOFFMANN-LAROCHE, the well-known international pharmaceuticals company, has its headquarters in Switzerland, but operates in more than 100 countries. It specializes in medical products. The international process for licensing new drugs causes the company recurrent problems, and it used to have particular difficulties with the FDA (American Federal Drug Administration). For years, the FDA repeatedly criticized the same procedural faults, which caused unnecessary delays in the approval of new products. HOFFMANN-LAROCHE lost valuable weeks and months in the licensing process because of missing data, incomplete forms, missed deadlines and failures to carry out sets of tests. This was losing the company estimated profit of a million Swiss francs a day. It therefore set up a task force to suggest measures for expediting the approval process. In the initial phase, the following questions were asked:

- Who in our company knows what *about the requirements of the licensing procedure?*
- What are the questions which the licensing officials repeatedly ask us, and why do they do it?
- What are the critical points in the licensing process, and what mistakes have we made at those points in the past?

The FDA was defined as a customer, whose needs HOFFMANN-LAROCHE had to satisfy as well as it could. Every single step from the basic research to the final approval of a drug was analysed and evaluated. Special attention was paid to the relationships among the scientists in different departments. It turned out that there was a lack of co-ordination at many points, leading to time-consuming adjustments in later phases of the approval process. The analysis team documented the specialist activities of the researchers involved and identified areas in which the sharing of knowledge was particularly important. The management of these critical interfaces appeared to be vital in speeding up the whole process.

The results of all the analyses were combined into a knowledge map. This showed the relationships and interdependencies between development departments and individual persons within the company. The critical interactions with the FDA were also studied. The map enabled HOFFMANN-LAROCHE to shorten the development and approval times. Not all the scientists were keen to disclose their skills; nevertheless, enough information was gathered to create a comprehensive picture of the product development process and to increase the transparency of the central production process. HOFFMANN-LAROCHE plans to computerize the knowledge map to make it even easier for the individual user to identify relevant knowledge. It is expected that new product development teams will derive particular benefit from this.

The production, maintenance and further development of knowledge maps of this kind take a good deal of effort,[11] and the expected benefits to the whole organization should be carefully considered. If the map enables the company to avoid costly delays in product licensing, as in the case of HOFFMANN-LAROCHE, then even a long-term project with highly paid experts may be worthwhile. However, in many cases, less expensive means will provide sufficient transparency within a particular area of knowledge.

Access to experience gained in previous projects

Competency maps illustrate processes, and these are an important part of the organization's knowledge base. However, most of the work of big organizations is carried out in a large variety of projects, and it is difficult to keep track of them all. The success of project groups is increasingly important to the success of the whole company, because project teams are usually the organizational form chosen for working on innovations. However, projects are temporary forms of organization: when the project is completed, the members of the project team usually disperse, taking their experience of the project with them. Especially in international organizations, it is often difficult to retrieve experience gained on projects which were completed some time ago. Because projects are initiated at decentralized levels, they may be duplicated in large companies. Consultancy firms are leaders in the management of project experience because their work is always project-oriented, and access to the experience gained on previous projects is a vital success factor.

The Rapid Response Network

McKinsey developed its internal Rapid Response Network (cf. Katzenbach & Smith 1994 and Peters 1992) as a solution to this problem. The network manages the experience gained on all consultancy projects and provides users with reports and contacts for specific problems which may arise in the course of a project. The introduction of a system of this kind can help an organization in the following ways:

- It safeguards project experience by making an automatic request for 'lessons learned' at the end of each project. This is an addition to normal project procedures.
- It increases the transparency of current projects, which helps to avoid duplication and can stimulate co-operation.
- It affords direct access to project workers and their experience.

The following example shows how a worldwide industrial concern has increased the transparency of its internal product development projects.

CASE STUDY: HOLDERBANK

Improving the transparency of research around the world
HOLDERBANK, which has its head offices in Solothurn
(Switzerland), is a world leader in cement and concrete. The
management pattern is decentralized: the global network of
subsidiaries and associates enjoy far-reaching freedom of
decision, while the headquarters regards itself simply as a
provider of services. Cement, which is the group's main
product, has a long life cycle compared with other industrial
products, so there is little pressure for innovation within the
industry. This, combined with the decentralized structure of
the company, led to a situation in which the head offices
knew very little about current product development
processes in its subsidiaries around the world.

Although HOLDERBANK had more know-how than any other
company in the cement industry, it could not focus its
strengths: chances for co-operation were lost, and senior
research workers in the subsidiaries were unknown in
Switzerland. This lack of transparency was the stimulus for
developing a system to increase utilization of the global
knowledge base during product development. Harry Brantz,
a recognized developer and marketing expert, was put in
charge of the project. In a little under two years, Brantz built
up a personal network. He located key people in the
subsidiaries ('Who is responsible for product development
in your company?'); he took trouble to make the personal
acquaintance of an appropriate product developer in each
subsidiary, and to win his/her confidence. He concentrated
on the leaders of the development teams or on persons
who were so close to the decision-making process that they
had an overview of current activities.

Brantz set up personal meetings to communicate his
mission, which was to promote better sharing of product
development knowledge throughout the whole HOLDERBANK
group. The meetings also helped him to build up a basis of
trust which enabled people to work together even though
they were thousands of miles apart. Gradually, information
came in about development projects all over the world. In

the USA, for example, the use of recycled materials in concrete was being investigated; in Germany, a procedure was being developed for reducing the amount of carbon dioxide used in cement production. The full range of HOLDERBANK's activities in the product development area became visible. This was Brantz's first achievement.

In order to gain systematic access to all projects, Brantz carried out a second phase in which he asked about the exact aims and current status of the projects. It was also important to establish a uniform language for talking about the development status of widely differing projects throughout the concern. Brantz therefore developed a product development and introduction plan (PIP), which allowed product developers in different places to evaluate their projects systematically.

By the beginning of 1995, Brantz had identified 283 product development projects around the world. He classified them according to development fields (alternatives, chemicals, durability, etc.) (see Figure 5.4). This matrix made the product development efforts of the whole concern visible for the first time. It also showed points where previously isolated units might join their research efforts. In an ideal situation, the matrix might be used as follows.

A development worker in company A, who is in the initial phase (stage 1.1) of a project on 'durability', discovers that a sister company C is already handling more advanced projects (2.1, 3.2, 4.1) in this area. He or she makes direct contact with the other developer in the network, and checks on similarities between the projects and in what areas it might be useful to co-operate.

HOLDERBANK's knowledge network is still in the experimental phase. Structural, personal, political and cultural obstacles to its use are currently being evaluated. It is, however, producing good initial results. A research group has been formed from HOLDERBANK companies in Mexico, North America and Europe, with a view to carrying out a large joint project in the future. The common interests of group members were revealed through the project database. The company hopes that in future there will be more co-operation in research, that the results of development projects will be made available internationally, and that global research circles will be established to deal with special topics. This would enable the HOLDERBANK group to make even better use of its enormous competency in all areas of the cement and concrete industry.

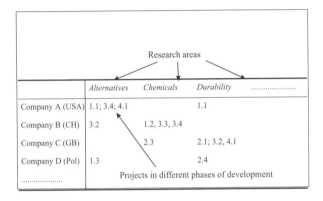

Figure 5.4 Product development matrix

Expensive systems are not always necessary; even small aids can be useful in identifying vital sources of knowledge in everyday activities. The next example is an intelligent solution of this kind.

Worldwide chart location

Consultancy firms make a living from the knowledge of their employees and the quality of their analyses and proposals. The presentation is the setting in which consulting teams communicate the results of their work to their clients. It is therefore not surprising that charts play a vital part in the daily work of large consultancy firms. They are the smallest 'units of knowledge' in the consulting industry.

Presentations must often be prepared in a short time. This means that charts – which are produced in various different offices and mostly exist only in outline – have to be completed as quickly as possible. Locating these charts is therefore of the greatest importance. Brook

Manville, the international knowledge director in MCKINSEY, has produced a solution to this problem. Every chart produced by the company's graphics experts anywhere in the world is given a code (e.g. 15-0002Y031.ZYJ), which is printed directly on to the chart. The chart can subsequently be located from anywhere in the world by means of this code. It can then be transmitted electronically to the appropriate MCKINSEY office, and developed there as necessary.

Non-material and legally protected knowledge

Companies and industries have various non-material resources which can help them to develop lasting competitive advantages (cf. Chapter 2). Many organizations have legally protected knowledge, in the form of patents, trademarks, brand names or licences. These rights are often little used, but they can be reactivated, as in the case of DOW CHEMICAL, and may then be of great value to the company.

Making informal structures visible

Patents and brand names are clear symbols of organizational knowledge; other knowledge structures, however, are more difficult to discern. Krackhardt and Hanson discuss the concept of informal organization. They describe this as a kind of central nervous system, which supports collective thinking and acting, but which is rarely understood (cf. Krackhardt & Hanson 1994, p. 16). Informal network structures can be made visible by asking employees with whom they discuss their work, whom they trust, and who gives advice to whom on professional matters.

Networks

This information can be used to draw advisory networks trust networks, and communication networks which show the various kinds of relationships in graphic form. Managers are often mistaken in their impressions of relationships, and this causes them to make serious mistakes when assembling project teams and assigning tasks.

In Figure 5.5, the arrows represent advisory relationships, e.g.

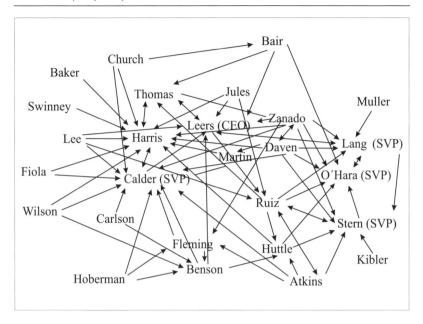

Figure 5.5 Advisory relationships in an organization. Adapted and reprinted by permission of Harvard Business Review. From 'Informal Networks: The Company Behind the Chart', by D. Krackhardt & J. R. Hanson, July/August 1994. Copyright © 1993 by the President and Fellows of Harvard College, all rights reserved

Kibler (below right) regularly asked Stern for advice when he had a problem with his work. Harris and Calder were the most frequently consulted experts in the network. However, the trust network involving the same people showed that these two were socially isolated. This had implications for the composition of project teams.

Teams as the bearers of organizational intelligence

Two teams whose members have the same formal qualifications may nevertheless differ enormously in performance. Some groups have a more intelligent approach to completing tasks or solving problems than others. Much has been written about the characteristics of high-performance teams (see e.g. Katzenbach & Smith 1994). One reason for the outstanding ability of some teams is the special quality of the relationships among the team members. Like nerve cells in the human brain, these relationships form a structure which some authors have called organizational intelligence (cf. Morgan 1986; Sandelands & Stablein 1987; Weick & Roberts 1993). The structure of relationships is difficult to describe. Weick and Roberts use the example of co-operation among different stations on an aircraft carrier to show the importance for flight safety of mutual trust among flight controllers.[12] Established flight control teams can draw on shared past experiences, and are aware of the connections between their various activities. They can thus operate at clearly lower rates of error than new teams which possess the same formal knowledge. Illness or movement of members quickly lead to an obviously lower level of 'intelligence' in teams of flight controllers. Disturbances in relationship structures can therefore easily result in serious accidents. This should provide food for thought for re-engineering experts.

Limits on transparency of collective knowledge

The performance of teams of flight controllers illustrates the limits on transparency of collective knowledge. Certain abilities of an organization are like a 'black box': one can see what abilities a group or organization possesses, but not why. The complex patterns of social behaviour make it difficult to understand. Organizations will continue to be surprised at the consequences of losing a richly networked expert.

Does this mean that understanding collective knowledge structures is impossible, and so not worth the effort? The answer is no. It is better to be aware that raising the visibility of organizational knowledge creates opportunities, but is subject to limitations. Trying to understand the 'unconscious' part of the organization's knowledge base can be useful, but it requires methods which are rarely used in companies today. Peter Scott-Morgan, an adviser in ARTHUR D. LITTLE, describes such a method in his book *The Unwritten Rules of the Game* (cf. Scott-Morgan 1994). The following example shows how these rules may operate.

Decoding the unwritten rules

A certain factory was perceived within the company as being exceptionally successful, and the employees who worked there were particularly proud of the good working atmosphere and the company image. However, it suffered a significant increase in near-accidents, *for reasons which nobody could understand.* An analysis by advisers from ARTHUR D. LITTLE showed that the increase was caused by a conflict between an unwritten rule of play and an official directive. Out of loyalty to their colleagues, employees had not reported critical incidents (the stage before near-accidents), even though officially, they were obliged to do so. There was an unwritten rule: 'Don't blow the whistle on your colleagues.' Reporting was considered tantamount to denunciation. The official rule, 'Report every critical incident', was therefore ignored. This meant that an important early warning sign for dealing with sources of danger was not operating, hence the increase in near-accidents. The situation was paradoxical: employees wanted to save their colleagues from getting into trouble, and as a result they put their own health at risk. It was only when they were made aware of the paradox that previous safety levels could be restored.

In this example, the identification of unwritten rules led to a better understanding of social dynamics within the workforce. The paradox was resolved by restoring and publicizing collective values.

Appropriate measures for creating transparency

Various techniques for creating transparency have now been described, e.g. knowledge maps (HOFFMAN-LAROCHE); advisory, trust and communication networks; research and development knowledge networks (HOLDERBANK). All these have helped to improve the visibility of organizational knowledge. However, they are not standard solutions. A medium-sized company in which all the employees know each other has no need of a rapid response network. A trust network drawn in a strongly politicized environment can be distorted because people do not trust those who produced it. It is extremely difficult to achieve genuine transparency in an environment of this kind. Large companies should consider whether the benefit to be derived from a global electronic knowledge base outweighs the expense of training, creating infrastructures, and tying up management capacity.

Ways of helping people to locate knowledge can nevertheless be found at all levels. Every employee can make his or her own skills better known, and thus more accessible to colleagues. Teams can provide information on the progress of their work. However, some measures affect the infrastructure of the company, and should therefore be implemented at organizational level. The best approach is to look for a solution which is appropriate to the context, builds on existing knowledge structures, and will not involve costs disproportionate to the expected benefit.

KNOWING WHAT IT IS THAT OTHERS KNOW

Pursuing trends in the knowledge environment

It is difficult enough for large international organizations to make their internal knowledge sufficiently visible; it can be even more difficult for them to follow developments in the external knowledge environment.[13] Many employees have no links with external experts or sources of knowledge, or they give up when faced with the flood of information. Nevertheless, companies must make sure that they know about major trends, and that they are able to identify important external experts and sources.

Knowledge selection by organizations and individuals

Individuals and organizations have developed a variety of filters which operate at the border between 'inside' and 'outside', and which allow only a part of the information available externally to pass through. These selection mechanisms protect individuals and organizations from a crippling flood of excessive stimulation. Not every applicant is interviewed; not every customer complaint will reach the product manager; not every patent that is protected somewhere in the world is checked by internal developers for its usefulness to the company. However, these natural and necessary forms of selection have their disadvantages. Organization theorists explain companies' failure or refusal to perceive certain realities in terms of cover-ups, defensive routines (cf. Probst & Büchel 1997 and Argyris 1990) or collective blind spots.[14] Rigid organizational frames of reference limit the company's search for knowledge to a few areas, which may not even be the most important ones. New sources of knowledge are thus often ignored, undervalued or simply overlooked. Individuals filter the daily flood of information and select those elements which confirm their own opinions and prejudices; psychologists call this selective perception (cf. Watzlawick, Beavin & Jackson 1993, p. 78). They describe the effects of the limited human capacity to process information in terms of selective attention (cf. Wessells 1994, p. 90).

Striking a balance

Both individuals and organizations need to achieve a balance between unhealthy and healthy ignorance, and between a stimulating and an overwhelming flow of information. The more clearly the knowledge goals are formulated and understood, the easier it is to achieve such a balance. We shall now examine the opportunities for creating better visibility of external knowledge, and the limitations on the process.

External Experts and Sources of Knowledge

Experts, professors, advisers, suppliers and customers are all bearers of knowledge; they possess competencies and information which are not necessarily present within the company. Associations of companies, archives, external data banks, specialist periodicals and the Internet are sources of knowledge which may hold information relevant to a company's problems. Time and energy are lost in trying to locate information because one asks the wrong people, or tries the wrong sources. The aims of the search for information are often vaguely formulated, or the seeker lacks experience in dealing with external experts and sources of knowledge.

Aids to dealing with the flood of external information

In large organizations, special centres have developed to support internal requests for information. Smaller companies, however, can rarely afford this luxury. They must often turn to external sources of help such as business consultants, market research organizations or other specialists, to gain access to the knowledge they need. This niche has been filled by knowledge brokers. They keep track of the kinds of knowledge which small and medium-sized companies cannot afford to pursue for themselves, and offer services such as patent research or finding partners for co-operative ventures.

Technology scouts help companies to find partners

STAEHLER is a medium-sized company located in Stade, in northern Germany. It was seeking an inexpensive substance for removing graffiti from underground stations, concrete walls and lift doors. The company was not large enough to afford an expensive research and development department, so it needed to find a partner with a product which could be sold under licence, or willing to co-operate in producing one. STAEHLER did not have sufficient resources to locate such a partner through its own efforts, though it was almost certain that the product it wanted must exist somewhere on the world market. It therefore employed a specialized technology scout, who used the Internet, CD-ROMs and relevant reference works to search the patent market. STAEHLER was put in touch with the Scottish company DECORARC LTD. DECORARC had developed a substance which not only removed existing graffiti, but also sealed the surface so that new graffiti would not stick. Without the services of the knowledge broker, the two companies would probably never have known that they had a common interest.

Listening posts

One way of identifying new developments as they appear is to maintain listening posts. Scientists, journalists and politicians who operate in special fields can be valuable sources of information on new trends. Contacts of this kind are institutionalized in many ways. Managers of the Swiss chemical multinational CIBA-GEIGY, for example, meet regularly to discuss new ideas with representatives of environmental organizations such as GREENPEACE, people who live near industrial installations, and local politicians. These 'risk dialogues' serve to identify the needs of important interest groups and build trust between them. Other organizations hold expert hearings on selected topics to gain in-depth understanding of new trends and to discuss them with outside experts.

Contacts with think-tanks

Contacts with think-tanks or think factories,[15] or with university departments, ensure that companies stay close to new technologies and theories which might in the long term help them to improve their own competencies. These contacts may be maintained on an informal basis or through joint projects or research contracts. Technical universities wishing to show their involvement with the world of applied technology, such as the FRAUENHOFER institutes of applied research, become trend seekers for the organizations which co-operate with them.

Transparency of outside partners

It is also important to monitor the competencies of suppliers and other service providers, especially in the area of information technology. As a result of massive outsourcing, many organizations have made themselves extremely dependent on external partners. Lean management policies have even led some companies to outsource parts of their core competencies. The monitoring of developments in key partner companies is therefore more important than ever to their own success. In the car industry, leading manufacturers carry out regular checks on the production processes of their suppliers – already carefully selected – to make sure that it would not be more efficient to produce the parts themselves.

Knowing the competencies of consultants

Consultants are the big winners of the 1980s and 1990s. Organizations have entrusted them with increasingly novel areas of management activity. In many companies, it is unusual for an important project to be started without the support of an external consultancy firm. Consultants have a special role in developing future competitiveness in the face of increasing pressure; companies are therefore anxious to know what the consultants can do before they commit themselves. Uncritical acceptance of these 'prophets of efficiency' seems to be a thing of the past; many companies now require detailed presentations, or make much more thorough enquiries about which consultants can best provide particular forms of expertise. Caution has reached a stage where contracts are no longer simply handed over to one of the big companies; people will now ask directly for Ms X, because it is known that she has handled similar business successfully in the past, or that she fits in with the company's internal culture. Consultancy firms react to these new demands for transparency by publishing details of their expertise in periodicals, at conferences, or in management hand-books;[16] this represents a deliberate move away from the low profile which they cultivated previously. It is also worth noting that many managers now bring consultants into the company not because they have superior skills, but in order to have someone to blame if things go wrong.

Building External Networks

Networks

Networks are an important aid to identifying experts and sources of knowledge. A network is characterized by a basic common interest among its members, a personal orientation and voluntary participation. The relationships among the participants are based on the exchange principle. Communication in networks therefore follows completely different rules from the 'regulated' exchange of information in companies with a hierarchical structure (cf. Boos, Exner & Heitger 1994).

Expert networks

Expert networks have developed in many areas of our society. They do not coincide with the boundaries of organizations or industries. As a source of information and contacts, they often provide their members with decisive informational advantages. The mutual trust which is built up and strengthened through personal contacts permits an informal and direct style of communication. This helps the members of the network to find their bearings in a rapidly changing environment. The system only functions when each person contributes his own knowledge, which for the others represents external knowledge. Networks are therefore polycentric structures which do not disintegrate when individual members are lost.

The problem for many organizations is that insufficient use is made of these expert networks. Organizations are often ignorant of their existence, of the areas of knowledge with which they deal, and of the fact that their own employees are members of multiple networks. Once relevant networks have been identified, efforts can be made to join them. Companies have a lot to learn from lobbyists and diplomats in this respect. The success of alumni networks (academic connections, alumni of American business schools, ex-McKINSEY employees) shows how networks can help people to master the increasing complexity of the external world.

Using a 'scene' network

Consider a European music producer looking for new rap talent in New York. Every day he reads special music magazines and contacts agencies, event organizers, fans, artists and colleagues from competing companies (who give him tips, thus building up mutual dependencies). He may have more in common with these people than with most of his colleagues in his own company. The 'scene' network provides him with a variety of opinions on the current rap scene; these help him to make a qualified selection and to identify interesting groups before approaching them directly. However, it is difficult to pass on all these contacts to others, because getting into the network takes time, and not everyone can do it. Especially in times of increasing movement of employees, it can be difficult to introduce new members of the organization satisfactorily into the complex network of relationships established by their predecessors. The organization thus loses quick and effective access to important reserves of knowledge which lie outside its own limits.

Networking with the external knowledge environment is an effective element in integrated knowledge management. It facilitates identification of high-quality sources and experts.

The Internet: The Universal Search Medium?

The Internet as an instrument of transparency

The Internet offers yet another way of identifying external information and sources of knowledge. It has developed rapidly since 1969, when it was established by the US Ministry of Defense to ensure communication between strategic points in the event of an atomic war. The system is now accessible to everyone. Its decentralized network, which joins different communications centres, today connects about 50 000 smaller computer networks and 5 million computers, and has about 30 million users worldwide.[17] At the heart of the Internet is the World Wide Web, which uses HTML (hyper-text mark-up language) to provide a single standard for the user-friendly transmission of text, graphics, sound and even videos. Individuals, universities and other state and private organizations have set up home pages in the World Wide Web to distribute information or to offer products or services to Web surfers.

Limitations of the Internet

For many users, the initial euphoria has dissipated. Searching for information on the World Wide Web proved ineffective and extremely time-consuming. It was almost impossible to find answers to specific questions. In the hypertext structure of the network, the user jumped from one Internet address to another. It could take hours to download interesting information, and the computer was blocked during this time.

Improved access to Internet sources

Light, however, is shining through the chaos. It is now becoming easier to search effectively for sources of information. On-line services such as AMERICA ONLINE, COMPUSERVE and MICROSOFT NETWORK structure the information market for their customers. They classify and update the immense flood of information and help their users to navigate it. Search engines help by combing the Internet with high-performance computers (web servers) to locate new information. Their real task is then to structure the masses of information in a meaningful way. The popular search engine YAHOO![18] has a web catalogue with over 12 000 categories into which the 20 employees organize the flood of new material to assist the 200 000 people who use the service every day. Like many other services, YAHOO! is hindered by its limited processing capacity, which can result in long wait times for the user.

Intelligent agents

Search engines or web robots belong to the wider class of intelligent agents. These are computer programs which carry out independent activities according to criteria supplied by the user. They may scan net news for particular keywords, obtain pages of interest and copy them on to the user's hard disk. They can provide an early indication of important trends, or filter the user's e-mail, thus preventing him or her from being overwhelmed by massive quantities of data. The intelligent agents of the future will be able to work even more closely to interests of their customers, who will be able to specify areas in which they want regular updates on the Internet. The navigation software (e.g. NETSCAPE, recognized as the market standard) is increasingly user-friendly and is now integrated into other applications. Downloading times will be shortened by rapid improvements in the performance of networks and hardware.

A meaningful Internet strategy

These trends mean that an increasing number of organizations will be able to make effective use of Internet resources. It will be possible to access external sources of knowledge rapidly from any PC in the network. In some areas of knowledge, public data banks have been established which are superior to traditional information services, archives and libraries. Swiss-Prot, for example, is a Swiss database which provides a 'Who's Who' of proteins. More than 52 000 proteins are described and illustrated, and can be downloaded in the form of three-dimensional graphics, with all supplementary information. In 1995, more than 200 000 researchers, doctors, laboratories, companies and students used this service, which is provided by the University of Geneva and the Cantonal Hospital.

The Internet is a new communications medium which offers another way of accessing and exchanging computerized data and information of all kinds; but it is nothing more than this. Like all other media (telephone, fax, conferences, etc.), it must be used in a meaningful fashion to achieve specified goals. It is of most use to those who already know more or less what they are looking for; it uses high-performance metamedia to offer them rapid access to information that they can use to improve their own competencies. Those who think that the Internet will solve all their problems are heading for disappointment. Many people still seem to have grossly exaggerated expectations.

Intranet

Many organizations use Internet technology to construct intranets. Internal documents such as market studies, the in-house magazine, yearly reports, presentations and press articles are entered on computers which are set up for the purpose, and can then be accessed by the employees. Effective intranets permit the user to research the company's internal computerized databases, thus providing rapid access to information internal to the company.

Protecting the intranet

Some pioneering companies have had to pay the price of not giving their intranet enough protection from the Internet. Lack of protection gives experienced hackers an opportunity to obtain confidential company information. According to HEWLETT PACKARD, the key factor in protecting internal data is the network configuration.[19] Figure 5.6 shows a configuration which distinguishes three network areas:

- The public network, with access to the full range of Internet services
- A private area on the Internet, which each employee can set up as he or she wishes
- The company's internal network, protected by firewalls

Home pages

Many organizations use home pages to introduce themselves on the Internet.[20] These pages provide interested outsiders with a quick and simple overview of the organization's activities. Home pages differ widely in quality; they can be worlds apart. In future, many of the

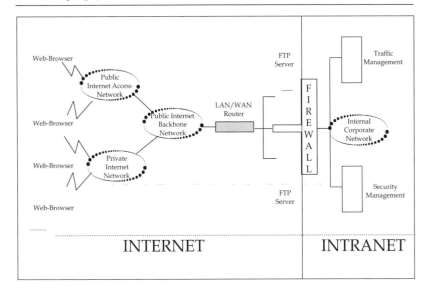

Figure 5.6 Relationships between intranet and Internet[18]

activities involved in maintaining the organization's external image could be carried out via this medium.

KNOWLEDGE GAPS

Consequences

The creation of knowledge inventories and knowledge transparency is not an end in itself. It only makes sense from the point of view of the goals of the organization. In our model of integrated knowledge management, the pursuit of transparency is guided by the knowledge goals described in Chapter 4. The outcome may take the form of increased knowledge about internal experts and their abilities, or an understanding of internal processes which support organizational competencies. The organization must not lose these existing competencies; it should find ways to secure them (Chapter 10: Preserving Knowledge).

The organization's interaction with its knowledge environment exposes its internal knowledge gaps and skills deficits. External

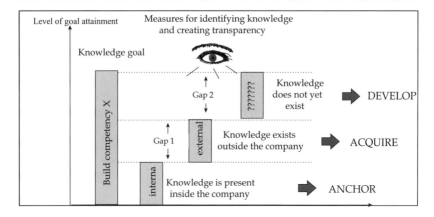

Figure 5.7   Types of knowledge gaps

sources of knowledge can be evaluated according to their contribution to developing the desired competencies. Analysing the competition can also lead to identification of best practices. This process is usually called external benchmarking. However, benchmarking can only close gap number 1 in Figure 5.7. Catch-up learning of this kind is seldom sufficient to build up organizational competencies that are difficult to imitate. These should be tackled by knowledge acquisition (recruitment, co-operation, imitation). The real challenge is to close gap number 2. This can be achieved through a range of knowledge development activities (research, market studies, quality circles, etc.).

Acquire or develop?

Once a company has recognized the gaps in its own knowledge and skills, it knows where to make a start on acquiring and developing knowledge. Do we need an external instructor for sales training, or do we have enough resources to do it properly ourselves? Should we give an external laboratory a contract to develop an intermediate product, or can our own research and development department do it? Should the new factory in China be developed by a relatively inexperienced young manager, or should we engage a different manager for a while? Shall we pay an external information service to provide us with concise information about the industry, or shall we let our managers choose for themselves? Shall we continue to do our own pure research, or shall we set up joint projects with universities? The basic decision in all these cases is: Shall we build up our own knowledge internally, or shall we use other (external) resources?

Conscious knowledge decisions

An excellent consultant might provide the desired information more quickly, and, at the end of the day, more cheaply. However, people who always turn to experts to sort out their difficulties may eventually lose the ability to think for themselves. Our discussion of the significance of acquiring, maintaining and developing organizational competencies has shown that decisions about importing knowledge or exporting skills cannot be made simply in the light of short-term financial considerations. Over-readiness to resort to outsourcing and a 'lean is beautiful' policy can be dangerous. An organization which contracts out its research to third parties may decrease its personnel costs in the short term, but even in the medium term it may find itself robbed of its unique product strengths. At the very least, it makes itself dependent on outsiders. Decisions on knowledge acquisition and knowledge development should be made in full awareness of these issues. To reduce the risk of making wrong decisions and possibly doing irreparable damage, knowledge managers should be aware of the general opportunities and dangers associated with acquiring knowledge as opposed to developing it. They need to know about possible approaches and appropriate instruments. Summaries may be found in Chapter 6 (on knowledge development) and Chapter 7 (on knowledge acquisition).

SUMMARY

- Organizations often know little about their internal skills, experts and networks; this hinders selective development of organizational competencies.
- Decentralization, globalization, lean management, restructuring and increasing employee fluctuation have decreased the internal transparency of many organizations.
- Internal and external networks permit rapid and effective location of information and experts. More use should be made of them.

- Organizations do not usually have persons or institutions charged with the task of increasing company-wide transparency of knowledge.
- Organizations need to find a healthy balance between ignorance on the one hand and excessive curiosity on the other.
- Information is increasingly something that employees have to find for themselves. The ability to handle the flood of information is becoming a key qualification. Organizations should support their employees by providing an infrastructure which will help them to find their bearings both inside and outside the company.
- Visibility of knowledge exposes existing gaps and helps organizations to decide between acquiring knowledge and developing it themselves.
- The worldwide exchange of computerized texts, graphics, etc., and the opportunities offered by the Internet, provide completely new search strategies and offer users who know what they are seeking a powerful means of locating external information and experts.

KEY QUESTIONS

- Do you know the internal experts in your company, and can you contact them easily?
- Do you often come across knowledge gaps? How often has the knowledge needed for important decisions been available in principle, but was not known about or not obtainable when it was needed?
- Do you know what projects are in progress in your company at the moment?
- How do you decide who is allowed to know how much? If information is held back, is it for security reasons, or because of excessive secretiveness?
- What systems are available to support you in your search for information? Are instruments such as knowledge maps in use?
- Do you have an Internet search strategy, or people who can help you to search?

6
Acquiring Knowledge

INTRODUCTION

We cannot acquire fluency in a foreign language by going out
and buying it. Companies, however, can buy knowledge in ways
that are not open to individuals. They can search the labour
markets for people with exactly the right skills – skills that the
company could not develop through its own efforts. They can
recruit experts, consultants or whole teams to fill internal
knowledge gaps. Unfortunately, investments such as these often
bring poor results. The experts once recruited may be avoided
and shunned by other employees. Consultants' reports may be
put into a drawer and forgotten. The newly acquired knowledge
is often incompatible with existing expertise, and so it is
rejected. We shall now consider how you can integrate 'outside'
knowledge into your company's knowledge base, how you can
use your customers as a source of information, and what
difficulties you may encounter when you recruit experts from
outside. We shall also discuss the effects of knowledge products
on the company's freedom of enterprise.

ACQUIRING KNOWLEDGE

The front line

We wanted to reorganize production on a process basis. We brought consultants in because they have theoretical knowledge and practical experience that we did not have in the company. Working with them was a lot of fun. We learned a lot, and the whole team believed that we would succeed. However, when the consultants left, the dynamism soon died down. Out of a hundred ideas for projects that we worked out together last year, only five remain, and even those five are losing momentum now. (*Manager of an industrial firm*)

We have a recruitment crisis. We get thousands of applications, but the best people don't apply to us. They never come on the market, because they are recruited while they are still students by consultancy firms, investment banks and a few big industrial companies. (*Personnel manager of a national commercial chain*)

We embarked on a joint venture with one of our competitors. We wanted to learn about a new technology, and our partners wanted to use our sales network. At the same time, we were developing a similar technology in our own company. This soon led to suspicion, and both sides became defensive. As a result, the joint venture eventually failed. (*Employee working on a joint venture*)

Growing importance of knowledge markets

The economic principle of division of labour holds true for knowledge too. Because of the rapid growth and fragmentation of knowledge, companies are often unable to develop for themselves the know-how that they need. Extra knowledge must therefore be acquired somehow. New technologies are developed in universities, state research institutions, and specialized private companies. Software, logistics systems and many other intelligent products are developed by outside agencies and offered for sale. Companies must still acquire capital and raw materials efficiently on traditional markets; now, they must also make the right choices on the knowledge markets, to gain access to essential experts and expertise. Companies may acquire the following on external knowledge markets:[1]

- The knowledge of external experts
- The knowledge of other firms
- The knowledge of stakeholders, e.g. customers
- Knowledge products

Features of knowledge markets

Knowledge markets are far from perfect. Their market transparency is usually minimal. The 'products' on offer are frequently extremely difficult to compare with each other, and trade is often in ideas that have potential rather than in ideas that have already been capitalized. The relationships between those seeking knowledge and those offering it are often personal, and are based on trust built up over a long period. This trust is necessary because the buyer does not always have the ability to evaluate the goods, and can only reach a considered judgement some time later.

Another peculiarity of the trade in knowledge is that in many cases, the most interesting items never appear on the official markets. Exceptionally gifted young scientists do not write applications, and revolutionary production processes are licensed long before they become operational. Other knowledge products bypass the open market in similar ways.

Successful acquisition of knowledge thus has a logic of its own. Would-be purchasers must play by different rules from those which apply to procuring the classic inputs. A few basic thoughts will help us to understand why it is often so difficult to import knowledge from outside the company.

Rejection of external expertise

Organizations and people have a basic stock of relatively safe knowledge that helps them to find their bearings in everyday situations. This everyday knowledge stabilizes our expectations and offers security. Importing new knowledge destabilizes this security, and often evokes strong emotions and defensive reactions within an organization. New

employees who do not fit the usual images, e.g. women in top management positions, or management experts as research leaders, have serious difficulties to overcome. Similarly, the ideas of external experts
may conflict with the results of internal studies, thus discrediting the
authors of the latter, or making them look foolish. Production licences
bought from outside destroy jobs in internal product development.
There is a complex set of interdependencies between inside and outside which determine how external knowledge will be received.
External discoveries are frequently rejected by product development
workers; this has been described as the 'not invented here syndrome'.[2]
Where this happens, an expensive internal development is preferred
to a cheaper, and possibly better, product from outside. This hinders
outsourcing of non-central development or value-creation activities.

Potential of investments

Importing different kinds of external competency pays off at different
rates. It may be years before the appointment of a young researcher
or an inexperienced but gifted manager brings results, because it takes
years for them to gain the experience they need to be high performers.
A company may have great difficulty in assessing what it is likely to
gain from the potential of a promising employee (see Figure 6.1). It
is much easier to estimate the output of a programmer who can write
a relatively constant number of lines per day in a special programming
language.

The risks of potential

What is true of people is also true of projects and non-material goods.
The effects of commissioning a consultancy project on internal culture
are much more difficult to predict than the effects of a routine analysis
of office overheads. Acquiring a patent for a piece of pure research
may secure a future market, but a licence to use a brand name in
Europe brings an immediate benefit. Who can say whether a patent
obtained today will really yield a product of marketable standard in
five years' time? This uncertainty makes it especially difficult to justify the acquisition of potential benefits. It is even more difficult if the
company's goal system has a short-term focus.

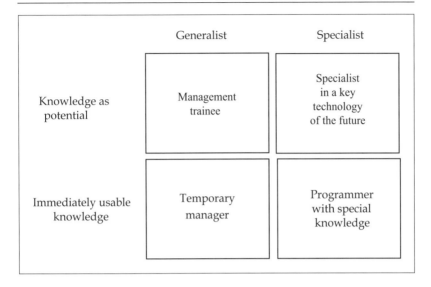

Figure 6.1 Types of knowledge holder

Making investments pay

We should therefore make a general distinction between investing in the future (acquiring potential) and investing in the present (acquiring immediately usable knowledge). Integrated knowledge management must employ suitable methods to support both kinds of investment. When formulating and monitoring knowledge goals, companies should bear in mind the likely differences in pay-off times between these different kinds of knowledge investment.

Role of the internal context

Standard formulae for acquiring knowledge are dangerous. American management researchers are particularly fond of them,[3] even though uncritical acceptance of standard solutions – such as decentralization, globalization, process orientation – is perilous. The attractiveness of standard formulae often rests on unreliable generalizations, which give a false impression that the authors have discovered universal truths. In individual cases, however, standard solutions have only a limited usefulness. When taken out of context, management ideas, skills and knowledge often lose their power to solve problems, thus losing their value. Knowledge is always tied to a particular context, and can only be extracted from it, or transferred to another, in a fragmentary fashion (cf. Müller-Stewens & Osterloh 1996 and Barney 1991). A Japanese sales genius will not automatically be a great sensation in the USA, and a consultancy firm that has been successful in the cement industry may have some difficulty in entering the media market. It may be better for a company to apply knowledge that already exists in its environment intelligently to its own history and competencies than to try to copy someone else's success story.

Absorptive capacity

The ability to use existing knowledge is described by Cohen and Levinthal as the 'absorptive capacity' of organizations (1990, p. 131). In their field research, they made the surprising observation that the main activity of many research and development departments lay not in developing new procedures and products, but in the intelligent acquisition of external knowledge. Research workers were more likely to find solutions by studying the specialist literature than by experimenting in their laboratories. This research highlights the enormous significance and the special potential of acquiring knowledge externally. The pursuit and adaptation of external technological trends thus become an important part of the work of research and development departments.[4] Before very specific knowledge is acquired, however, its suitability for supporting the company's goals must be checked. Uncritical import of knowledge can lead to rejection by the organization.

Outsourcing as substitution

Outsourcing, lean management, and make-or-buy are ways in which companies can try to optimize selected links in their value-creation chains. The basic idea is to entrust value-creating activities to market partners who can produce a better-quality result, or do the work more cheaply or more quickly. From the point of view of knowledge management, outsourcing may be described as substituting external know-how for internal know-how. Substitutions of this kind should not be made simply to save money in the short term, since they can have other consequences. Engaging an outside company to clean the building will not normally have any drastic effects. However, a company can seriously weaken its core competencies by outsourcing all its logistics, or the production of intelligent components[5] (cf. Chapter 4).

We shall now describe in more detail the main potential sources of external knowledge.

BRINGING EXPERTS TO THE COMPANY

Recruitment

As a rule, companies employ people in order to use their skills to manufacture products or provide services. People with skills to offer and people who need those skills find each other on various labour markets. The process of recruiting experts is a vitally important part of an integrated knowledge management policy, since appointing people with certain kinds of expertise involves deciding what kinds of competencies the company will develop.

Linking recruitment to knowledge goals

The recruitment policy should therefore be closely linked to strategic knowledge goals. Many companies put a great deal of effort into recruitment, using multi-stage selection procedures and staff-intensive testing methods (assessment centres etc.). In spite of all this, personnel officers are often dissatisfied with the abilities of those they select (cf. Risch & Sommer 1996). The 'ideal candidate' often turns out to be unsuitable as a banker, or the programming specialist cannot communicate with the customers and requires expensive training.

Vague candidate profiles

Candidate profiles are often imprecise. Companies in different branches of industry differ widely in organization, culture and activities, yet their advertisements for staff are very similar. The ideal candidate is often described in vague, woolly terms.[6] Taking the time to translate normative and strategic knowledge goals into clear search profiles (see building block 'Defining knowledge goals') pays off at this point. Companies can only search the labour market systematically and act proactively if they have a clear picture of what they are looking for.

CASE STUDY: BERTELSMANN

Proactive recruitment

BERTELSMANN[7] is a media company with a proactive recruitment strategy. The company is decentralized into largely autonomous profit centres. To ensure that these centres contain sufficient management potential, it seeks highly gifted, self-reliant young people who can work under stress. Finding entrepreneurial talent of this kind is a high priority. Even the vice-presidents and the CEO are involved in the process.

The qualities of currently successful employees yield a relatively clear skills profile for potential employees. Whatever candidates have attempted, they must have shown determination in driving it forward and bringing it to a successful conclusion. The company looks for evidence of enterprise in the lives of future employees. Rather than relying on detailed applications, it puts a great deal of effort into broadening areas of contact so as to identify suitable people in advance of the applications process. With the assistance of previous graduates, professors, and other contacts, selected educational establishments are systematically searched for candidates with the right potential. The system permits competent (and often exclusive) contact with candidates, and acquaintance without obligation before the application process starts.

Significance of the applicant profile

The fight for the best grows fiercer, and companies should set themselves realistic recruitment goals. State authorities follow current trends by seeking entrepreneurial talent, but they do themselves no favours if they recruit people whose skills they cannot use. The candidate profile should therefore be carefully prepared, and should concentrate on the competencies which the organization wishes to develop in the long term. McKINSEY, for example, wished to strengthen its expertise in chemistry, so in 1994, its German talent seekers bought up a large share of the available chemists who had obtained a doctorate 'summa cum laude' (cf. Balzer & Wilhelm 1995).

Diversity recruiting

The question of equal employment opportunities for ethnic groups in the USA has caused management literature to focus on diversity in organizations. Diversity recruiting means the appointment of employees with widely different professional and cultural backgrounds. The policy is thought likely to bring new backgrounds, approaches and values into organizations. This variety can help an organization to consider problems from several different points of view, thus leading perhaps to a better formulation of knowledge goals. At the same time, the organization gains more transparency of knowledge regarding the sections of the population from which their new employees come. The policy carries potential for conflict, making internal routines more visible and causing questioning of things that were previously accepted; however, it is claimed that the increase in internal diversity can ultimately improve the effectiveness and reactivity of the whole organization (cf. Schneider 1997). A private bank, for instance, which in the past has appointed only economists and lawyers, may find that recruiting a Sinologist or a physicist brings fresh approaches to its Far East activities or its technological pursuits, and it thus closes gaps in its knowledge.

Headhunting

Companies which cannot develop special knowledge for themselves, or do not wish to do so, must buy it on external markets. In the USA, the movement of individual researchers, or even of whole research teams, from universities to the laboratories of drugs companies is an everyday occurrence (cf. Schülin 1995, p. 306). However, trying to recruit the employees of other companies is still considered unacceptable behaviour in many areas of industry. Some industries even have rules, and impose sanctions on aggressive recruitment, thus preventing key experts from being bought or increasing their income by bargaining. However, gentlemen's agreements of this kind can no longer necessarily be relied upon, as illustrated by the sudden move to VOLKSWAGEN of López, the purchasing manager at GENERAL MOTORS. Good people in executive positions receive calls and offers from headhunters at least once a month. Headhunting is now an established occupation. Recruitment agencies cannot take over the appointment decisions, but they can locate companies' blind spots, and thus improve their selection process. Headhunters and personnel advice bureaux thus improve transparency and create efficient labour markets in various segments. They also make the competition for the best even fiercer. Legal requirements are no longer much of an obstacle to changing jobs, and many firms are more willing to accept some conflict in times of fierce competition. However, companies do need to consider not only how to attract new experts, but also how to keep the ones they have.

Limited contracts

Temporary contracts are an interesting alternative to the traditional permanent appointments. Particular skills are often in short supply only in the short or medium term. Temporary managers or contract agencies can help companies through the bottleneck. Some skills rapidly lose their value, or are of uncertain significance for the future of the company; in these circumstances, limited contracts are an attractive way to secure the knowledge in the medium term.

The kinds of experts who are employed on limited contracts will thus have less job security. This means that in future, the number of permanent knowledge employees will fall, since more people will become entrepreneurs in their own field. Contractors must market their own services, and anticipate future needs. It is essential for them to maintain and develop their portfolio of skills, since it is this which enables them to survive on knowledge markets, and will enable them to do so in the future. Companies can use these markets to fill their knowledge gaps selectively, without having to enter long-term employment contracts.

Specialized and general consultants

Business consultancy follows similar principles. Specialized consultancy firms employ a number of experts whose skills could not be used by a single company. If companies make selective use of these specialists, they gain access to high-quality expertise without the disadvantages involved in making a permanent appointment. Consultancy contracts can also include success-related categories. Patent lawyers, engineers' offices and network supervisors are consultants of this kind. General consultants often offer a more general service, and may concentrate on strategy development or organizational structure. In these areas, the import of knowledge is less specific in nature. A company which employs general consultants is buying itself some extra problem-solving capacity for the duration of the contract. The value of this extra capacity depends on the quality of the consultancy team and the use made of the consultancy firm's global knowledge base.

Boom in consultancy

The rapid growth in the consultancy market – in knowledge management as in other areas – indicates that consultancy is becoming an increasingly important way for companies to import knowledge. One consequence of this is that some of the top experts in various industries are no longer working in the traditional way, but are selling their experience by working as consultants. They can often earn more that way. Many organizations have become dependent on their consultants, and now seem incapable of making important decisions without their advice. The consultants are usually interested in follow-up contracts, so companies should look carefully at the reasons why they need them.

TAPPING EXTERNAL KNOWLEDGE BASES

Forms of co-operation

Another way of acquiring knowledge is through forms of company organization. Rather than recruiting individual experts or 'renting' their expertise for a while, companies can gain access to the knowledge bases of others by setting up various forms of co-operation. The co-operative forms shown in Figure 6.2 give some idea of the options for acquiring knowledge in this way (based on the diagram in Müller-Stewens & Gocke 1995).

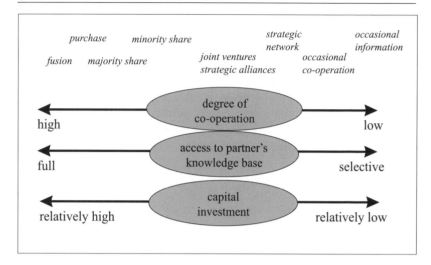

Figure 6.2   The co-operation continuum

Taking over hot shops

Large companies that are having internal difficulties with innovation often choose the most radical way of acquiring knowledge, namely, acquisitions. In recent years, Wall Street has seen a wave of take-overs of small communications companies by large, established companies such as MICROSOFT or IBM. The large companies hoped to secure access to Internet products of the future, and to acquire gifted product developers and programmers from the hot shops for their own strategic projects. However, when they tried to integrate these people into their own organizations, their creativity dwindled, and the best of them left the company. In the worst scenario, they left to form a rival company. Taking over the whole knowledge base of another company, with all rights of access, can devalue and destroy that knowledge base by precipitating a brain drain (cf. Schülin 1995, p. 308).

Selective closing of knowledge gaps

Acquiring small, innovative companies is often a way of investing in potential. Take-overs can also close particular knowledge gaps. Under favourable circumstances, acquiring a trading company with an established sales network in a particular market can dramatically improve the purchasing company's chances in that market. It profits from distribution capabilities which have been built up over a long period. In practice, however, the outcome is not generally so favourable, since the cultures or competencies of the two companies often prove incompatible. Where this happens, two knowledge bases in combination add up to less than the two when kept separate. Competencies are destroyed.

Importance of the take-over process

The way in which the take-over is conducted is critical to the future use of the acquired knowledge base. An unfriendly take-over is often followed by lengthy internal power struggles, which destroy part of the acquired company's knowledge base. Employees who feel they have been 'sold' may not be willing to make their expertise available to the new owners; in extreme cases, they may use it for sabotage or disinformation. These phenomena are part of the well-known 'merger syndrome'; they should be taken into account when plans are made to take over the knowledge base of another company.

Strategic alliances

Take-overs are only one of the ways of acquiring knowledge that belong to other companies. Most firms now choose less radical forms of co-operation, which often involve a lower level of risk and less financial commitment. Strategic alliances, in which the participants commit themselves to common goals, are a popular form of co-operation. Each partner company can partly compensate for its own weakness by acquiring the other's physical resources, markets, know-how or capital (cf. Probst & Büchel 1997, p. 134).

Product links

There are various kinds of strategic alliance. 'Product links', for instance, can be used to fill gaps in a company's product range.[8] The partners in the product link use each other's know-how, and this helps them to counter the increasing mobility of knowledge. The aims of product links are to reduce costs and risks, shorten the time to market, control movement of knowledge, and watch and neutralize the competition. Product links lead to short-term advantages rather than long-term increases in the expertise of a company.

Knowledge links

Knowledge links are a form of co-operation which goes somewhat further.[9] Mutual learning and acquisition of knowledge are declared aims of the relationship. This distinguishes knowledge links from other types of co-operation, which are based on strategic interests such as economies of scale. IBM, for example, strengthens its own strategic competencies by forming multiple knowledge links with partners in different fields, e.g. universities, unions, competitors. Managers should remember the following rules when setting up knowledge links:[10]

- Before entering the alliance, make sure you have a clear strategic understanding of the current competencies of your own company, and that you know which ones it will need in the future.
- Before entering the alliance, consider plenty of other possible alliances.
- Before entering an alliance, examine critically the values, the commitment and the competencies of the potential partner.
- Understand the risks of opportunism, leakage of knowledge, and gradual wear and ageing.
- Avoid over-dependency on alliances.
- Structure and conduct your company's alliances as separate companies.
- Build mutual trust between the partners.
- Change the core activities and the traditional organization of your company so as to make it open to the learning processes taking place in the alliances.
- Lead the alliance, do not manage it.

BRINGING STAKEHOLDER KNOWLEDGE INTO THE COMPANY

Management of stakeholder knowledge

External knowledge can be acquired by selective and careful management of contacts with the company's stakeholders. Stakeholders are the groups in the environment who have particular interests in the company's activities, or make particular demands on it (cf. Bleicher 1992, pp. 105, 139). The knowledge potential and knowledge assets of these groups are of the greatest importance for the company, though the particular relevance of individual groups depends heavily on the organizational context and the field of knowledge in question. The most important stakeholders mentioned in the literature are usually customers, suppliers, owners, employees/employees' representatives, politicians, media and opinion leaders, the financial world and the general public (see Figure 6.3).

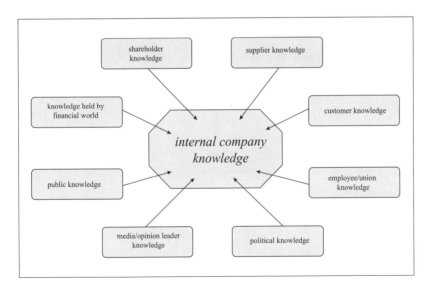

Figure 6.3 Stakeholder relationships

Example: acquiring knowledge from customers

Import channels

Establishing import channels for stakeholder knowledge is an important element in the 'knowledge acquisition' building block of knowledge management. Any stakeholder group can be important; we shall discuss customers as an example.

Knowing about customers

Traditionally, analysis of demand for products is one of the three main fields of market research activity.[11] It involves ascertaining income level and consumption in households, examining purchasing habits and mapping the distribution of demand across the sales area. Key functions of market research are to calculate elasticities of price, advertising and income (cf. Wöhe 1990, p. 663). Companies need this information to work the market successfully, and many specialist institutions now exist to supply it to them.

What customers know

Companies also need access to the knowledge and beliefs held by their customers. The innovation researcher von Hippel has pointed out that customer ideas are now the main source of innovation for companies in the processing industry.[12]

Use of key customers

Key customers, that is, customers who are particularly intensive users of a product, often know more about its strengths and weaknesses in daily use than the people who developed it. Some car manufacturers have set up 'customer workshops', where certain customers are invited to work with designers on factors which are difficult to measure, such as smell or acoustics. The designers thus learn from regular users how the lock should click when the door is shut, or how the car interior should smell. In Japan, powerful product managers are responsible for the whole production process from the initial concept to the mass production of a new car (cf. Clark & Fujimoto 1992, p. 252). These 'heavyweight' product managers follow their customers into department stores, museums and discotheques, and form an overall picture of them based on their own observations as well as on quantitative marketing data. Observing customers when they are using the product gives product managers ideas for layout, design or other features which influence purchasing behaviour, and promotes a fuller understanding of complex customer needs. In HILTI, it is the mechanics who pick up useful ideas during their many customer contacts; they then pass the ideas on to the research and development department.

Involvement in customer activities

METTLER-TOLEDO, a manufacturer of precision weighing scales, arranged for the developers of the next generation of the product to work in a large bakery for a week. When the developers had to use the scales every day, they found weaknesses that had not been mentioned in customer surveys. One problem was that the fresh bread dough stuck fast to particular parts of the scales, and was extremely difficult to remove. The various discoveries were fed directly back into the next generation of the product.

Involving the customer in the development process

Dissatisfied customers can be seen either as a thorn in the flesh or as a source of valuable information about customer needs and product features. A printer manufacturer invited an argumentative customer who complained constantly to work occasionally with the development team on the next generation of printers. By involving the troublemaker in this way, the manufacturer gained prompt and competent feedback on customer needs, and was able to incorporate many of his ideas into the new prototype.

Pilot projects

Pilot projects are another way for producers to benefit from customer knowledge. Especially when products are not yet mature, companies are dependent on customers who are prepared to take part in pilot projects. Knowledgeable input from pilot customers is particularly important for software companies; modifications based on customer feedback can then be built in before the final version is launched. A common method is to release 'beta versions' on the Internet. Users can then load the prototype of a new piece of software on to their own computers, and the developers receive free feedback from computer enthusiasts all over the world.

Understanding customer language

If a company wishes to satisfy the needs of its customers, it must know what those needs are, and be prepared to use customers' ideas. Basic to all this is the ability to communicate with clients in a meaningful language. It is not just a case of hitting the right note with the advertising messages. Customers must also feel that they are understood when they make enquiries or complaints. TELTECH found an effective way of studying customer language.

CASE STUDY: TELTECH

A terminology map of customer language
TELTECH (headquarters in Minneapolis) maintains a network of technological specialists.[13] It puts customers with special technological problems in touch with an appropriate expert. Since customers rarely express themselves clearly in technical language, TELTECH experienced some difficulty in finding the right specialist. The company therefore developed an on-line search service, in which customers could use a 'knowledgescope' to identify a suitable specialist. The knowledgescope is in fact a thesaurus, with over 30 000 technical entries. It is maintained by several full-time knowledge engineers who feed between 500 and 1200 new terms into the system every month and remove outdated ones. Every term used by a customer has several synonyms; if the customer refers to these, there is a good chance of being put in touch with an expert who can solve

the problem. Every day, the knowledge engineers receive a list of all unsuccessful search manœuvres made by customers, and they build this information into the map. New terms and new synonyms are added to the knowledgescope; this provides TELTECH with a relatively accurate picture of the technical language used by customers at any particular time.

Mass-produced import channels

We have just considered some of the unusual methods that organizations now use to gain vital knowledge about their stakeholders – in this case, their customers. The channels which conduct external knowledge into the organization's knowledge base will be differently structured in each case. The design should be appropriate to the importance of the stakeholder groups, and the channels should be organized creatively.

ACQUIRING KNOWLEDGE PRODUCTS

Recorded knowledge

Companies may import knowledge in ways which do not depend on people, e.g. by buying software or CD-ROMs. However, buying recorded knowledge in these forms does not automatically provide a company with organizational competencies. The potential of the material can usually only be realized through human activity and meaningful integration into the existing knowledge base. The purchase of suitable knowledge products can be a valuable tool in knowledge management; in practice, however, companies often buy resources which are incompatible with what they have. It is therefore most important to test the products before buying them.

Acquiring intellectual property

Acquisition of intellectual property is frequently cited as a way of acquiring knowledge products. The research and development results of many companies are patented; they can then be used by third parties under licensing agreements of various kinds. Acquiring licences is a suitable way for a company to fill gaps in its knowledge base when capacity, time or capital are limited (cf. Schülin 1995, p. 305). Franchise agreements enable companies to benefit from proven marketing systems, and the knowledge which is stored in them.

Substitution by software

The introduction of software packages is the most visible kind of intervention in a company's knowledge base. A fully developed program often represents many person-years of development time, and these can be imported into the company in the form of a program code. This code changes the way in which the organization deals with data, information and knowledge. ANDERSEN CONSULTING, for example, networked all its consultants by means of the groupware LOTUS Notes. This communications program enables consultancy teams around the world to access the same data and process them in parallel. The use of this package thus had a strong influence on knowledge-sharing processes, and radically changed the information flow in the organization.

The effects of powerful software packages are even more obvious when they are used to take over processes which were previously controlled by people. Enterprise resource planning (ERP) systems, such as SAP-R3, require an expensive customizing phase, but they then standardize and program processes, from purchasing through storekeeping to production and bookkeeping. Formalizing the main processes in this way often increases efficiency, but it can also have disadvantages. As we have already seen, experts are seldom able to make their knowledge completely explicit, and collective knowledge is difficult to understand. There is therefore a risk that formalizing and programming a process that was previously carried out successfully by many employees working together will rob it of the very features that made it what it was.[14]

Acquiring designs

Another group of knowledge products contains construction plans, blueprints and other design drafts.[15] 'Knowledge packages' of this kind are recorded in a form which is directly usable by third parties; this makes them ideal items for knowledge acquisition, but also, unfortunately, for industrial espionage. In 1982, six Japanese computer experts were arrested for passing the next generation of IBM mainframe designs to HITACHI (Badaracco 1991, p. 36). As a manufacturer of IBM-compatible products, HITACHI gained a considerable lead from this, and was able to bring a competing product on to the market earlier than would otherwise have been possible. This case of proven industrial espionage ended with a fine of $300 million for HITACHI, and an undertaking to give IBM access to its own designs in future.

Legal copying

Illegal acquisition of knowledge is not always so easy to prove, and it is not always covered by legislation. At the Paris fashion shows, multinational fashion chains such as HENNES & MAURITZ have their representatives by the catwalks, to note the latest trends and pass them quickly to their production centres in Asia. Within a few weeks, the main designs and motifs from the Paris fashion designers are well established in the mass-produced collections.

Reverse engineering

Today, most products and machines can be obtained legally. They contain 'frozen knowledge', which competitors can often obtain by taking them to pieces and analysing them. This method of acquiring knowledge is called 'reverse engineering' (Badaracco 1991, pp. 50–51), and it may go far beyond simple copying. In the household equipment industry, for example, a development team scrutinized various features of the products of three competitors. They compared the results with their own production processes, and identified cheaper individual components that competitors used without affecting the quality of the product. By combining these cheaper alternatives – e.g. by using snap fasteners instead of screws – they were able to reduce the cost of the next generation of products by about 6%. (For a detailed account see Rommel *et al.* 1993, p. 107.)

Acquiring technical storage media

Software is not the only storage medium which can be bought on the knowledge market. CD-ROMs, books, data banks, videos and computer-based training (CBT) offer solutions to special problems. They are particularly suitable if the solution will be used frequently within the organization, i.e. if there is a quantitative rather than a qualitative knowledge gap to be filled.[16]

Limits on knowledge acquisition

Companies can now buy many kinds of knowledge that they could not develop for themselves. For suitable pay and incentives, they can employ highly competent experts to implement their knowledge goals. However, the same solution is also open to their competitors. This is the reason why it is still important to be able to develop knowledge from one's own resources, and why this is often the deciding factor in the competitive knowledge environment. In the next chapter, we shall discuss opportunities for targeted knowledge development, and the limits on this process.

SUMMARY

- Knowledge can be acquired on many knowledge markets.
- We draw a distinction between acquiring knowledge that is directly usable and acquiring knowledge potential.
- The acquisition of 'outside' knowledge often elicits defensive reactions. Acquired knowledge should be as compatible with the company as possible.
- Outsourcing is the substitution of external skills for internal ones. It becomes dangerous when vital skills are relinquished.
- One of the main tasks of research and development departments is to keep track of the knowledge in the organization's environment, and to import this knowledge into the company's own products and services.
- Organizations increasingly use consultants as catalysts of external

knowledge. Use of consultants should be carefully planned from the knowledge point of view.

● Knowledge links are strategic alliances in which mutual learning and acquisition of knowledge are important objectives of co-operation. Knowledge links can be made with institutions of all kinds.

● There are many channels for bringing the knowledge of important interest groups into a company.

● Knowledge products, e.g. blueprints, software and high-tech equipment, contain 'frozen knowledge'.

● Knowledge media such as CD-ROMs offer a way of replicating solutions to particular problems quickly and efficiently throughout an organization.

KEY QUESTIONS

● Before starting a development project, do you check whether you could acquire this knowledge from outside?

● What are your main ways of acquiring knowledge? Which channels do you use often, and which very little, and why?

● How has your company failed to integrate external knowledge – e.g. consultancy reports, scenarios – in the past? What have you learned from this?

7

Developing Knowledge

INTRODUCTION

Innovative ideas, bubbling creativity and a Nobel prize for the head of the research laboratory. This is how some companies picture successful knowledge development. However, developing new competencies – like genius – is generally 10% inspiration and 90% perspiration. In other words, it has little to do with luck, and a great deal to do with systematic hard work. Knowledge developers operate in a zone of conflict between creativity and systematic problem-solving. 'Invention' should take place not only in departments of research and development, but in all areas of expertise that are important to the company's success. How can you learn more about your customers, suppliers and competitors? How do you work with the various think-tanks? We shall show you how to give a free rein to new ideas without bringing chaos down on your head. We shall argue that it is not advisable to become too dependent on individual experts: companies must also develop collective skills, such as the ability to solve problems, in heterogeneous teams.

DEVELOPING KNOWLEDGE

The best opportunities for growth are in areas where we can add new procedures and products by extending our knowledge. New knowledge is the basis of innovative products and thus of value creation. (*CEO of a chemicals company*)

We have taken on as partners a number of excellent scientists who are now paid by us, but have complete freedom of action in their pure research. We don't know how their research will develop, but we hope that it will give us access to pioneering discoveries. (*Manager of a computer manufacturing company*)

New knowledge arises in dialogue amongst all the people who are affected by an issue. Our organization is decentralised, and in the past it has been impossible for all the employees who were involved to take part in the preparations for major decisions and to contribute their knowledge. We have therefore introduced special workshops for making important decisions. All those with potentially useful expertise attend the workshops, and can take part in the collective process of knowledge development before the decision is made by the appropriate managers. (*Manager of an energy company*)

Significance of knowledge development

Knowledge development is a particularly important building block of knowledge management. It focuses on the development of new skills, new products, better ideas and more efficient processes. Knowledge development includes all those management efforts through which the organization consciously strives to acquire competencies that it does not have, or to create competencies that do not yet exist either inside or outside the company. If a company decides to develop knowledge internally even though it could be acquired outside, there must be extremely good economic or strategic reasons for doing so. Internal development makes economic sense if it is cheaper than buying knowledge on the market. It makes strategic sense if the company must at all costs retain control of certain essential competencies.

LABORATORIES ARE NOT THE ONLY SOURCE OF INNOVATION

Research and development

Traditionally, knowledge development is seen as the preserve of research and development departments: new drugs come from the laboratories of the pharmaceuticals industry, while the next generation of computer chips is designed in the development laboratories of computer firms. In reality, however, research and development departments – where they still exist – are no longer able to develop new competencies by themselves. They usually need competent external partners who take over parts of the knowledge development process, either in collaboration with the company's own research and development facilities or independently (see Figure 7.1).

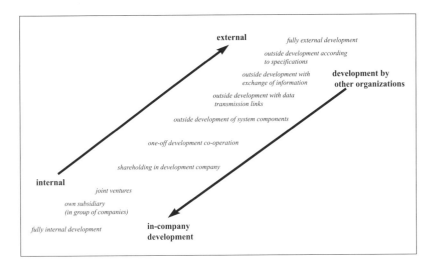

Figure 7.1 The continuum of development co-operation (based on Picot & Reichwald 1994, p. 561)

Types of research co-operation

There are many different structures for research co-operation. Activities range from sharing research with competitors (cf. Brockhoff 1992, pp. 45f.) to contracting out pieces of research (cf. Schülin 1995, pp. 309ff.). Companies increasingly seek external sources of ideas; universities and research institutes with high reputations are the organizations which profit most from this development. At the Massachusetts Institute of Technology (MIT), more than 50 chairs in high-technology subjects are sponsored by industry. Japanese companies alone, which support about a third of all the positions, pay 40 million DM per year to retain their connections with world technological leadership.[1] NESTLÉ has built up a network of about 20 research centres around the world, which work in close co-operation with outside experts in relevant fields.

Dominance of the research and development angle

Laboratories are not, however, the only sources of innovation. Organizations cannot improve their competencies simply by acquiring and applying new discoveries in the natural and engineering sciences. Knowledge managers must also analyse other company activities and innovation processes which create new knowledge vital to the whole organization.

Types of innovation

It is helpful to distinguish between product innovation, process innovation and social innovation. This distinction underlines the fact that innovation can take different forms. A manufacturer of computer chips is completely dependent on the next generation of the product, i.e. on product innovation. A chain of restaurants on the other hand may make a critical difference to the performance of its staff by introducing a new system of remuneration; this is social innovation.

Types of research

Organizations often concentrate on one type of innovation, e.g. product innovation, and take no interest in other forms. The traditional goal of research and development is usually product innovation, and the distinctions it makes are between pure research, applied research and development (cf. Brockhoff 1992, p. 37). Process and social innovation often receive much less attention. This is unfortunate because the different forms of knowledge development enrich the organization's knowledge base; many more sophisticated distinctions are drawn in the literature on innovation.[2]

In the following section, we shall examine some of the general difficulties which beset knowledge development.

BARRIERS TO KNOWLEDGE DEVELOPMENT

Barriers to innovation

Innovation takes place in a conflict area because of tensions between the existing order and the new one (cf. Waldenfels 1991, p. 100). Change is destabilizing, since old norms and beliefs must be sacrificed, often before it is certain that the new solution will work. Innovations also change power structures, because they devalue traditional skills and strengthen the positions of those who hold the new ones. Defensive reactions to innovation are therefore natural, and they endanger the formulation and development of new ideas.

Some barriers to innovation are person-centred and some are object-related, for example incompatibility of a new product with the existing range, or departmental egotism. There are also environmental barriers, e.g. strict legislation, or a shortage of workers with the desired expertise (cf. Schülin 1995, p. 25).

Planning versus self-organization

Innovations can be planned only to a limited extent. No one can make a researcher have a brilliant idea. Doubling the research budget is not a magical way of increasing creativity. At the same time, there is a difference between active, deliberate development of knowledge towards particular goals, and the passive, incremental and fortuitous appearance of new competencies. The processes by which knowledge emerges and develops are extremely difficult to describe, and therefore to control. In many ways, they are self-organizing.[3] The knowledge manager must recognize the areas in which he can influence the organization's production of knowledge. Where it cannot be influenced directly, the role of the knowledge manager is to create positive conditions in which knowledge can develop. A learning-friendly atmosphere increases the likelihood that individuals or parts of the organization will develop useful knowledge.[4]

Disconnected development of knowledge

Even though many knowledge development processes cannot be directly controlled, the main processes should nevertheless be linked to the organization's knowledge goals. If professional developers have too much freedom to pursue their technological ideas, this can be extremely inefficient for the company as a whole. Recently, in the car industry, interest in the technical feasibility of various features was allowed to take precedence over what was needed to sell the product; this led to expensive development projects which brought little market return[5] (see Figure 7.2).

Duplication

Duplication of development processes cannot always be attributed to lack of transparency. There are some activities – such as the production of certain reports or studies – which take place automatically and are no longer questioned. They have become detached from existing knowledge goals, and often from the needs of knowledge users. In exceptional cases, duplication can be efficient, because it may lead to internal competition to find the best solution, or to the building up of development reserves. However, it is usually just a waste of resources, and could be reduced by focusing development efforts.[6]

Knowledge leads are now more difficult to protect

Effective management of innovation becomes more important as competitive pressure grows. In the pharmaceuticals industry, it is accepted that only the fastest innovator, i.e. the first company to offer a new drug on the market, can recoup its development costs. Companies that

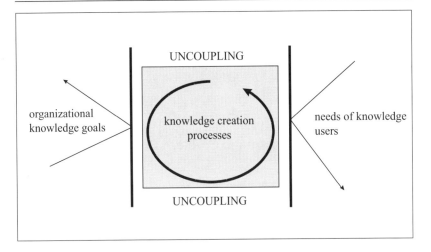

Figure 7.2 Uncoupling of knowledge creation processes

enter the market too late are often left with nothing but costs. At the same time, the period during which the winner can profit from its monopoly position grows ever shorter because of ingenious imitation techniques.[7] The increasing mobility of experts and the availability of 'packaged knowledge' levels out the advantages that companies build up through their own development efforts.

We shall now describe ways in which the knowledge development process can be managed at individual and collective levels. This will provide a basis for tackling the problems described above.

DEVELOPING THE KNOWLEDGE OF INDIVIDUALS

Replication versus development

For the individual, every learning process is one in which new personal knowledge is developed. If a production apprentice learns how to grind a piece of metal, he has acquired new knowledge. For the organization as a whole, however, no innovation has taken place, because grinding skills are already present at other places in the organization. For the purposes of this book, we are more interested in the kind of learning by individuals that also represents an innovation for the whole company. We shall therefore introduce some theoretical approaches to knowledge development, describe circumstances which favour innovation and finally present a series of techniques which many organizations now find helpful in encouraging their employees to produce new ideas.

Creativity versus Systematic Problem Solving

Creativity

How do people come to have ideas and inspirations, or to perform creative acts? Everyone knows what it feels like to be suddenly struck by a new idea, or to have a brainwave. These metaphors present ideas as things that occur to us spontaneously, not things that we can summon at the push of a button. We can rarely say in retrospect exactly how we came to have a bright idea, or how we discovered an unusual solution to a problem. The reason for this is probably the way our brains work. Patterns of information are formed in neural networks as a result of interactions between internal and external data, and new and old data. These patterns combine to reveal new meanings, thus generating new ideas (cf. Wessels 1994, pp. 66f.). The ability to produce new ideas and solutions is what we call creativity. It is an important – and unequally distributed – quality of individuals, but it leads to the appearance of knowledge that is useful to the whole organization.

Individual ability to solve problems

Another important source of new knowledge is the ability of individuals to solve problems of various kinds. Creativity can take the form of single acts of creation; problem-solving on the other hand is a process which may consist of several phases. We may think of creativity as the chaotic strand in knowledge development, and problem-solving ability as the systematic strand.

Problem-solving processes may be divided into simple, compound and complex, according to the type of problem.[8] In companies today, we see a move away from simple problems and towards increasingly complex ones. Simple and compound problems can often be solved by managers using standard solutions. Complex problems, however, differ in that they are dynamic in nature. They are characterized by the rapid appearance of new patterns, and the presence of interactions which are difficult to comprehend. All this means that a complex problem can rarely be solved without developing new knowledge or new skills. In these circumstances, the ability of individuals to solve problems involving knowledge development becomes a key qualification.

Conditions That Support Innovation

Shaping the context

We have already argued that in the knowledge development phase, knowledge management is more likely to consist in shaping the context than in exercising direct control. The next question is, what are the contexts or situations that encourage innovation? Many organizations adopt various measures in the attempt to increase their employees' creativity. Conference rooms are painted in stimulating colours, coffee areas are installed to encourage discussion, and many other techniques are applied to stimulate creative thinking. Most managers have taken part in brainstorming or synectics sessions. All of these measures are expensive and they often prove fruitless. There is no general formula for generating ideas. Nevertheless, it is worth considering some basic conditions which do seem to influence knowledge development.

Creating freedom

Many authors agree that giving people the freedom to have new ideas is one of the most important conditions for innovation. Good ideas are often suffocated at birth by the existing culture. 'But it has always been like this.' 'We have tried it before, and it didn't work.' It is 10 times easier to throw out a novel idea than to develop it constructively. However, many companies have now learned their lesson. They protect new ideas by running innovation projects in subsidiaries, or providing them with strong sponsors. IBM, for instance, sets up 'skunk works' for innovations; the vulnerable new ideas are thus protected by their geographical separation from the main company.

Freedom from other activities

People also need time to think. In the everyday running of organizations, short-term activities often take priority. Innovations and ideas for improvement are frequently lost in the rush to get things done. Pressure can be relieved by creating situations where people are free of everyday constraints and can work together on long-term projects (cf. Kirsch 1992, pp. 82ff). Some employees may take sabbaticals, as in universities. Others may be freed from their normal duties in order to prepare publications or lectures. Physical space for creative activity can be provided in the shape of 'creative zones', which are spatially separate from the normal working environment. We have already seen how members of development departments in 3M have the right to work for a substantial proportion of their time on projects of their own devising (see Schmitz & Zucker 1996, p. 108).

Congruence of interests

People who work on projects of their own choosing are generally more motivated than those who are given a set of targets to meet. Highly competent and creative workers often put enormous effort into their own projects, and a certain amount of 'bootlegging' occurs in development departments. This means that research workers continue to work in secret on projects from which management has withdrawn support and resources. Projects which had been officially 'killed' have sometimes led to revolutionary discoveries. If management succeeds in reconciling individual and collective knowledge development goals, it can tap this considerable source of self-motivation.

Tolerating mistakes

The way in which an organization treats its employees' mistakes has implications for creativity. A culture in which mistakes must be avoided at all costs suffocates innovation, since the man who never made a mistake never made anything. In an atmosphere where errors are seen not as failures, but as a necessary apprenticeship on the way to a viable solution, employees will be more inclined to look for unusual answers. Tolerance of mistakes is therefore conducive to innovation; but it must be demonstrated convincingly and over a long period, otherwise, there will be a double-bind situation: 'Mistakes are allowed – but they won't do your career any good!'

Aids to Innovation

Planning creativity

Knowledge does not appear from nowhere. Research into innovation has produced a number of efficient and tested methods for planning and guiding innovation processes. Even creativity can be learned to some extent (cf. Binnig 1992, p. 134). However, the application of a particular technique is not a guarantee of success. The following is a useful rule: 'Techniques are not in themselves suitable or unsuitable for achieving a particular end. One and the same technique may stimulate or hinder learning; its effects always depend on the way in which it is used' (see Probst & Büchel 1997, p. 177).

Techniques for stimulating creativity

It is therefore unsurprising that the growth in the number of techniques for stimulating innovative activity is not accompanied by a corresponding increase in the actual rate of innovation. Various methods of stimulating creativity, such as brainstorming, the morphological method and synectics, have now become established (cf. Probst 1993, pp. 350ff). Even so, organizations often fail to gain access to employees' ideas. Anyone who has taken part in a brainstorming session that was badly run, or held at the wrong time, knows that such things can be counter-productive, especially when the promoters are not credible, i.e. when they do not really want to risk doing something new. We therefore need to know not only the principles on which a technique is based, and its area of application, but also a great deal about the conditions in which it can be used. The same applies to search and screening methods, Delphi methods, relevance tree methods, and the use of computer-supported algorithms.[9]

The following are SONY's principles for stimulating creativity (cf. Gomez & Probst 1995, pp. 158f.)

- Small, easily comprehensible units encourage enterprise
- Mobility across the whole company increases creativity
- A sense of family is a source of energy
- Creativity requires goals
- The attitude to mistakes must be made clear
- A long time span creates freedom
- A fair way of dealing with disputes stimulates innovation

Employee suggestions

Organizations have various ways of encouraging and rewarding suggestions from their employees; many are now introducing new structures for making decisions on suggestions, acting on them and rewarding them. However, no technique will be effective unless it suits the company's particular circumstances. If a company has a traditional culture which resists innovation, there is little point in putting a 'suggestions box' on the intranet unless the employees can first be persuaded that risk and new ideas are now acceptable. It may not even be necessary to introduce new techniques, because existing ones can be adapted. In many organizations, for example, there is an established system for receiving suggestions. The function may be institutionalized as a specific position. The person who holds the position has the task of gathering new ideas and rewarding them with bonuses of all kinds. Many of these systems have lost impetus over the years, and no longer work well. They can even have negative effects, if they give the impression that creativity is not expected as a normal part of work, and that there ought to be a prize for everything which goes beyond routine. However, it may be possible to update the system.

CASE STUDY: METTLER-TOLEDO

From suggestions system to innovation management
METTLER-TOLEDO (headquarters in the small German city of
Albstadt) is a company that manufactures weighing scales.
It dispensed with its traditional method of gathering
suggestions and replaced it by an innovation management
system. This new system was based on faith in the
creativity of the company's employees. First, the old
centralized method of taking in suggestions, then evaluating
and rewarding them, was completely abolished. Instead, it
was expected that each employee would bring about a
small improvement in his or her personal sphere of work,
and that this would happen once a week, or at least once a
month (see Figure 7.3).

Suggestions are no longer handed in; instead, they are
implemented immediately. This cuts out the bureaucratic
process of evaluation. Now, as soon as the improvement is
in place, the employee fills in a form giving a short
description of it, specifying its effects in terms of cost,
quality, time, etc., and listing all the people who helped to
implement it. What started as the idea of an individual thus
immediately becomes a matter for the group. Following the
same principle, ideas are not rewarded on an individual
basis. For each person who has helped, a 20 DM note is put
into a prize fund, which is used at the end of the year for a
joint action on behalf of the whole staff. The company tries
in this way to make creativity part of normal working life,
and to show that in the end, everyone profits from
innovation.

Problem-solving by individuals

The techniques described above support the chaotic component in
individual knowledge development, that is, creativity and the
production of new ideas. The systematic component – the ability of
individuals to solve problems – can also be supported by the use of
suitable techniques. Some steps in the problem-solving process can be
formalized, and this helps to ensure that important factors are not left
out of account from an early stage (see Figure 7.4).

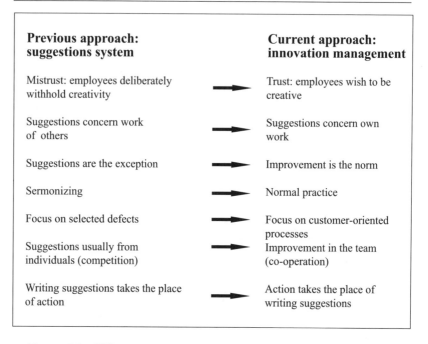

Previous approach: suggestions system		Current approach: innovation management
Mistrust: employees deliberately withhold creativity	→	Trust: employees wish to be creative
Suggestions concern work of others	→	Suggestions concern own work
Suggestions are the exception	→	Improvement is the norm
Sermonizing	→	Normal practice
Focus on selected defects	→	Focus on customer-oriented processes
Suggestions usually from individuals (competition)	→	Improvement in the team (co-operation)
Writing suggestions takes the place of action	→	Action takes the place of writing suggestions

Figure 7.3 Different approaches to generating ideas (cf. Gomez & Probst 1995)

Systematic approach to problem-solving

A system for solving problems of different kinds makes the work of individuals easier. It can also improve communication among individuals and groups who are working on different aspects of the same problem area. For some time now, XEROX has been systematically training its workers in problem-solving techniques that can be applied in all areas of the company and at all levels in the hierarchy (cf. Garvin 1993, pp. 81f.). They learn to develop ideas and to gather information by brainstorming, interview techniques, and various forms of data collection. To improve their skills in analysing and presenting data, they learn the basic rules of cause-and-effect diagrams and force-field analysis. They learn to describe planning processes more clearly with the aid of flow charts. Employees practise using these techniques on real problems in 'family groups', i.e. groups from a particular department or business unit; the techniques are thus anchored in their every-

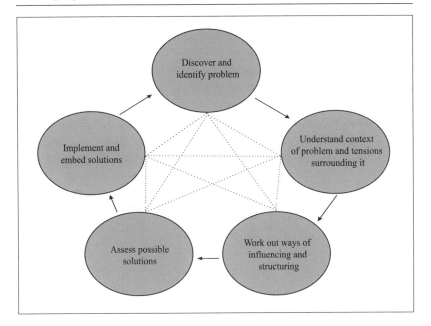

Figure 7.4   Steps in the integrated problem-soving method (see Gomez & Probst 1995)

day working life. This has led to the development over the years of a standard 'problem-solving language', which greatly simplifies communication across departmental and hierarchical boundaries.

Knowledge through action

A large part of our personal knowledge comes neither from the conscious application of innovation techniques nor from systematic use of problem-solving methods. In normal working life, knowledge comes through everyday activities. A mechanic who has been servicing a particular machine for years often knows the meaning of every little noise it makes, and he also knows what to do about it. He has a skill which no one else in the organization possesses; he even has abilities of which he himself is not aware. This is tacit knowledge; we have already discussed it in the chapter on knowledge identification. It makes an important contribution to the process of knowledge development.

Ways of externalizing knowledge

The expert, in this case the mechanic, is often not aware of the valuable knowledge which he possesses, or at least, he cannot describe it in clear and comprehensible language. This means that if he were to resign, retire or die, the organization as a whole would lose the knowledge, unless ways can be found to externalize it. Metaphors, analogies and models are useful ways of expressing tacit knowledge (cf. Nonaka & Takeuchi 1995, pp. 64–67 and Schüppel 1996, pp. 263f.). Metaphors offer a clear and lively way of expressing ideas that the individual cannot put into precise and logical terms, for example, 'The look on your face reminds me of when I was in the army.' Analogies are more structured. They express functional similarities between different areas of knowledge, and transfer an idea directly from one to the other, as in: 'This suction tube works like an elephant's trunk.' If tacit knowledge can be described even more precisely, it may be possible to construct a model. This involves deriving variables from the metaphors and analogies and testing their interdependencies. If the model has sufficient explanatory power, it can be distributed throughout the organization as a form of explicit knowledge.

Limits on making knowledge explicit

All techniques for making knowledge explicit depend on the willingness of experts to externalize what they know. However, this is often regarded as tantamount to sacrificing one's livelihood, and arouses anxiety. If a company robs its experts of their vital knowledge in order to be less dependent on them in the future, or in order to make them redundant, it gambles away the trust needed for any subsequent attempt to externalize knowledge.

In spite of all efforts, a substantial part of the knowledge of valuable experts will never be made explicit. Every loss of such an expert therefore means a loss to the organizational knowledge base on which it is difficult to place a value. Attempts to externalize the knowledge cannot prevent this; they can only attenuate the effects of the expert's departure. An organization's ability to make the knowledge of its experts visible and transfer it to other members is therefore a vital aspect of making individual knowledge collective.

ESTABLISHING ROUTINES AND BUILDING TRUST

Collective knowledge

What distinguishes knowledge development processes in the individual from collective learning or knowledge development? Teams or whole organizations can develop characteristics which cannot be explained in terms of the skills of individual members. Groups in which there is daily sharing of experiences and in which the members are interdependent develop behaviours which can only be explained in terms of group interactions. This suggests that some types of innovation cannot be achieved by individuals, but only by the team.

Processes which combine the efforts of many employees now form the distinctive core competencies of companies. The mechanisms of innovation must also be sought at group level. In this section, we shall describe separately the processes involved in the development of group knowledge, the contexts in which it takes place and the techniques that may support it.

How Knowledge Develops among Individuals

To avoid isolating the knowledge of individuals, and to make it available to group processes of knowledge development, certain conditions must be met. Only where there is interaction and communication, transparency and integration can individual knowledge become collective knowledge, which in turn reacts upon the individual knowledge (cf. Klimecki, Probst & Eberl 1994 and Probst & Büchel 1997, p. 21) (see Figure 7.5).

Interaction/communication

Without communication among individual bearers of knowledge, there can be no comparison of each person's ideas and experiences with those of others. Organizations in which there are significant barriers to communication between departments have difficulty in developing joint solutions, and contain inefficient islands of knowledge. Interaction is the first essential in developing organizational intelligence, because '. . . the collective mind resides in the processes by which

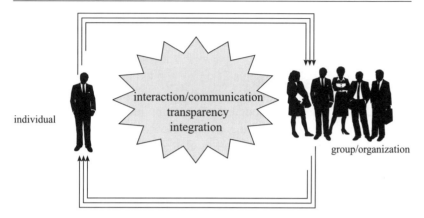

Figure 7.5   Key dimensions in emergence of collective knowledge

people influence each other', and we find 'intelligence . . . in patterns of behaviour rather than in individual knowledge' (cf. Weick & Roberts 1993, pp. 359, 365). For the organization to succeed, therefore, the knowledge of individuals can be less important than the relationships and interdependencies among them, which constitute the knowledge 'between' individuals. However, these relationships can only be established and maintained where there is interaction and communication.[10]

Transparency

We have already devoted a whole chapter to the importance of transparency of knowledge and effective processes of knowledge identification. An organization's centres of knowledge development cannot keep track of all the information and competencies which are in principle available, both internally and in the environment. Knowledge development is held back or made more expensive because of unused publications, unknown experts or parallel activities. Experts who are ignored, whether deliberately or not, may become defensive, thus reducing the chances of successful innovation.

Integration

The third key factor in the development of collective knowledge is the integration of individual skills and knowledge components into a functional whole. We have already emphasized that interaction between members of a group can lift the limitations on individual minds and often leads to the solution of problems which the individual could not have solved alone. Two-way feedback between the individual on one hand and the group or the whole organization on the other is central to this process of integration (cf. also Müllen-Stewens & Pautzke 1992, p. 137). Individual skills can be integrated into group competencies in various ways and with varying levels of freedom. In 'machine bureaucracies',[11] the individual is virtually programmed by the organization, which defines clear rules for behaviour and catalogues of required skills. In other types of organization, the integration of individual knowledge follows self-organizing principles. In the latter case, novel group solutions are more likely to appear, but at the same time, the processes of knowledge development are less predictable.

High-Performance Teams and Their Skills

In modern organizations, the most likely setting for the appearance of collective knowledge is the team.[12] We shall concentrate on teams in our attempt to identify conditions that promote knowledge development. Teams research new technologies, analyse cultures, work to improve the efficiency of workshop processes and develop new sales strategies. They are increasingly entrusted with important tasks and projects. The performance of these tasks generally brings new knowledge to the organization as a whole, and extends the skills of individual members.

The trend away from the solitary thinker or decision-maker is based on the recognition that top-quality teams can achieve things that are impossible for individuals. We should therefore look to established research on groups and teams to find conditions and circumstances conducive to collective knowledge development.

Conditions for team success

MCKINSEY advisers Jon Katzenbach and Douglas Smith studied nearly 50 exceptionally successful teams, and identified conditions which were particularly favourable to success (see Table 7.1). The same situational variables are unlikely to work for all processes of collective

Table 7.1 Favourable conditions for teamwork and key questions for team planners (Katzenbach & Smith 1994)

Small enough in number
- Can you convene easily and frequently?
- Can you communicate with all members easily and frequently?
- Are your discussions open and interactive for all members?
- Does each member understand the others' roles and skills?
- Do you need more people to achieve your ends?
- Are sub-teams possible or necessary?

Adequate levels of complementary skills
- Are all three categories of skills either actually or potentially represented across the membership (functional/technical, problem-solving/decision-making, and interpersonal)?
- Does each member have the potential in all three categories to advance his or her skills to the level required by the team's purpose and goals?
- Are any skill areas that are critical to team performance missing or under-represented?
- Are the members, individually and collectively, willing to spend the time to help themselves and others learn and develop skills?
- Can you introduce new or supplemental skills as needed?

Truly meaningful purpose
- Does it constitute a broader, deeper aspiration than just near-term goals?
- Is it a *team* purpose as opposed to a broader organizational purpose or just one individual's purpose (e.g. the leader's)
- Do all members understand and articulate it the same way? And do they do so without relying on ambiguous abstractions?
- Do members define it vigorously in discussions with outsiders?
- Do members frequently refer to it and explore implications?
- Does it contain themes that are particularly meaningful and memorable?
- Do members feel it is important, if not exciting?

Specific goal or goals
- Are they *team* goals versus broader organizational goals just one individual's goals (e.g. the leader's)?
- Are they clear, simple, and measurable? If not measurable, can their achievement be determined?
- Are they realistic as well as ambitious? Do they allow small wins along the way?
- Do they call for a concrete set of team work-products?
- Is their relative importance and priority clear to all members?
- Do all members agree with the goals, their relative importance, and the way in which their achievement will be measured?
- Do all members articulate the goals in the same way?

Clear working approach
- Is the approach concrete, clear, and really understood and agreed to by everybody? Will it result in achievement of the objectives?
- Will it capitalize on and enhance the skills of all members? Is it consistent with other demands on the members?
- Does it require all members to contribute equivalent amounts of real work?
- Does it provide for open interaction, fact-based problem solving, and results-based evaluation?
- Do all members articulate the approach in the same way?
- Does it provide for modification and improvement over time?
- Are fresh input and perspectives systematically sought and added, for example, through information and analysis, new members, and senior sponsors?

Sense of mutual accountability
- Are you individually and jointly accountable for the team's purpose, goals, approach, and work-products?
- Can you and do you measure progress against specific goals?
- Do all members feel responsible for all measures?
- Are the members clear on what they are individually responsible for and what they are jointly responsible for?
- Is there a sense of 'only the team can fail'?

knowledge development, but they provide a good basis for checking one's own organization.

Complementary skills

Groups seem to be better at creative problem-solving if their members possess different skills. However, too much diversity can destroy the cohesion of the group: if there is no basic consensus, the team's creative power is tied up in political manœuvring. In group learning processes, the balance between consensus and diversity must be constantly readjusted.[13] One way to achieved balance is to seek a consensus on the cognitive framework to be used, while accepting divergent viewpoints. Katzenbach and Smith offer a more concrete formulation. They believe that successful teams contain a balanced mix of relevant professional or practical knowledge, skills in problem-solving and decision-making, and interpersonal skills. All team members should possess these three basic qualities, though with different emphases. This seems a reasonable approach, since there cannot always be an equal division of labour within the team, especially when it comes to applying social skills.

Meaningful and realistic goals

Meaningful and realistic goals which provide a common guideline are essential for co-ordinating and integrating group activities. Vague abstractions, such as 'We want to be a learning organization', create problems because it is left to the team to put them into practical terms. Team cohesion is also strained if individual performance criteria are put before real team objectives. If the chosen development goals are not clearly defined, not readily measurable or not fully supported by top management, then conditions will be unfavourable to innovation. The goals must be reformulated in more precise terms, or success is endangered from the outset.

Openness versus defensive routines

One of the greatest obstacles to innovation takes the form of 'defensive routines' (cf. Argyris 1987, 1990). These are collective behaviour patterns which make it unlikely that individuals, groups or organizations will give up damaging routines, or discover and eradicate their own errors. The reason is that facing up to one's own errors is threatening, and can bring uncertainty and unpredictable changes. Certain possible solutions are thus subtly made taboo, and not pursued, which can seriously damage the innovation process. These information pathologies[14] are less likely to occur if there are clear rules of play within the team, and if members have the right to express their ideas freely and without fear of adverse consequences. A clear but non-dogmatic approach to work helps to integrate non-standard opinions throughout the innovation process, rather than excluding them.

Intensity of communication

Intense communication works against defensive routines and supports the development of group skills.[15] If all members of a team meet frequently and exchange ideas in an open atmosphere, each person learns to understand the abilities of the other members. It then becomes clear who could or should adopt what role in different situations, in order to meet the group objectives most efficiently. In an atmosphere of this kind, confusing concepts can be clarified by careful discussion. This 'languaging' process[16] helps the group towards a common understanding of central concepts and distinctions, and future communication becomes substantially more effective. The value of such a group atmosphere also shows the limits on electronic aids such as video conferencing or groupware. While these are effective means of transferring data, they cannot replace direct personal contacts.

Finding Room for Something New

Existing approaches

There are now many management techniques for guiding the development of collective knowledge. They are often rooted in existing management concepts such as business process re-engineering or total quality management. Instruments for knowledge development are widely used and accepted, whether as systematic and gradual innovation in the context of continuous process improvement (CPI), or in setting up experience groups or communication forums on particular topics. We shall now present examples, and ideas for developing the basic approaches to support the development of collective knowledge.

CASE STUDY: GENERAL ELECTRIC (GE)

Concentrating knowledge in a 'Work-out'[17]
In 1981, GE, the energy giant, adopted a new strategy, in response to threats arising from a strong inward orientation, insufficient internationalization and concentration on markets characterized by weak growth. The strategic about-turn radically changed the structure of the company, since it involved spectacular acquisitions and sales of whole business areas. This had serious effects on knowledge: core competencies were sold at a stroke, whereas the knowledge of the newly acquired firms initially remained unconnected with GE's competencies. In an effort to endow the new conglomerate with a common and dynamic culture, GE introduced a programme of cultural change which it called 'Work-out'. The driving force behind the change process was to be an organizational dialogue which would affect all levels in the hierarchy. It would focus on critical events and lead to rapid decisions; it would also eliminate unnecessary steps in work, and thus make space for creativity and communication.

A Work-out session usually consists of three phases. In a 'pre-meeting', topics are delineated, and participants and relevant experts identified. The core phase is the 'town meeting', in which 40–100 people from different functional areas and levels in the hierarchy take part. Ideally, they represent GE's assembled expertise in relation to the topics and processes under discussion. Solutions are developed in small groups, in which the knowledge of individuals is brought forward and combined with other viewpoints. In this way collective solutions are found. During the discussions, a common language develops, which makes the solutions easier to integrate.

The assembled management must give immediate

decisions on the solutions suggested by the small groups, and must give their reasons. Decisions may be postponed only in exceptional circumstances, e.g. lack of data. The whole Work-out is monitored at a 'post-meeting', at which the implementation status of the agreed activities is checked.

The whole Work-out system is probably an efficient way of bringing together people who have relevant knowledge to discuss specific themes. It is a process of open communication in which participants combine their knowledge in a joint problem-solving exercise. Prompt decisions ensure that their knowledge is fed into future management decisions.

Think-tanks

Methods such as GE's Work-out programme are clearly circumscribed in time and place. Think-tanks are quite different: they are groups in which the organization concentrates its intelligence and which it entrusts with the development of knowledge and skills that are critical to the organization as a whole. Expert groups and research and development departments are traditional forms of the think-tank; more recently, new and interesting forms have emerged. MOTOROLA, for example, has set up its own university, where employees are trained and core business areas researched. There is also a McDONALD's university, where the company's future products are designed, and where the quality standards of the leading fast-food chain are taught to future branch managers.

Learning at work

The main criticism of think-tanks and panels of all kinds was – and still is – their remoteness from everyday activity. For this reason, many organizations have made radical cuts in the number of employees involved in them. Today, many companies concentrate on techniques which support the emergence of knowledge during the normal work process. The Harvard Professor Leonard-Barton believes in the factory as a research setting, and offers suggestions on how to turn production processes into a learning laboratory. All participants must make a continuous effort to integrate external and internal knowledge, to solve problems independently and to look for new possibilities. However, collective learning processes can only be achieved if certain values are respected. Real innovation only takes place under conditions of equal treatment, common ownership of the knowledge gained, acceptance of risk and openness to the knowledge of others. The Product Clinic approach, which we shall now describe, is based on a similar philosophy. It aims at systematic improvement of products, procedures, structures and the supply structure.

The Product Clinic as the germ cell of learning processes (for details see Wildemann 1996)
Wildemann, a production expert at Munich University, calls for organizations to institutionalize innovation by means of a 'germ cell' which can invigorate the innovation process and keep it moving. The basic idea of his Product Clinic is 'to compare the company's own current products and processes directly and physically with those of competitors, using market, competitor and customer data' (cf. Wildemann 1996, p. 39). As an example, one might take 10 different toasters to pieces and compare them in terms of technology (e.g. screws or welding) materials (e.g. steel or plastic) and individual parts (e.g. make of screws). The functions and performance characteristics of one's own product can then be systematically analysed in relation to the corresponding parts. In this way, best practices can be identified and incorporated directly into one's own product (see Figure 7.6).

Specialists from all functional areas are involved, so the implications for processes, performance and technology can be analysed directly. This procedure can radically accelerate the innovation process. It also improves general understanding of the complex interactions between production, research, marketing, purchasing and other functional areas (see Figure 7.7).

Learning arenas

Germ cells for learning and knowledge development are not limited to production. It is useful to establish 'learning arenas'[18] for all those learning processes or fields of knowledge which are especially import-

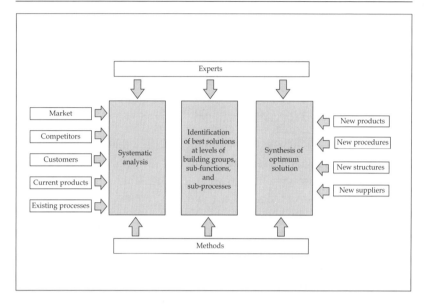

Figure 7.6 Outline of product clinic procedure

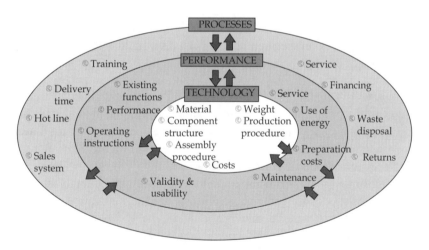

Figure 7.7 Levels of analysis in the product clinic

ant to the company's goals. The learning arenas can be successfully integrated into the company by setting clearly operationalized learning objectives, providing suitable resources and assigning personal responsibility unambiguously. Learning arenas overlap the usual structural and sequential forms of organization, without replacing them.

This is illustrated by the organization of knowledge development in the following example.

CASE STUDY: McKINSEY

Creating internal centres of competence for selective knowledge development[19]

In the 1970s, competitive pressure increased in the business consultancy sector. Competitors such as BCG and AT KEARNEY were challenging McKINSEY for the most attractive customers and the best graduates and employees. Functional knowledge in company practice was becoming increasingly differentiated. Consultants therefore needed to specialize more, and to some extent they needed to move away from a general approach to consulting. Furthermore, increasing internationalization necessitated special regional knowledge and more knowledge of the process of internationalization itself (see Figure 7.8).

McKINSEY responded to these challenges by forming internal groups of experts, or think-tanks, which they called 'practices'. Today, these exist for functional divisions (manufacturing, etc.), for selected branches of industry (cars, banks) and for topics currently of special interest (e.g. Eastern Europe). In the practices, experienced specialists – in addition to carrying out normal project work – concentrate project experience, develop it further and communicate it to others. For young consultants, this is an opportunity to gain sound knowledge of a special area and to apply it to suitable projects. Members of the 'Energy' practice, for example, work on visions and concepts for the energy industry of tomorrow. The knowledge they develop is then made available in condensed form, as 'lessons learned', to the whole organization.

Lessons learned

In every project, the team members learn things which can be of great interest to future teams addressing similar questions. However, it often happens that at the end of a project, no one collates these experiences systematically or makes them available to the whole organization (see Figure 7.9).

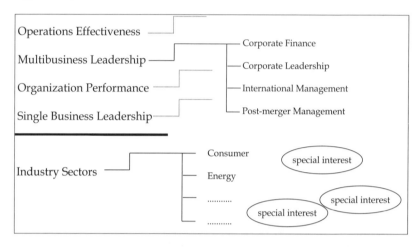

Figure 7.8   Structure of competence centres in McKINSEY

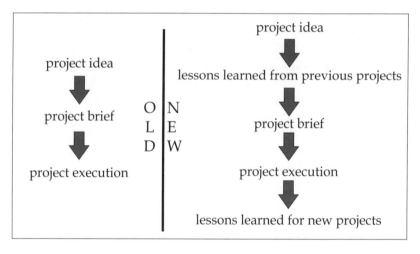

Figure 7.9   Integrating lessons learned into the project process

Reflecting on the work

After a project has ended, team members may meet to discuss the work, what they have learned, and what future teams addressing similar problems should bear in mind. Different assessments of the project are often not visible until this stage, but they can provide a valuable stimulus for members to reflect on their own efforts. More companies are now using a 'lessons learned' procedure to criticize and incorporate past activities, and to learn from previous successes and mistakes. Lessons learned represent the essence of the experience gained in a particular project or position.

CASE STUDY: Coop

Strategic lessons learned
The Coop Group, which has a turnover approaching 12 billion Swiss francs, is one of the leading trading companies in Switzerland. In recent years, it has succeeded in raising its competitive profile considerably, especially with innovative ideas for its ecological products.

The company recognized that the different strategic projects in ecologically oriented product areas were achieving different levels of success. It therefore started a knowledge project to determine what lessons had been learned. The aim of the project was to assess the possibility of using knowledge gained in successful strategy projects to support the less successful ones.

For the purposes of the study, a series of interviews was carried out, and case studies were made of individual projects. A number of success factors were identified in the formation, organization and conduct of strategic projects. Lessons were learned about aspects of organization and staffing that could be applied to other projects; they included modifying project organization and establishing specific training programmes.

Preserving experience

If companies are to make use of lessons learned, they must have suitable ways of preserving them. Organizations often fail to appraise and record their activities systematically because of lack of time, conflicting priorities or unwillingness on the part of participants; yet unless the knowledge is preserved, it cannot be used later.

High-reliability organizations

Much can be learned about conditions that favour learning from 'high-reliability organizations'.[20] Nuclear energy plants, chemical works and flight control centres are examples: the smallest accident must be followed by a careful investigation, and any sources of error eliminated. A study of high-reliability organizations has revealed a number of conditions which help to safeguard lessons learned. They are:

● Disclosure of all mistakes, without reservation
● Immediate evaluation of operations or projects and debriefing of staff
● Participation of the whole team
● Examination of processes or standard operating procedures for any errors
● Mutual supervision without loss of trust (see LaPorte & Consolini 1991, p. 29)

Learning from the past

Research at a more abstract level is carried out at MIT's Center for Organizational Learning. This is a research institute which works with partner companies on ways of setting up infrastructures for learning (cf. the account in Senge & Scharmer 1996). The Center experiments with learning laboratories and dialogue projects to create learning-friendly environments. There is also a certain emphasis now on documenting and using learning histories. Key events in organizations, such as major successes or failures, are studied in respect of their effects on the behaviour of the whole organization. The members of the 'Consortium of Learning Organizations' hope to gain insight into the learning history of their own companies and their basic learning mechanisms.

Use of scenarios

When companies wish to consider possible future developments, the scenario technique can be useful (cf. also Gomez & Probst 1995, pp. 126f.). The participants in a scenario workshop work out joint models of the future during a communication process which is structured in several phases. The department of research, society and technology at DAIMLER-BENZ has developed a version in which participants are taken from different parts of the company. First, the participants clarify and agree on the topic for the workshop. In the next step, they identify factors which affect the issue; the future development of these factors is then networked by computer. The networking yields scenarios, which are presented as consistent model worlds. Hypotheses can then be derived and supported, and can include unforeseeable events or changes in trends. Typical applications are the development of company visions, strategies, products and services. The following is an example.

CASE STUDY: DAIMLER-BENZ

Air Traffic Project 2015: the scenario technique as a tool for developing knowledge in Daimler-Benz
The department of research, society and technology at DAIMLER-BENZ organizes 'laboratories of the future', based on the scenario technique, for parts of the company and for external clients. The research department thus takes on a knowledge management function, since many forms of knowledge about the organization's environment are identified and networked, focused and made available to the organization. A company-wide team was set up with DAIMLER-BENZ AEROSPACE to form a 'laboratory of the future' on air traffic in 2015.[21] The parts of the organization that developed, produced and sold aircraft were brought together to combine their knowledge. The aim was to achieve a complete description of air traffic, including factors which influence the whole system, and environmental relationships and effects. Finally, a picture would be created of air traffic in the year 2015, and strategic implications would be derived from it.
    The present situation was taken as the starting point. World air traffic is currently dealing with growing numbers of passengers and increasing amounts of freight. Many airlines operate at a loss because of price wars on transatlantic and transpacific routes. Increasing business

integration and dynamic developments in the industry
mean that suppliers of products related to air travel must
have a thorough understanding of interactions within the
air traffic system.

Strategic planning is difficult. Faced with this situation,
DAIMLER-BENZ AEROSPACE decided to develop a business
strategy which would reach far into the future. The
process consisted of five steps, in which several
major scenarios were developed.[22] The two scenarios
summarized in Table 7.2 have completely different strategic
implications.

The 'laboratory of the future' yielded results at different
levels. First, a far-reaching business strategy was developed
on the basis of the scenarios. Experts and participants in
the laboratory of the future used the descriptors and the
scenarios themselves as a basis for critical analysis of their
assumptions about air traffic development. One result was
that old planning approaches were re-evaluated and partly
rejected. The laboratory of the future also helped to solve
communication problems among the divisions which took
part, viz. organization, airline companies and airports.

The scenario experts in the DAIMLER-BENZ department of
research, society and technology assess the knowledge
management potential of their method as follows:
The scenario technique develops knowledge. The individual
knowledge of workshop participants, experts and moderators
is combined and modelled into pictures of the future. The
shared process of building future 'model worlds'
systematically changes the knowledge structures which are
brought to bear upon it. First, the group develops an
alternative mental representation of reality, to which every
participant contributes. Each person's own assumptions
about the subject are thus brought face to face with those of
experts and other participants, and this provides a stimulus
for analysing individual habits of thought. Second, the
scenario refers to the future, which puts present knowledge in
a different light. The knowledge which the organization
currently has about present clusters of problems is seen in a
new context. Alternative plans and actions become possible.

The potential which the scenario technique has for developing knowledge is limited in time to the period of the exercise. However, the process of communication in the group has strong and lasting effects. Long after the workshop ends, the participants are still a group of people who have shared a special experience. They form a kind of knowledge community, and often maintain frequent contact with each other. The results of the process can also be spread throughout the organization by the use of suitable transfer techniques. They thus become accessible to others and make a contribution to continuing knowledge management.

Table 7.2   Air traffic scenarios, 2015

Scenario A: 'By air, how else?'	Scenario B: 'Air travel is limited'
• Passenger numbers increase because of low ticket prices, attractive services and improved connections • There is a comprehensive air travel network that offers convenient services • The market is shaped by strong demand for aircraft and other components of integrated travel systems • Air traffic control, airlines and passengers interact smoothly	• Flying is much less attractive • Difficult market conditions lead to falling aircraft prices • There is a lack of integrated traffic systems • Air travel stagnates

SUMMARY

- Knowledge development is the deliberate production of competencies which were not previously present within the organization. It is not restricted to research and development departments; it happens in all areas of the company where vital knowledge is generated.

- Knowledge is not always the result of deliberate effort. It can also be a by-product of daily activities in the organization. We must therefore be aware of the limits on the extent to which development of competencies can be controlled.

- If the processes by which knowledge is created are detached from knowledge goals, resources are wasted.
- Creativity and individual ability to solve problems interact in the development of individual knowledge.
- Innovation can be supported by influencing working conditions, e.g. by giving people freedom and time away from other duties.
- Vital tacit knowledge must be externalized, so that it becomes visible, and exists at a conscious level. It can then be used by the whole organization. However, we must recognize that not all knowledge can be made explicit, and that the costs will be high.
- Key conditions for the development of collective knowledge are interaction, communication, transparency and integration.
- Methods of collective knowledge development include think-tanks, learning arenas, lessons learned and scenario techniques.

KEY QUESTIONS

- Where are the centres of knowledge development in your company?
- How are they linked to the knowledge goals of the company?
- Are there continuous efforts to make tacit knowledge conscious and explicit?
- Do you support the establishment of cross-company centres of competence, which focus scattered know-how and develop it further?
- Do you lack creativity or systematic problem-solving ability? What are you doing about it?

8
Sharing and Distributing Knowledge

INTRODUCTION

'Divide and conquer.' This may work in politics, but it is dangerous to play politics with knowledge. Information and experience can only be used to benefit the whole organization if they are available to those who have to make the decisions. Do people often keep knowledge to themselves in order to preserve their own power and prestige? Is the most important knowledge vested in certain individuals because it is bound up with their duties and experience, and cannot be described and passed on to others? E-mail makes it easy and cheap to send masses of irrelevant information; but there are some kinds of knowledge that can only be shared in personal discussions, or by copying the way someone else works over a long period. In this chapter, we shall examine some techniques for distributing knowledge. We shall describe the setting up and running of knowledge networks, which make effective use of the computer revolution. Finally, we shall consider how to increase employees' willingness to share knowledge, and we shall describe instruments that can support the transfer of 'best practices'.

SHARING AND DISTRIBUTING KNOWLEDGE

The front line

In our business, rapid distribution of knowledge and global use of 'best practices' are absolute musts. To survive the competition among top consultancy firms, we have made long-term investments in these areas. Now, every employee can obtain the existing materials on certain topics in a very short time. Contacts with experts are also provided, so employees have access to first-hand knowledge. (*Senior consultant in a global business consultancy firm*)

There is no way that people would share knowledge willingly in our company. Especially since management pushed the last re-engineering project through, everybody guards his patch for all he is worth. The motto seems to be: 'Don't make yourself unnecessary. Somebody might believe it next time'. (*Department head in a supplier to the car industry*)

In our pilot factory, a certain foreman has been fine tuning our product tests for decades. He is retiring this year, and all of a sudden people are starting to ask: 'What shall we do, when we can't ask Mr X any more?' It is absolutely essential to us that Mr X should pass his knowledge on to others in the time he has left. (*Research and development manager in an international food company*)

Key questions

It is vital that knowledge should be shared and distributed within an organization, so that isolated information or experience can be used by the whole company. The key question is: Who needs to know (or be able to do) how much of what, and how can we facilitate knowledge sharing?

Presence of knowledge

The first condition is that knowledge should exist. It can come from internal sources (knowledge development) or external ones (knowledge acquisition). If the existing individual or organizational knowledge assets can be recognized and located by the potential user (knowledge identification), then the conditions for the sharing and distributing of knowledge are in place.

Difficulty of knowledge distribution

However, many companies find that this is where the real problems begin. One of the most difficult tasks in knowledge management is to distribute knowledge to the right people, or make organizational knowledge available at the point where it is needed. This difficulty is often underestimated. Recent surveys have shown that in many companies, more than half the available intellectual capital is not used. Many also report difficulty in transferring knowledge to the point where it could be utilized. In most cases, vital elements of knowledge were concentrated in a very small number of people (see Lester 1996 for these survey results).

Meaning of 'knowledge sharing and distribution'

We have called this building block 'knowledge sharing and distribution' to underline the fact that it is not just about the mechanical distribution of packaged knowledge from a central co-ordinating point. On the contrary: knowledge is a commodity which is often only transferable in personal exchanges between individuals.[1] According to the context, knowledge sharing and distribution can mean either a centrally directed process of distributing knowledge among a particular group of employees, or it can be the transfer of knowledge between individuals, or within teams or working groups.

THE RIGHT CONDITIONS FOR KNOWLEDGE SHARING AND DISTRIBUTION

Knowledge distribution as an economic necessity

In recent times, the opportunities and risks inherent in the global exchange of data, information and knowledge have become a social issue (cf. Kupfer 1996 and Willke 1996). Politicians have visions of the data highways of the future. Scholars of the humanities are concerned about the threats posed by a networked society to social inter-action and the private life of the individual. Technology has changed so much, with the advent of global data networks and powerful hard-ware and software, that companies are now experimenting with new ways of sharing and distributing knowledge. The growing trend towards international teamwork is putting many companies into virtual reality. Team meetings are held in cyberspace; even so, they cannot replace direct personal contacts.

Trend towards group work

In a parallel development, growing numbers of employees are spending more of their time working in teams or project groups (cf. Katzenbach & Smith 1994). Teamwork is now the fashion. At one time, a worker was judged according to his ability to solve problems using his own knowl-edge; today, he is judged according to his contribution to the team. What does his input do for the whole project? How does he share his knowl-edge with his colleagues, and how does he make use of their knowledge? Employees increasingly depend on each others' help to perform com-plex tasks successfully. The success of a project or of a team is closely related to the efficiency of knowledge sharing in the group.

Virtual teams and offices

The move towards the virtual organization does not facilitate knowl-edge sharing and distribution. In virtual teams, the members are working on the same problem, but they are scattered amongst different locations. HEWLETT PACKARD, for example, has used virtual teams as a form of organization. Development specialists in several European countries place their skills at the disposal of all branches by means of a European network. In more extreme cases, this form of organization is used not just for teams, but for whole departments or companies.

VERIFONE

VERIFONE is a Californian company which produces authorization equipment for credit cards. It is a much-quoted example of the virtual office.[2] Production is concentrated in India and Thailand. The top managers are spread all over the USA, and work mostly from home. The typical salesman works wherever his customers are. The whole company is held together by a powerful computer network. All the employees – almost 2000 of them – have laptop computers with modems, so they can communicate and exchange knowledge across all levels in the hierarchy. VERIFONE works in 90 countries; employees' experiences with customers and competitors in all those countries are entered in the data banks, which are accessible throughout the company.

Virtual companies

The extreme case of this form of organization is called the virtual company. This is a conglomerate of organizations, mostly connected by data networks, which co-operate in complicated ways to perform a function, and which present a largely unitary appearance to outsiders. Individual members of the network concentrate on their own core competencies, and leave other parts of the process to the other members.[3] In a network of this kind, one member often takes on the role of organizer, co-ordinating the activities of the rest.[4] The exchange of information and knowledge is a basic essential. Instead of setting up management functions to run the conglomerate, a virtual company relies on exchange through intensive use of information technology.[5]

Dangers to cultural knowledge

Abrupt changes in company structure pose a threat to effective distribution of knowledge. Acquisitions or disinvestments can destroy accustomed channels for the spread of knowledge, or necessitate completely new infrastructures. Excessive growth has similar consequences. Consultancy firms, some of which have annual growth rates of more than 50%, find it particularly difficult to maintain consistency in the internal flow of organizational knowledge. Where there is growth on this scale, knowledge about the company culture is particularly affected. Cultural knowledge teaches new employees the rules of the game and how they are expected to behave; in other words, it socializes them.

Loss of natural contexts for sharing

The growing popularity of teamwork makes knowledge sharing and distribution increasingly important as a success factor. However, virtual forms of organization and abrupt discontinuities in company development pose obvious threats to the efficiency of these processes. Natural situations for sharing knowledge are those in which colleagues are physically present at the place of work. Where there are fewer opportunities for working together or meeting informally, efforts must be made to arrange social situations in which knowledge can be shared.

Approaches

Fortunately, there are plenty of aids to knowledge management. The more difficult circumstances are partly offset by considerable advances in methodology. Instruments to support the sharing and distribution of organizational knowledge cover all the physical, technical and organizational aspects of individual and group working contexts.

Organizational and technical approaches

With regard to organization, traditional functional or divisional forms can be supplemented by parallel structures to support knowledge management. In the technical area, the main implications are for communications and information technology. Recent advances have been considerable, and in many cases have made a virtual form of organization possible for the first time. The most important recent advance is 'groupware' technology, of which LOTUS Notes is the best-known example. Groupware applications offer consistent management of shared information, and thus provide substantial support for group working processes.

Space management

Knowledge sharing can also be affected by the spatial arrangement of work areas. By careful space management, knowledge flows can be reflected in physical arrangements: people who regularly work together, and for whom exchange of knowledge is especially important, should be relatively close. At present, offices tend to be arranged along functional lines, and little attention is paid to the distances between people who need each other as knowledge partners. Intelligent layout can physically reproduce the whole business processes, thus facilitating cross-functional co-operation (cf. Ogilvie 1994).

LEVERAGE THROUGH KNOWLEDGE SHARING

Time and quality

Time-based management and total quality management (TQM) are two of the dominant management concepts of recent years. From both practical and theoretical viewpoints, it is now clear that companies which fail to keep their delivery times, are late in bringing new products to market, or are defective in product quality or customer service, will not remain competitive in the long term. Knowledge sharing and distribution have powerful effects on both time and quality, and thus influence important competitive factors.

Distributing knowledge to co-ordinate processes

As product life cycles have shortened and technology has advanced, time has become more important as a competitive factor. Meanwhile, research and development are increasingly expensive. The combined effect of these changes is that speedy development and prompt marketing often have a greater influence on final profits than strict observance of the development budget. Delays in internal processes are less likely to be due to the shortcomings of particular employees than to problems in co-ordination. The re-engineering approach can be helpful here: it eliminates co-ordination problems by comprehensive restructuring of processes. However, the problem can sometimes be solved in a less radical and interventionist manner by introducing measures to promote the sharing and distribution of knowledge. This approach involves helping individuals, groups or organizational units to understand their role in the whole process, and creating the necessary channels of communication. Sequences of activities can be accelerated in this way.[6]

Second time right

Quality management is also critically dependent on successful knowledge sharing. 'First time right' is a well-known TQM slogan. 'Second time right' would make a good measure of successful knowledge distribution. If knowledge were distributed efficiently, errors would not be repeated, the organization would learn, and it would save the costs of making the same mistakes two or three times over. All this could be largely achieved by systematically recording the lessons learned and distributing them to the right people. Knowledge distribution is not just about sharing recipes for success; it also means passing on knowledge about how to avoid mistakes (see Figure 8.1).

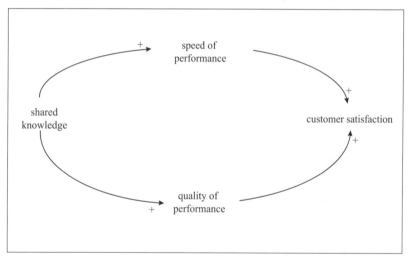

Figure 8.1   Sharing and distribution of knowledge as an indirect effect on customer satisfaction

Direct benefits

In addition to improving time and quality management, knowledge distribution can also yield direct customer value. Distribution of intellectual assets enables employees to use them at many points in the company. Knowledge is on the spot. Staff can give quick and competent answers to customer enquiries without having to ask head office. Many of us have been annoyed by branch employees who seemed to know nothing about the latest products of their own company. A customer-oriented organization attaches great importance to the distribution of such critical information. It signals competence, and can give the company a critical competitive advantage, especially in service industries.

Consistent image through knowledge distribution

Multinational companies can draw a further advantage from knowledge sharing. A company which operates in a number of countries must preserve a consistent image and comparable quality standards worldwide. McDONALD's food should taste exactly the same in Singapore as it does in Lima. A first-class international consultancy must apply similar standards everywhere in selecting personnel and fulfilling its mandates, if its image is not to suffer. In both cases, the distribution of knowledge – for example by training and socializing employees carefully and intensively – can point the way to success.

Importance for use of knowledge

The process of sharing and distributing knowledge makes its effective application possible or impossible. We cannot use what we do not get, and it will not affect our decisions or products. Much that seems self-evident and boring to one person is a novelty to another, and might make the second person's work easier or better. We often lose sight of the valuable skills or knowledge that we possess, thus preventing other groups from making use of them. To promote better knowledge distribution, organizations should foster an awareness that the value of knowledge is a relative matter.

NOT EVERYBODY NEEDS TO KNOW EVERYTHING

General principles

How much knowledge should be shared? Which of the organization's knowledge assets should remain secret, and protected from large-scale distribution? Before we start thinking about techniques for distributing knowledge, we must have principles for deciding which kinds of knowledge should be distributed and which should not. If this is not done, we have no right to be surprised if the company's secrets appear on the Internet. We also need to decide in principle between a centrally controlled strategy for knowledge distribution and decentralized infrastructures.

Limited provision of knowledge

Not everybody needs to know everything. There is a difference between effective distribution of knowledge and aimless spreading of any and every piece of information to all employees. Knowledge distribution is only possible and meaningful within certain limits. Its real purpose is to give individuals or groups access to the knowledge that they need to perform their own tasks. In this way, it contributes to a smooth sequence of processes within the organization. This need not involve telling everybody everything. In any case, there are a number of natural limits on the spread of knowledge.

Economic limits on knowledge distribution

The first of these limits is economic in nature. Universal distribution of knowledge would destroy all the advantages of efficient division of effort. First, it would most probably fail because of the expense. Second, even if it could be done, it would be counter-productive. The limited range of skills which any individual can master makes specialization unavoidable. Universal sharing and distribution of knowledge would place senseless limits on the range of possible competencies that an organization might develop.

Confidentiality and secrecy

The need to protect certain areas of knowledge also places important limits on knowledge distribution. There may be a duty of secrecy, i.e. as part of legal obligations to customers or contractual partners. However, knowledge is more likely to be restricted for competitive reasons. Certain core intellectual assets may be essential to the company's competitive position, and must be protected from imitation by rival companies. This is easier if the circulation of knowledge is restricted. In both these cases, certain knowledge assets are excepted from circulation from the outset.

Relationship with organizational structure

The extent and scope of knowledge distribution should be appropriate to the company's organizational form and its personnel policies. In a strongly hierarchical, 'command and control' organization, it is easier to establish what knowledge is needed by which persons or departments, and to limit its circulation accordingly. There is, however, usually a price for this, in terms of lower flexibility and longer reaction times. The more flexible the organizational structures, the more important it is to distribute knowledge so as to create certain redundancies in intellectual assets. These redundancies have a co-ordinating role at critical interfaces, as described above. The extreme case is the virtual organization, in which the co-ordinating function of redundancies is necessary for survival.

Human barriers

People do not automatically pass their knowledge on to others; there are individual barriers which make people less willing or less able to do so. Employees usually regard certain areas of their personal knowledge as part of their power base within the company, or as their private business. In both cases, willingness to share the knowledge is limited.[7] Other knowledge assets may not be passed on because individuals are not able to describe and communicate them.[8]

Positive side of limited distribution

Limits on knowledge distribution are not entirely a bad thing. Some studies have found that differences in knowledge can also have positive effects. This is especially true of 'peripheral' knowledge. There should be a high level of agreement on core elements of organizational knowledge, that is, those that concern the mission and vision, and enable people to understand the competitive situation. In peripheral areas of the company's knowledge base, however, a certain level of dissent is perfectly acceptable. Loose links between the two kinds of knowledge help the organization to react more quickly to changes in its environment. In other words, disagreement in peripheral areas of knowledge can promote flexibility.[9]

REPLICATION OF KNOWLEDGE

Replication of knowledge

Replication of knowledge is a centrally controlled form of intervention; its function is to distribute certain knowledge assets quickly among a large number of employees. The new knowledge should be quickly available, in lasting form, to all the employees involved. Teaching all employees who work outside the office to use a new standard software is an example of knowledge replication. Another might be a workshop entitled 'Organizational change', to teach employees about a new strategic direction for a part of the company. In both cases, the use of the term 'knowledge replication' is justified if the process is centrally directed.

Creating a knowledge network

Knowledge replication, then, is marked by an element of central control and permanent access to new knowledge. Knowledge networks, on the other hand, work according to decentralized principles. Instead of providing permanent access to a prepared stock of knowledge, they offer knowledge according to need. This kind of distribution requires conditions in which knowledge can be delivered 'just in time'. It is based on movement of knowledge between employees via the infrastructures of the organization's knowledge network.

Socialization

Replication of knowledge is used in two major areas of organizational activity: socializing employees, and the continuing process of training and educating them. Socialization involves familiarizing employees with the organization's norms and values, and communicating basic behaviours and role expectancies. In short, it means teaching them the company culture.[10] The purpose of socialization may be to acclimatize new employees, or to convey a new strategy or culture.

Methods of socialization

In the simplest case, initial socialization takes place through contact with colleagues, and informal exchanges about 'how we do things here'. However, especially in large companies, the acculturation of new employees may be an occasion for seminars, or even retreats lasting several days, in which the basic features of company culture are taught. These activities provide a basic level of knowledge that can be refreshed subsequently. During periods of serious upheaval, companies often undertake major initiatives to present and justify a new strategy, or a change in company culture. GENERAL ELECTRIC's Workout programme, described above, is an initiative of this kind.

Professional training

Professional knowledge can also be spread by knowledge replication. It is important to keep employees' competencies at a constant high level, especially in dynamic, knowledge-intensive industries. Professional training is part of employee development. In ARTHUR ANDERSEN, each employee receives up to four weeks' training per year to learn about new standard tools.[11]

Personnel development measures

Knowledge replication is an important part of all techniques for employee development. Training programmes replicate knowledge, and the programmes themselves can also be replicated, as in the 'train-the-trainer' approach. This is a technique which enables people who are not themselves professionals to train others. Increasing numbers of companies now use self-learning procedures (cf. Rieker's article, 1995). Employees work in small groups, usually consisting of four participants and a moderator; simple graphic tools are used to aid the discussion of new initiatives, and ways of implementing them are developed. The four participants then become the moderators in four more groups. If the process is repeated a few times, knowledge can be spread rapidly throughout the company, thus creating a broad base for organizational change. BASF successfully carried out a TQM initiative using this technique. SIEMENS used the '4 plus 1' method to implement a comprehensive re-engineering programme. DAIMLER-BENZ stopped production in a whole factory and used the snowball method to familiarize all the workers with the new vision and mission statement.

Documentation

The methods described so far have been person-centred. Other techniques for knowledge replication are based on documents or data. Company manuals, whether computerized or in traditional form, are still an indispensable source of knowledge in many companies. Their main functions are to acclimatize new employees by familiarizing them with rules and regulations pertaining to routine work processes. Documented standard operating procedures are also a useful way of passing on knowledge about processes that have proved successful.

Preserving knowledge

All methods of replicating knowledge automatically support knowledge preservation. If knowledge is shared among a number of people, it is much less likely to be lost when someone leaves. This can be a way of avoiding serious problems.

CREATING KNOWLEDGE NETWORKS

Controlling knowledge distribution

It is often impossible for management to control knowledge processes directly. In previous chapters, we have repeatedly drawn attention to the need for companies to establish conditions favourable to knowledge development. Creating a knowledge network is one way of moulding the context to facilitate knowledge sharing and distribution.

It is true that employees cannot be compelled to share their knowledge with others; but the presence of a suitable infrastructure at least makes it possible, whereas this may not have been the case previously.

Moulding the Infrastructures

'Push' strategies

Knowledge replication works on 'push' principles. Decisions are made centrally about what knowledge to distribute, and who should receive it. The knowledge is then 'pushed' into the organization through clearly defined channels, such as training sessions, or employees whose job it is to circulate the knowledge. The success of a 'push' programme depends on the choice of material to be pushed, and on finding the right media. A hierarchical, top-down approach of this kind has no need of a decentralized information infrastructure.

Creating infrastructures

The 'pull' principle starts from the knowledge user and his needs. He must be able to obtain knowledge quickly when necessary; making selective requests for knowledge should be second nature to him. Information is something that the user must locate for himself. In these circumstances, the systematic distribution of information through a hierarchical system is not helpful, because the knowledge which is needed may be in another business area, or another functional division. A hierarchical path to it would put so many obstacles in the way that the knowledge seeker would never reach it. The 'pull' principle works where there are no difficulties about contact between the knowledge seeker and the source of knowledge. A knowledge network is the appropriate infrastructure here.

Advantages of horizontal infrastructures

Knowledge infrastructures that run horizontally, i.e. across rather than with the hierarchical pathways, have a number of advantages.

They permit selective access to organizational knowledge according to need. If the infrastructures are user-friendly, and the company incentive system is favourable to sharing and distributing knowledge, then distribution will organize itself. The information overloads that can result from automatic knowledge distribution are thus avoided.

Organizational Support for Sharing and Distribution of Knowledge

Parallel structures

Organizational structures are not generally formed to suit the needs of knowledge management. Geographical or functional barriers which have developed in the company's past may make efficient knowledge distribution difficult or impossible. The marketing and production divisions may have little direct contact with each other, while subsidiaries in China and Canada rarely share their experiences with the parent company or with each other. In addition to functional and geographical structures, therefore, companies need structures based on interests or particular topics, such as centres of competence or learning arenas. These can pave the way to an efficient knowledge network. Many companies have introduced structures of this kind in recent years.

Examples from business consultancy

The large business consultancies were among the first companies to recognize the need for intensive distribution of knowledge. Many years ago, McKinsey introduced functionally oriented practices, and industry groups for certain industries. The practices and industry groups focus the company's know-how in certain areas and develop it further. Employees from offices all over the world meet regularly to exchange experiences and – in addition to their normal project work – they develop their professional knowledge of special functions or industries. Arthur Andersen employees organize themselves into 'competence centres'. The BOSTON CONSULTING GROUP also has global practice groups.

Experience groups and learning arenas

Other companies have similar arrangements, often called 'experience groups' or 'communication forums'. Learning arenas are a special kind of infrastructure for knowledge distribution. A structure may be termed a learning arena if it overlaps the normal structural and process-based forms of organization without replacing them. It serves to steer learning processes in the company, and, if leaders and organizers are carefully chosen, it supports targeted distribution of knowledge.[12]

Benefits of central structuring

Infrastructures of this kind are an excellent way of integrating personal, functional or geographical islands of knowledge into the mainstream of company knowledge. They help to bring in the knowledge of employees who hold minority views, or specialized departments that are seldom heard, or out-of-the-way locations. However, they presuppose a certain decision in favour of integration, at least in the early stages of creating the infrastructures.

Support through employee development

Knowledge networks can be developed selectively by careful job rotation or assignments to special teams (cf. Harrigan & Dalmia 1991, p. 7). International assignments in multinational companies are not simply a means of developing the individual employee; they also develop the organization. Multifunctional or multicultural project groups can overcome natural barriers to the sharing of knowledge. The resulting development of knowledge networks and the socializing effect of assignments support knowledge distribution and strengthens cohesion within the company.[13]

CASE STUDY: MCKINSEY & COMPANY

The 'Rapid Response Network': a hybrid solution
Knowledge sharing and distribution in MCKINSEY depended
for a long time on informally developed personal networks.
The MCKINSEY advisers knew the fields of activity of most of
their colleagues, and usually only needed to make a few
enquiries to locate the leading experts and the current best
practices for dealing with a particular problem. The
organizational infrastructure, based on practices and industry
groups, also facilitated selective sharing of knowledge.

Strong growth pushed this system to the limits of its
efficiency. At the end of the 1980s, MCKINSEY had over 2000
advisers in more than 50 offices. It was no longer possible
for employees to share knowledge on a personal basis,
without the support of a specialized function. This problem
was particularly serious for the organization practice, the
competence of which was of great importance for most
MCKINSEY projects. The company therefore decided to set up
a system in that area which would give prompt information
about internal experts on a particular topic and documents
relevant to it. This was the start of a project called the
'Rapid Response Network'.

The system owes its present success to three vital factors.
First, a special computer system manages the document
library and the personal skills profiles of the advisers.
Second, two permanent employees answer telephone
queries and identify experts and documents when possible.
Third, special experts from the organization practice are on
call to deal with complicated requests. These experts are
the ultimate channel through which knowledge passes from
one person to another.

Even though the experts tend to be overloaded with
normal project work, most of them are able to answer
queries and offer their specialist knowledge within a
relatively short time. In the second year of its existence, the
Rapid Response Network answered more than 1000
enquiries from about a quarter of the company's employees
worldwide. This is a testimony to the quality and speed of
the service. It now serves as a model for other practices.[14]

Limits on organizational infrastructures

As MCKINSEY discovered, when a company experiences rapid growth and globalization, existing ways of sharing and distributing knowledge no longer work. In large companies, it is impossible for everybody to know everybody else personally. In these circumstances, computer networks are useful. Their introduction can form a basis for computerized knowledge distribution on a larger scale.

Knowledge Distribution via Computer Networks

Compatibility

If a company wishes to distribute knowledge by computer, certain conditions must be met. The first is that the company's technology should be internally compatible. It makes no sense to talk about high-quality technical infrastructures for efficient knowledge distribution, if the organization is not yet capable of transferring simple text or graphics files internally. However, once a certain level of compatibility is reached, significant achievements are possible.

Simple solutions

A company does not need the latest intranet technology to enable employees to communicate best practices to each other. In ARTHUR ANDERSEN, for example, global best practices (GBPs) are regularly sent on CD-ROMs to all the company's offices around the world. The CD-ROMs contain selected presentations and documents of which advisers on the spot can make direct use. This method complements the much costlier intranet. It is a relatively simple way of circulating knowledge, and could be used in many other companies, even where the technical infrastructure is very limited.

Data networks and groupware

The current debate about technical infrastructures for knowledge distribution focuses on a number of high-quality solutions. These are basically of two kinds: company-wide data networks, and applications which come under the heading of groupware, or computer-supported co-operative work.

CASE STUDY: ARTHUR ANDERSEN

Knowledge sharing on a technical basis
Since the end of the 1980s, ANDERSEN WORLDWIDE has been divided into two separate strategic business units. ANDERSEN CONSULTING is concerned mainly with IT consultancy, while ARTHUR ANDERSEN operates in three areas: accountancy, business consultancy and tax and legal advice. The whole global organization now has almost 90 000 employees working in 361 offices in 76 countries. Its yearly turnover is 8.1 billion US dollars.

ARTHUR ANDERSEN describes its role in relation to its customers as that of a 'supplier of knowledge'. In view of this self-image, and the continual growth of competitive pressure in the consultancy business, knowledge management is essential. Furthermore, as a provider of advice about knowledge, the company feels obliged to practise exemplary knowledge management.

Internally, ARTHUR ANDERSEN uses a simple formula to express the strategic significance of knowledge for the company's success:

$$K = (P + I)^s$$

where K = knowledge and P = people and I = information. People and information are joined by technology, which is represented by the plus sign. The combination is raised to the power of s, which stands for sharing. The formula makes no claims to mathematical exactitude, but it performs two basic functions. First, its global circulation throughout the company drew attention to the importance of knowledge as a basic parameter of competitive success. Second, it emphasizes the special role of sharing in knowledge management.

ARTHUR ANDERSEN's internal knowledge management system has been constructed in a series of building-blocks. The success of the system springs largely from the interplay of technical infrastructures and the special attention paid to knowledge distribution.

ARTHUR ANDERSEN presents a 'one firm' image. The company regards itself as a consultancy with a global presence and globally uniform performance levels. It therefore attaches great importance to circulating lessons learned among its organizations and widely scattered offices in many countries. A CD-ROM entitled 'Global Best Practices' is distributed globally at regular intervals. The principle dates back to the foundation of the company at the beginning of this century. The material was initially distributed in paper form; now, it is sent electronically.

The 'GBP' CD-ROM contains complete project presentations which document global best practices for a wide range of business processes. The material comes from internal project reports, which are initially circulated mainly without commentary. Comments are then added, and finally, ARTHUR ANDERSEN's individual competence centres condense the reports plus comments to best practice levels. The CD is arranged according to core processes, and knowledge is organized hierarchically within this framework. However, information on a specific topic can also be found by searching the full text. The CD contains problem-solving knowledge (methods and instruments), knowledge about the content of solutions (standard solutions, causal relationships), and identifies experts and forms of knowledge (persons, documents, data banks). In addition to stored knowledge, therefore, the CD also enables users to make contact with experts or people who have worked on earlier projects, thus permitting a direct exchange of experiences.

The technical basis of knowledge distribution in ARTHUR ANDERSEN includes a comprehensive intranet. The 'AA Net' is a global data network (WAN) which connects all the local networks of the individual offices. It gives each ARTHUR ANDERSEN employee access to more than 1000 groupware servers.

The company also has another medium called 'AA On-line'. This is a data bank based on LOTUS Notes. It was created especially for the purpose of knowledge distribution, and consists of three components which correspond to the main distribution functions. The 'announcements' section is devoted mainly to replicating knowledge. Announcements from top management and daily news are sent by a few people and received by many. The 'resources' section has an identification function similar to that of the 'GBP' CD-ROM: it can be used to obtain standardized and edited company knowledge in the form of presentations, work papers, brochures, and so on. Finally, the 'discussion' section supports an almost simultaneous exchange of information. It contains forums on specific problems and provides a medium for distributing and developing knowledge independently of time and place.

AA Online is maintained by professional knowledge managers. Although new files become available every day, the absolute size of the system remains more or less stable. Irrelevant or outdated knowledge is removed regularly.

Parallels to expert systems

The technical infrastructures of knowledge distribution can link many different sources and users of knowledge. A similar function has been performed until now by expert systems. GENERAL MOTORS developed a system called CAMS (Computer Aided Maintenance System) to help their authorized mechanics in diagnosing faults and repairing vehicles (cf. Davis & Botkin 1994, p. 168). In addition to the usual technical details, which were previously to be found in various repair handbooks, the system also stores the personal knowledge of its users. Experienced mechanics can use the expert system to pass on hints and tips for dealing with particularly awkward problems. The system is thus a regularly extended knowledge base containing the expertise of all the repair experts in GENERAL MOTORS. It creates a direct link between the sources of knowledge and its users.

Advantages of quasi-simultaneous exchange

A serious drawback to expert systems is that they must be updated at regular intervals, and this introduces an element of delay. In dynamic competitive environments, where it is important to transfer knowledge rapidly, delays can tip the balance. The GRAPEVINE system, described below, supports quasi-simultaneous distribution and use of knowledge assets, thus providing extra leverage.

Intranets

Intranets, such as AA Online, have the same potential. An intranet is a data network based on the same principles and standards as the Internet, but it is limited to a particular group of people, usually the employees of an organization. An intranet also offers a higher level of data security than the Internet, so it is easier to keep material confidential. Guidelines for using an intranet can be defined by the user or the administrator, whereas the Internet cannot be controlled because it is universally accessible. Unlike expert systems, intranets permit modified knowledge assets to be used without appreciable delay.

Groupware as a catalyst

A group of applications called groupware, or computer-supported co-operative work, have recently become extremely popular.[15] They offer extra functions in distributing knowledge by means of technical infrastructures. Groupware technology is generally thought likely to act as a decisive technical catalyst in the future distribution of information. Its main advantages are that it helps to ensure the consistency of the knowledge that it distributes, and it has special mechanisms for co-ordinating distribution.

Problems: consistency and co-ordination

When knowledge is distributed through e-mail systems or intranets, there can be problems with consistency and co-ordination. E-mail sends communications in specific directions. Messages are only sent to certain addresses, which must be known to the sender. Even prepared mailing lists are only a partial solution. Furthermore, e-mail systems do not provide any check on the consistency of the information sent: many contradictory messages relating to a given topic may be in circulation at the same time.[16] An intranet allows better control of consistency, since all users are in principle accessing the same information. With intranets, the problem is the undirected nature of distribution. The search for relevant information is left to the potential user, who is often swamped by the quantity of knowledge on offer.

Types of groupware application

The special strength of groupware applications is that they co-ordinate processes of knowledge distribution within a particular group of users, and largely ensure the consistency of that knowledge. The classification of groupware applications is controversial; nevertheless, a number of tasks can be distinguished which can now be performed by groupware systems.[17] 'Group schedulers' co-ordinate the diaries of several users: they can locate, for example, a time when they could all be free to attend a meeting of a given length. If this function is combined with one that produces and checks task lists, the systems can be used in project management.

Work flow management

Work flow management is the name given to a different category of groupware applications that follow a previously modelled work flow and can initiate the next communication or stage in the work if, for example, the previous stages have been completed. The efficiency of these systems depends heavily on how far the work sequence can be modelled, and the extent to which rules can be formulated to deal with exceptional cases. Work flow management systems can be based on messaging or on data banks.

Lotus Notes

The Lotus Notes software can link very different types of servers and desk-top computers into a network; it supports interactions analogous to those that take place via the synapses in the central nervous system. It keeps track of the files distributed on the network and checks them regularly for consistency. This enables users to work on documents, spreadsheets or other files simultaneously and independently of each other (cf. Kirkpatrick 1996).

Complementary technology

A range of complementary technologies can be used to support different groupware applications. The use of paper, for example, can be almost eliminated by scanning documents into the system and adding appropriate document management. OTICON, an innovative producer of hearing aids with its headquarters in Denmark, is a well-known example of the paperless office. Many other firms are also moving towards increasingly systematic computerization of incoming paperwork, after which they destroy the originals. Documents can thus be stored according to multiple criteria, and can be retrieved quickly and easily by means of appropriate search functions. The system can also be complemented by electronic document publishing (EDP) and various multimedia and hypermedia applications.

GRAPEVINE for Notes: An Electronic Knowledge Network

Simultaneous knowledge distribution in multinational organizations

Some companies have technical infrastructures that can distribute knowledge almost simultaneously to a large number of people, who use it, and, in the process, develop new, improved knowledge. This new knowledge can then be distributed in its turn. This situation is a marginal case of knowledge distribution. In small working groups or in well-run departments, it should be the norm; in large, multinational organizations, however, it presents considerable technical and organizational challenges. GRAPEVINE for Notes is an example of how electronic knowledge networks can help meet these challenges.

CASE STUDY: GRAPEVINE TECHNOLOGIES

Collaborative knowledge management using GRAPEVINE for Notes
One of the first applications specifically designed for knowledge management was created by the Australian software company GRAPEVINE TECHNOLOGIES. GRAPEVINE for Notes is based on the existing LOTUS Notes system. It supports targeted distribution of internal and external knowledge, and collaborative development of new knowledge within companies.

GRAPEVINE consists of several elements. A knowledge map contains a hierarchical arrangement of the keywords used in the system, and thus provides a classification of the company's knowledge base. Using these keywords, users define their personal interest profiles, in which they specify areas of knowledge, and grade them according to personal level of relevance.

At the heart of the system lies the 'GRAPEVINE profiler', which classifies external files and internal Notes documents, and distributes them to users according to the interest profiles. The individual user then receives – either by e-mail or via a special in-basket – a message giving the keywords and interest levels of the documents. The documents can be read by means of a DocLink, and the reader can add comments. He or she can also raise the relevance level of the document, to bring it to the notice of other interested users.

Benefits of GRAPEVINE

Systems such as GRAPEVINE show how different knowledge management processes can be combined through the use of technical knowledge networks. In this case, the processes of identifying, sharing, distributing, using and developing knowledge are all linked together. Knowledge identification is supported by the inclusion of external knowledge, and the possibility of evaluating external and internal documents. Experts add comments to documents that fall within their field of knowledge, and can raise the relevance levels if they wish, which is helpful to non-experts. Knowledge is thus made transparent, and can then be distributed and used within the organization. Since the process can be repeated almost without delay, the rapid addition of comments and the raising of the interest levels of useful material can quickly generate new knowledge which is relevant to the company's needs. Finally, the new knowledge structure may be reflected in changes to the knowledge map; this adds to the corporate memory, and is therefore an element in knowledge retention.

The Potential of Hybrid Systems

Hybrid systems as catalysts

We should not lose sight of the main tasks that technical infrastructures for knowledge distribution are designed to perform, even though they may offer other interesting possibilities. They should not be allowed to develop a technology-dominated dynamic of their own; their function should be restricted to that of a catalyst, facilitating smooth interaction between bearers of knowledge in the organization.[18] Even on this limited interpretation, problems can still arise.

Limits on efficiency of technical solutions

Empirical studies have shown that new technologies are only used efficiently in companies that are culturally receptive to them. Organizations with a learning-oriented culture, where the sharing and distribution of knowledge are explicitly encouraged, can implement groupware more quickly and comprehensively than organizations where such a culture is lacking.[19] Empirical observations also suggest that a limited use of technology often brings greater benefit than a complete technical solution. In a study of 50 multinational companies, the return on investment of a limited installation of LOTUS Notes in one function was higher than that on installing the system across the whole company.[20] For various reasons, technically sophisticated infrastructures proved more or less superfluous, or difficult to implement. The reasons included lack of motivation on the part of potential users, complexity of problems, the presence of successful low-tech mechanisms for sharing and distributing knowledge, and difficulty in measuring the benefits of technical systems.[21]

Training and communication

A move towards technically more sophisticated solutions generally requires a considerable investment in supporting measures. Organizational mechanisms are sometimes fundamentally changed by new technologies, as in the case of the virtual office. Where this happens, training and communication are essential to calm employees' fears of change, and perhaps to help them to enjoy new ways of working. Central processes such as assessment, pay, employee development and career planning must usually also be adapted to fit the new circumstances.

Benefits of hybrid systems

Technical systems for knowledge distribution still yield the greatest benefits when they are combined intelligently with conventional methods. The combination of technology and people in 'hybrid systems'[22] is important in this context. There are many ways of introducing a human element into the technical infrastructure. One way is to make internal experts available as advisers to support the users of the system. The efficiency of Internet use, for example, can be increased considerably if an Internet specialist is available between the Net and the end user, offering tips and helping to reduce the search costs of less experienced users.

Uniform structures

Experts are also needed to maintain the infrastructures. Although many companies agree that knowledge distribution is better served by market principles than by central planning, nevertheless certain aspects of the market should be defined. It can make excellent sense to have an internal 'supervisory body' to oversee the system and to correct any faults. HEWLETT PACKARD did precisely this with Knowledge Links, its web-based knowledge management system. The specialists do not interfere with the basic functions of the system, but they edit, format and classify individual contributions, giving them a more uniform structure which simplifies access to the system and makes it easier to use (cf. Davenport 1996, pp. 38–39).

Consistent terminology

TELTECH, the technological advisory company, takes a similar approach. Its service operates through an on-line search system called Knowledgescope, so it is clearly technology-based. However, the en- tries – which number more than 30 000 – are maintained by the com- pany's 'knowledge engineers'. A particularly important feature is the thesaurus of specialist terms, which is continuously updated to include the expressions which customers and experts really use. As with Knowledge Links, the knowledge map is maintained by human inter- vention, which ensures that the system is user-friendly .

Service orientation

The fear that users might be dominated by technicians can be largely allayed if the role of information departments or special knowledge management groups is clearly formulated in terms of service to the user. This can often be supported by symbolic acts. In BUCKMAN LABORATORIES, for instance, the information systems department was transformed into a nucleus of internal knowledge management. Instead of its old name, however, it is now called the knowledge transfer department, which clearly expresses its customer-oriented mission (cf. Davenport 1996, p. 36).

Contacts with experts

The value of hybrid solutions is increased if technical distribution systems contain references to human experts wherever possible. In G.M. HUGHES ELECTRONICS, for example, the data bank containing edited versions of best practices from internal re-engineering pro- jects provided the names and locations of persons who could give more information. The project descriptions in the data bank were kept to a minimum, to prompt the interested reader to contact the experts.[23]

Creating new infrastructures

Finally, the human component in knowledge distribution can lead to the creation of new infrastructures. Following a successful contact and an initial exchange of knowledge, employees may discover a common area of interest. They may pursue it by creating a new infrastructure, such as a new practice or an experience group, which directly supports the sharing of knowledge in the common area. Ideally, this will lead to joint development of new knowledge.

ENCOURAGING WILLINGNESS TO SHARE KNOWLEDGE

Barriers to sharing

Organizational and technical infrastructures are needed for efficient distribution of knowledge. However, creating the infrastructures is not in itself enough to set the process in motion, since there are a number of individual and cultural barriers to sharing knowledge.[24] They may coincide with functions or levels in the hierarchy, and may lead to a splintering of the organization's knowledge base which is difficult to reverse (see Figure 8.2). To eliminate the barriers, companies need to create the right conditions, primarily in the areas of employee management and company culture. The aim of all interventions will be to create sufficient willingness to communicate knowledge.

Individual willingness to share knowledge

At individual level, barriers are of two kinds: those affecting the ability to share knowledge, and those affecting the will to do so. The ability to share knowledge depends primarily on the individual's talent for communication and his or her social behaviour. Willingness, on the

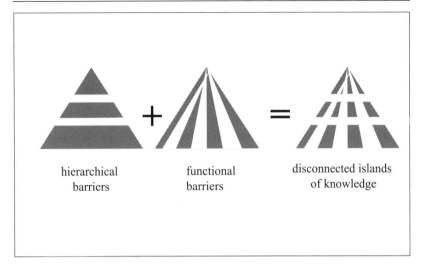

hierarchical   functional   disconnected islands
barriers   barriers   of knowledge

Figure 8.2   Barriers to knowledge

other hand, is influenced by many factors. Pride in the ownership of one's own expert knowledge may play an important part. Lack of time resulting from real or imagined informational overload can also reduce preparedness to take part in knowledge-sharing activities. Finally, employees often fear that if they pass on their knowledge to others, they will endanger their own position in the organization.

Influence of company culture

Cultural barriers to sharing knowledge exist in the absence of elements of company culture that would legitimize or support such sharing.[25] Company culture can affect both the scope and the content of knowledge transfer. The definition of important areas of knowledge is often a significant indicator of the company culture. In a quantitatively oriented culture, it is likely that only financial figures and related aspects will have official significance, whereas a strong marketing culture uses the vocabulary of customer value. The less relevant areas of knowledge are almost automatically excluded from intensive sharing and distribution. A related point is that the knowledge of employees who do not speak the dominant business language is largely ignored.

Power

Political or power-based barriers are of great significance. If the sharing of knowledge might weaken the position of its owner, there is a serious obstacle. This happens mainly in strongly politicized organizations where knowledge serves as a power base; under these conditions, efficient sharing of knowledge is usually impossible. The company should take steps to build up the trust of the owners of knowledge by relating sharing of knowledge to pay and incentives. Equally, these mechanisms must support requests for knowledge, which should be regarded not as an admission of weakness and incompetence, but as an expression of openness and constructive curiosity.

Dangers to the atmosphere of trust

An atmosphere of trust is essential for efficient sharing of knowledge, but it is difficult to create. Trust can only be established slowly, through positive example, but negative events can destroy it abruptly and for a long time. When important decisions are made which could affect the climate in which knowledge is shared, this aspect should be expressly included in the calculations. If, for example, an outstanding knowledge broker is sacked in the course of redimensioning, this will have a direct and generally lasting effect on trust.

Management

Employee management has an important part to play in creating the right culture. It is difficult to increase the sharing and distribution of knowledge in the absence of knowledge-oriented incentives and assessment mechanisms. The general attitude to knowledge distribution in companies today is that there is a duty of collection on the part of the person who wants it. Management systems that make clear to employees the importance of sharing knowledge can transform this into a duty of provision. Both positive and negative incentives may be provided. In the LOTUS DEVELOPMENT CORPORATION, the assessment and pay of customer service employees have been made up to 25% dependent on their activities in support of knowledge sharing and distribution. A low level of activity automatically affects performance ratings. BUCKMAN LABORATORIES have kept a traditional system of employee assessment, but there are special incentives for particular efforts at knowledge sharing. One such incentive is that the 100 best knowledge sharers fly to a seminar held at an attractive holiday resort (cf. Davenport 1996, p. 37).

TRANSFERRING 'BEST PRACTICES' – TODAY'S CHALLENGE

Internal benchmarking is valuable as a knowledge identification process,[26] since it reveals areas where there is potential for increasing efficiency. However, additional measures – such as adopting best practices – are needed if this potential is to be realized. Best practices can only be spread through different areas of a company if there is systematic sharing and distribution of knowledge.

The benefits to the company of implementing best practices are often impressive. BUCKMAN LABORATORIES, for example, achieved a 10% increase in turnover on the basis of new products; they attribute this increase to systematic implementation of best practices. In CHEVRON, a best practice transfer within the energy management area brought savings of $150 million. The company estimates that its best practice teams have been responsible for savings of $650 million to date. Finally, TEXAS INSTRUMENTS succeeded in generating extra production capacity worth $1.5 billion as a result of a best practice project (cf. O'Dell & Grayson 1998, p. 156)

Given their potential value, we might ask why best practices are not systematically shared and distributed in all companies. The answer lies partly in the many obstacles that stand in the way of best practice transfer. A large-scale study by Szulanski produced many new and surprising findings on this subject.[27] Previous research had attributed difficulties in best practice transfer primarily to lack of motivation among participants. Reasons for lack of motivation include rivalry between departments or areas of the company, general resistance to change, and the well-known 'not invented here' syndrome (NIH). Szulanski's study questions the importance of these phenomena in hampering best practice transfer. His results emphasize knowledge-related factors, and he identifies two main obstacles to successful transfer of knowledge; these are lack of 'absorptive capacity' in the receiving unit, and 'causal ambiguity' of the knowledge to be transferred.

In ordinary language, this means that the transfer of best practices most commonly fails because the receiving unit does not have sufficient knowledge to recognize the value of the best practice, and to use it meaningfully for its own purposes. Secondly, transfer may fail because of uncertainty about which factors determine the functioning of the practice, or are responsible for its success. The quality of the relationship between the unit where the best practice originates and the receiving unit occupies third place, behind the knowledge-related factors. It embraces the motivational issues that were previously thought to be of primary importance.

How can the transfer of best practices be improved? The following is a summary of possible techniques; they are often used in combination.

Transfer of managers; information trips

If managers are in regular contact with the different company locations, this increases transparency of knowledge and creates the conditions for identifying and transferring best practices. The contact may take the form of information meetings or of longer-term transfers.

Benchmarking teams and best practice teams

Benchmarking teams prepare the ground by looking for best practices outside the company. They provide continuous support for the transfer of internal best practices, giving priority to the core processes of the organization.

Best practice networks

Unlike formal teams, best practice networks are based on informal exchanges among the members of a 'community of practice'. Communications and information technologies often play an important part in supporting these networks.

Internal Audits

A system for evaluating internal best practices may lead to outstanding performances being honoured in some way, and thus made public. This approach is often combined with best practice conferences, at which the winners present their successful practices and have an opportunity to make contact with interested parties.

The experiences of companies where best practices have been successfully transferred generally confirm the efficacy of the knowledge distribution structures recommended in this chapter. From their study of best practice transfers, O'Dell and Grayson derive a number of ground rules, which we interpret as follows:

- Internal and external benchmarking are useful techniques for creating pressure that can trigger best practice transfer.
- Critical business processes where there is high potential for increasing efficiency should be given priority for best practice transfers.
- Best practice transfer programmes should not be so large or numerous that it is impossible to keep track of them all.
- Evaluation is necessary. However, attempts to measure and evaluate individual practices too accurately can lead to measurement becoming an end in itself, and may hold up the actual transfer process.
- Systems of pay and incentives must be consistent with the goals of best practice transfer.
- Technology can act as a catalyst, but it is not a solution in itself.
- Motivation and the support of top management are deciding factors.

SUMMARY

- The trend towards group work, co-operation between companies, and the virtual organization makes the distribution of knowledge a matter of priority.
- Ways of structuring the processes of knowledge sharing and distribution multiply with the development of more mature technologies and sophisticated organizational methods.

- The sharing and distribution of knowledge holds a prominent position in knowledge management. They support vital competitive factors such as time and quality, and possess leverage because of their significance for other aspects of knowledge management.
- Sharing and distribution of knowledge only make sense within certain limits. They may be restricted in any case by economic, legal and organizational barriers.
- The tasks involved in sharing and distributing knowledge are of three kinds: (1) the replication of knowledge, by transferring it quickly to a large number of employees; (2) the safeguarding and sharing of previous learning; and (3) the simultaneous exchange of knowledge, which leads to the development of new knowledge.
- The sharing of knowledge meets with barriers at individual and cultural levels. These primarily involve issues of power and trust.
- The increasing networking of companies with their environment and the trend away from individual work and towards collective forms make the sharing and distribution of knowledge a precondition for effective and efficient management.
- Recent developments in information and communications technology offer many new opportunities. However, there are still few criteria for using them rationally.
- Knowledge distribution must balance many conflicting interests. It is not just a question of finding the correct medium; companies must also decide on the proper scope of the application.
- Depending on the type of knowledge and the type of organization, knowledge may be distributed through centralized mechanisms (replication of knowledge), or by the use of more decentralized techniques (creating infrastructures).
- Practical experience up to the present suggests that the combination of people and technology in hybrid systems is a promising approach.
- The transfer of best practices is a vital part of knowledge distribution in companies. If best practices are successfully spread throughout the company, considerable increases in efficiency can be achieved.
- There are obstacles to the transfer of best practices both at the motivational level and in the nature of the knowledge to be transferred. Necessary success factors include adequate absorptive capacity in the receiving unit and a thorough understanding of the best practice.

KEY QUESTIONS

● What information and communications technologies are currently used for sharing and distributing information and knowledge in your working environment?

● Who provides the impetus for the use of these technologies? Was there broad agreement among employees on the purposes for which they were to be used, or is the technology allowed to develop an uncontrolled dynamic of its own?

● Do you use all the available ways of communicating knowledge that concerns everyone promptly and widely to your employees?

● Do you exchange information and knowledge systematically with other parts of the company or other functional areas?

● If you want internal access to knowledge, do you have to go through the hierarchy, or are there parallel infrastructures which offer quick and non-bureaucratic access?

● Do these infrastructures work mainly on a technical or mainly on an interpersonal basis? What are the advantages of the current solution, and where do you see problems?

● Do you believe that the employees in your organization would be willing to share their knowledge if asked? If not, why do you think that is?

● Do you have an overall picture of the best practices for core processes in your company? What measures could you take to improve transparency in this area?

● Are you exploring thoroughly all possible ways of increasing efficiency through transfer of best practices? What specific obstacles have you noticed in your company?

9

Using Knowledge

INTRODUCTION

You have identified gaps in your company's knowledge base.
You have bought and developed knowledge to fill them, and put
it at the disposal of the decision-makers – and nobody uses it!
There are numerous barriers, structural and psychological, which
make people slow to use 'outside' knowledge. They are reluctant
to give up the familiar routines that help them through their daily
tasks. Applying new knowledge means accepting uncertainty,
and taking a step into the unknown.

One of the functions of knowledge management is to ensure
that the company uses its know-how. Knowledge is of no value
if it is not applied. Those who make knowledge available must
therefore pay greater attention to the needs of potential users,
whom they should regard as their customers. Workers will only
accept 'outside' knowledge, or develop new skills, when they
see clear advantages in doing so. We shall now show how you
can overcome the barriers that prevent your colleagues from
using the knowledge that is available to them. This will increase
the use of knowledge in ordinary work situations.

USING KNOWLEDGE

I don't think that we have a problem with lack of knowledge. We have enough capable and experienced employees. But when I look at the projects that failed, I am always surprised to find that we do in fact have the knowledge to avoid making those mistakes. We just don't use it! (*Section head in a mechanical engineering company*)

Understanding something is by no means the same thing as doing it. We have found that even when we have made the right knowledge available, we still have to keep on rubbing our employees' noses in it. We have found it extremely helpful to demonstrate its relevance in the normal work setting. (*Divisional head in a multinational industrial concern*)

We are almost always at odds with our research department. For years they have treated us as engineers of an inferior kind. Now that we finally have a recognised development department, we tinker around with a problem for weeks, rather than use the existing knowledge produced by the 'researchers'. (*Development engineer in an electronics company*)

Knowledge utilization as a measure of success

A company can have first-rate processes for identifying and developing knowledge, and still fail. If it does not apply its new knowledge, no benefit is achieved and the effort was in vain. Countless programmes have failed because of the mistaken belief that designing better knowledge infrastructures automatically leads to mastery of knowledge management process. All the building blocks of knowledge management must be directed towards using individual and organizational knowledge efficiently in order to reach the company's goals. 'Knowledge in action' is the most meaningful measure of successful knowledge management, since the productive application of knowledge is the only way to translate it into visible results.

Knowledge utilization in relation to other building blocks

In our diagram, knowledge utilization comes almost at the end of the cycle of knowledge management. However, the whole diagram could be turned around, since the processes of identifying, developing, acquiring, sharing and distributing knowledge should always be geared to the needs of potential users. Where management information systems are left unused, or project reports unread, it is often because they were not designed to meet the needs of the users. The reports are too long, or not practical enough. The management information system is not compatible with other applications, or it ignores vital management considerations.

CASE STUDY: HEWLETT PACKARD EUROPA

User-friendly presentation of information
HEWLETT PACKARD's European headquarters chose an unusual way of presenting important indices of general business performance. The company had had a management information system for a long time, but it was not used as much as it might have been. HEWLETT PACKARD therefore introduced a system that presents the most important information in a particularly user-friendly fashion. It can also be used in a variety of ways because it combines different media forms.

The 'management cockpit', created in collaboration with the consultancy firm NET-RESEARCH, builds on existing data warehouses and management information systems, rather than replacing them. The central idea is to present a few main indices in simple graphic form, and to arrange them in groups like the instruments in the cockpit of an aircraft (see Figure 9.1).

Selected 'cockpit' displays are shown on large boards in the different work areas, and are regularly updated by a computer technician. Special software allows data to be viewed on individual computers; this function is supported by special software. Depending on his or her needs, the user can view particular indices in the context of the whole hierarchy, or filter out critical ones in the form of 'traffic

---

lights', or analyse individual variables in more detail ('drill-down'). A major advantage of the system is that it concentrates relevant information, which can then serve as a basis for focused discussion of important trends in general business development. The cockpit can be shown in a special conference room, for example, as an aid to team meetings. It is also a useful tool for virtual teams, since it can be shown on screen.

When systems of this kind are designed, the needs of the end user are sometimes included at a surprisingly late stage in the process. Knowledge management activities aimed at the needs of the user ('pull') have a much better chance of being used than activities which are not linked to those needs ('push').

ENCOURAGING PEOPLE TO USE KNOWLEDGE

Barriers to using knowledge

Having taken the trouble to ensure that the right knowledge is available, managers must then create conditions in which employees will actually use it. The working environment should support the application of new knowledge, and should encourage both individuals and groups to access the company's intellectual assets. For many years, German car manufacturers were not willing even to look at Japanese production methods, let alone use them in their own factories. Psychological barriers of this kind are often due to overestimating one's own skills, or fear of losing one's expert status. These factors can block the use of new knowledge. Just as people must be willing to share their knowledge to some degree, they must also be prepared to use new knowledge.

Organizational blindness

Using 'outside' knowledge – like sharing our own knowledge with others – can seem unnatural (cf. Davenport 1996, p. 37). One reason

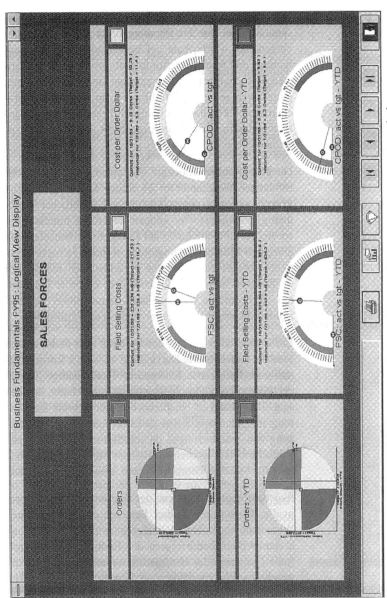

Figure 9.1 Instruments from HEWLETT PACKARD management cockpit

for this is that work sequences become routine. In general, the more familiar and automatic the task, the more difficult it is for us to recognize the importance of new knowledge, or to exchange ideas with colleagues about new ways of performing it. As routines become more familiar, we usually grow more reluctant to believe that new procedures might improve our efficiency. The knowledge of individuals thus becomes 'set'; this is called 'organizational blindness'.

Cultural barriers

In addition to the general inertia which inclines people to continue in the old, familiar ways,[1] there are often hidden rules of play which block the use of unfamiliar knowledge. If an employee requests and uses new knowledge, he puts himself in a vulnerable position. He admits to a gap in his knowledge, and feels – often with justification – that this puts him in a bad light among his colleagues. The way in which the knowledge is requested, and from whom, conceals further hazards. If knowledge is sought from a different department, the head of one's own department may be discredited. Colleagues may also believe that they could have answered the question themselves, and this leads to bad feeling. The combination of all these factors tempts the individual worker to do nothing and to keep quiet about the problem. He is thus prevented from using knowledge that is scattered through other parts of the organization.

Leadership

Management measures aimed at cultural variables may help employees to use new knowledge. Individuals should be encouraged to maintain a critical attitude to existing methods, and the 'not invented here' syndrome should be avoided. Questions must be interpreted not as a sign of incompetence, but as an indication of willingness to learn and to accept change.

At organizational level, knowledge should be seen as a resource which must be used by all for the general benefit, regardless of its provenance. The important question is not where the knowledge came from, but how it can be used well and efficiently to profit the organization.

THE KNOWLEDGE USER AS CUSTOMER

User-friendly infrastructures

Countless studies have shown that whether individuals make use of knowledge depends primarily on convenience. People are likely to seek knowledge if it only takes a short telephone call, or perhaps an informal request to a colleague who is close enough to hear, or only a short walk away. They are less likely to make an independent search in a library or a data bank. If employees need to use more remote elements in the organization's store of knowledge, the best way of encouraging them is to make the knowledge base and knowledge infrastructures user-friendly.

Challenges

The main features that make systems user-friendly are simplicity ('easy to use') good timing ('just in time'), and compatibility ('ready to connect'). Ideally, information and knowledge can be localized and transferred simply and quickly, and are available in a form that permits prompt application and continued use. One way of making knowledge infrastructures simpler and more user-friendly is to use a software system like GRAPEVINE, which allows for simultaneous distribution, use and development of knowledge. If all the building blocks of knowledge management are planned together, there is a good chance of setting up infrastructures that are consistently user-oriented. GRAPE- VINE offers rapid distribution, and it uses compatible formats, which permits direct use of the information packages.

Integrated approach

The organizational knowledge base will be used with much greater efficiency if the building blocks of knowledge management connect seamlessly. There should be a system for knowledge identification that offers the user ready access to interesting information and knowledge. Listings of material should also give information on archiving and on ways in which items can be retrieved. References to experts are more effective when they contain a current telephone number or some other way of making contact. LANGNESE-IGLO have set up an Info-center based on these principles.

CASE STUDY: LANGNESE-IGLO

Info-centers increase knowledge utilization
LANGNESE-IGLO uses Info-centers as a way of increasing communication among employees. They are located at central points in the office building. The graphic presentation of material and an abundance of seating makes them inviting places to linger (see Figure 9.2).

Information is presented in different media, ranging from simple wall displays to video equipment and interactive computer terminals. The contents include messages from management and news from different departments and project teams. The Info-centers have various features to encourage interaction, for example, an 'ideas market', which is a terminal for entering non-personal comments on the various topics that are currently displayed.

Using newly acquired knowledge

The extent to which new knowledge is used depends mainly on its quality, that is, on the potential benefits of using it. There is usually a clear positive correlation between value of knowledge and level of use. A complicated piece of software which offers no real improvement in efficiency, or a barely noticeable one, will usually be ignored. The same applies to a highly scientific memo on a largely irrelevant topic. More promising are knowledge elements that strike a balance between the costs of searching and learning on the one hand, and the benefits of using the knowledge on the other. This balance usually depends on the quality of the knowledge, its level of aggregation, and the media in which it is available.

Developing knowledge on the job

A practical context can be valuable in developing knowledge. On-the-job training is based on the belief that employees acquire new knowl-

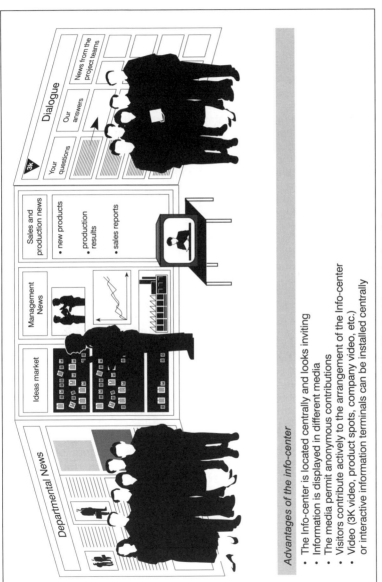

Figure 9.2 Typical layout of an Info-center

Advantages of the info-center

- The Info-center is located centrally and looks inviting
- Information is displayed in different media
- The media permit anonymous contributions
- Visitors contribute actively to the arrangement of the Info-center
- Video (3K video, product spots, company video, etc.) or interactive information terminals can be installed centrally

'User unfriendly' document structure

This text summarizes the main propositions of the cognitive sciences and explains their implications for the structuring of texts and documents. It makes special mention of the structure of hypertext documents, and how they can be made 'brain friendly', i.e. easy to use. The last 20 years have seen rapid development both in the cognitive sciences and in information technology (IT). However, the two disciplines have developed not in tandem, but in relative isolation from each other. Until recently, co-operation between them was restricted to particular topics. The principal driving force behind the growing collaboration between psychologists and information scientists has been, and remains, research on artificial intelligence. Co-operation between cognitive psychology and IT is essential for constructing efficient representations of knowledge and information. Psychology improves the structuring of computer processing of symbols, since it examines the cognitive requirements for efficient transmission and storage of information. Information technology on the other hand makes it possible to manipulate these units of information, i.e. it processes the symbols. In the list given below, individual findings of cognitive psychology are linked with the corresponding informational techniques. The following list should be regarded as an extract from a more comprehensive catalogue of requirements: pictorial coding of information and unconscious construction of cognitive maps are converted by IT into clickable knowledge maps (combination of visualization technique and data bank technology); the improvement in retention that can be achieved by involving both cerebral hemispheres is achieved in IT by using visual and structural metaphors to construct interfaces; information is stored in the brain more than once, in different ways, and often linked by associations, which corresponds to hypertext as an associative storage technique; sequences of information can help or hinder information processing, so it is important to bring out the distinctions between sequential items of information, and this can be ensured by sequencing algorithms or thematic archiving techniques. These techniques can be classified under four headings: search for information, storage of information, information management and use of information. There are instruments for use in all these fields, for example the thesaurus, which serves as a rationale for queries and storage when knowledge is being used. Hypertext is a technique that chiefly supports use of knowledge; it supports knowledge development only to a limited extent. Sequencing algorithms also facilitate use of knowledge, since they guarantee meaningful storage of information. Search languages and knowledge maps are tools which support the search for knowledge during use. For knowledge development, the main techniques are co-operation with others and continual training. From these remarks one can draw the general conclusion that cognitive psychology. . . .

Figure 9.3 User-friendly preparation of documents (cf. Eppler 1998)

'User friendly' documents

Requirements and rules for structuring readable texts and creating ergonomic documentation

Overview   This text summarizes the main propositions of the cognitive sciences and explains their implications for structuring texts and documentation. It makes special mention of the structuring of hypertext documents and how they can be made 'brain friendly, i.e. easy to use.

Introduction   During the last 20 years, both the cognitive sciences and IT have developed rapidly. However, they have developed not in tandem, but in relative isolation from each other. Until recently, co-operation between the two disciplines was restricted to selected topics. The driving force behind increasing co-operation has been, and remains, research into artificial intelligence.

Relevance   Collaboration between cognitive psychology and IT is essential for the structuring and efficient representation of knowledge and information. Psychology improves the structuring of computer processing of symbols. The following diagram shows the intersection between the two disciplines.

knowledge processing
cognitive processes   symbol processing

psychology   information technology

Cognitive techniques   The following table shows insights from cognitive psychology and corresponding IT techniques. The list should be regarded as an extract from comprehensive set of requirements.

Insights

Cognitive psychology	Information technology
• pictorial coding of information and unconscious creation of cognitive maps	• clickable knowledge maps (linking of visualization technique and data bank technology)
• material more intelligible if both cerebral hemispheres are involved	• text organized by means of visual and structural metaphors (graphics)
• information stored repeatedly in different ways, often with associative links	• hypertext as associative storage system for information
• Information sequences can support or hinder information processing. The brain needs to emphasize differences between sequential items	• Sequencing algorithms or subject-based archiving techniques can ensure that items of information are clearly distinguished and can be retrieved

edge more readily in a context where it can be directly applied. Material learned in this way is easier to remember. In training and development, a number of techniques are used – such as action learning[2] – which require simultaneous development and use of knowledge in the context of a collective problem-solving process. Scenarios, simulations and planning games also put the application of knowledge in a practical context.[3] Training is more effective when carried out in a motivating learning environment of this kind. Knowledge development in groups can also broaden employees' views of organizational processes. Contact with colleagues from other departments or units reduces the danger that isolated, routine work sequences will lead to organizational blindness.

Intuitively appealing documents

Small things can sometimes make a great difference to whether knowledge assets are used. A large part of company communication still takes place by means of documents, memos and internal publications. Many of these documents, however, are not intuitively appealing or user-friendly. Graphics, short summaries and other similar devices can make a clear difference to levels of utilization (see Figure 9.3).

WORKING CONDITIONS INCREASE USE OF KNOWLEDGE

User-friendly working conditions

If the workplace is made more user-friendly – and there are accepted ways of doing this – then use of knowledge also increases. The most important factors are the positioning of workstations and sections within the building, and a more user-friendly arrangement of individual workstations. In both cases, the deciding factor is the physical proximity of workers to the knowledge they need.

Examples of space management

Space management in this context means translating relationships that involve communication or exchange of knowledge into the shortest possible physical distances between individuals or sections. This deals directly with failure to use knowledge because it is too far away. Coopers & Lybrand have been particularly successful in reorganizing the work environment according to this principle. Their premises were previously arranged to reflect the prestige of the partners, who had large offices on the best side of the building. This arrangement was changed to a more open and flexible layout, with fewer offices but more work rooms and conference rooms, and workstations that can be used by several people at different times, depending on who is in the office.[4]

Arrangement of workstations

Individual workstations in offices and workshops can be made more attractive, often by simple means. In Ericsson, for example, ordinary screen savers on computers were replaced by an automatic blend of Reuter News and a ticker tape with the price of Ericsson shares. This directs workers' attention to one of the main purposes of their activities, and reminds them regularly that they can draw on a global range of information. ABB (see below) have used other ways of creating an atmosphere that encourages use of knowledge.

CASE STUDY: Asea Brown Boveri (ABB)

Increasing the use of knowledge by better structuring of working environment
As part of its 'customer focus' programme, ABB implemented a total quality management (TQM) initiative. To give this initiative a broad base within the company, they started by teaching employees to understand problem-solving methods and to apply them in their daily work. This was supported by documentation of the ABB six-step problem-solving process, and the 'memory jogger', which contains a concise guide to the most important tools of TQM.

The company discovered, however, that developing knowledge by these methods was not enough. Consistent application of knowledge is a much more important success

factor in quality management. Work areas were therefore
arranged so as to facilitate the use of TQM techniques. Each
production island is now equipped with a large whiteboard
on which the main quality measures are shown. Problems
are analysed in regular group sessions held in the
production area itself. The results of these sessions are
shown on the whiteboard in the form of Pareto or fishbone
diagrams. In this way, the analysis of the problem, the
agreed action and the measures of success all remain in the
production area. The knowledge is always accessible, and
its presence in the working environment means that it is
more likely to be used.

SUMMARY

- It is by no means enough to acquire, develop and accumulate
  knowledge. The knowledge must be made usable, and ultimately
  it must be used.
- Utilization of knowledge can be increased by appropriate structuring of group and individual work environments.
- The use of knowledge can be seen as the 'implementation phase'
  of the knowledge management process. It is at this stage that
  knowledge is transformed into concrete results.
- There are barriers to using knowledge, just as there are barriers to
  sharing it. They may arise from 'organizational blindness', fear of
  revealing one's own weaknesses, or a general mistrust of 'outside'
  knowledge.
- The ultimate application of the knowledge must be considered at
  all stages in knowledge management. The needs of the user must
  be taken into account in all the building blocks of knowledge management.
- Integrating knowledge management methods into the immediate
  working environment encourages employees to use knowledge.

KEY QUESTIONS

- In your organization or department, is it possible to question the
  content of the work? Is knowledge requested from other functional

areas or other organizational units, and is it then used? Or are requests usually made only within the department?

- Are your preferred technical sources of information (such as data banks, management information systems) structured in a user-friendly way? When searching them, can you combine different sources of knowledge (internal and external documents, project workers, experts), or are these kinds of information held separately?

- Can information and knowledge that you need be found close to your own working area, or must you go a long way to find it?

- Is your own workstation equipped and arranged so as to encourage you to use relevant knowledge on a daily basis?

- Is there an area in your department where topics of current interest are documented or shown graphically, where information 'crystallizes' and where people can develop knowledge together?

- Do the documents that you receive every day have a user-friendly design? If not, how do you give feedback to the people who produce them?

10
Preserving Knowledge

INTRODUCTION

'We used to be able to do it, but we seem to have forgotten how.' Parts of an organization's memory may be lost, temporarily or permanently, as a result of re-engineering, outsourcing or lean management policies. Does your company suffer from amnesia? Do knowledge gaps appear when employees leave, whether or not their departure was planned? How do you retain the things that your organization has learned? Do you maintain contact with former employees, and make use of their experience even after they have left? At the end of a project, do you compose 'lessons learned', to preserve the main advances in knowledge for future project teams? In this chapter, we shall show how you can keep important experts even after they leave the company. We shall also discuss the role of the collective memory in preserving knowledge, and how you can use the rapid advances in storage media to build an electronic memory for your company.

PRESERVING KNOWLEDGE

The front line

In our research centre, we have a small number of people who are real experts on our products. The most experienced and highly regarded of them retired a few days ago. We know that with him, we are losing an extremely important part of our product competence; but we don't know how to preserve his experience for the future. (*Head of research and development in a foodstuffs company*)

A few months ago, I realised what it means to work for a company that knows how to preserve valuable knowledge and use it again. I sat in a presentation and watched a young colleague show some slides that I had made myself some time previously. For the presenter, they had become knowledge that belonged to the company, and he had no idea where they came from. (*Partner in a business consultancy firm*)

In our company, there are many project groups working at different levels to create an electronic memory for their special area. However, there is no integrated solution for the whole organization, and this will lead to interface problems. I am afraid that in the end, we shall only have access to a fraction of the knowledge that now exists, and of all that we have learned up to this point. (*IT Manager in a large service company*)

We are constantly told how important the organizational memory is, yet in most approaches to management, deliberate preservation of the company's own past plays a minor part. In general terms, memory may be described as a system of knowledge and skills that preserves and stores perceptions and experiences beyond the moment when they occur, so that they can be retrieved at a later time.[1] The organizational memory is the point of reference for new experiences: without memory, no learning is possible.

Undervaluing experience

For these reasons, preserving knowledge is an important part of knowledge management; yet when companies reorganize, the value of organizational memory is often underestimated. Managers may decide that the company should be leaner, or that it needs rejuvenating. Decisions of this kind are often the prelude to outsourcing. Useless ballast is thrown overboard; but the decision to discard parts of the company's past (outdated?) experience should not be taken lightly (cf. Davenport 1996, p. 35)

Irreversible losses

Removing employees who resist change may ease the general flow, but at the same time, there are always costs to the organization in terms of personal experience. Many companies have made the bitter discovery that a rigorous lean management policy, complete with redundancies and outsourcing, has taken away valuable know-how. They then have to pay high consultancy fees to buy it back. Certain kinds of knowledge that are specific to the company, for example about the architecture of old industrial plants, are irreversibly lost. The loss of certain critical information can affect the functioning of whole areas of a company.[2]

The company memory

Andy Miller is a good example of the importance of company memory. For 30 years, he worked in the sales department of a large American firm. In a department of about a 100 people, everybody knew and liked him. He spent most of his working day chatting informally with his colleagues, and on most days, he talked with all the other sales staff in the department.

Following a change of management, the new managing director brought in an external consultant to analyse the sales figures. Andy Miller, who had never sold very much, and was over 50, was dismissed after the next quarter. The consultant's personal comment was: 'Miller is seldom to be found at his desk. He spends a large part of his time chatting about things that have nothing to do with sales.'

After Andy's departure, unaccustomed difficulties began to appear. Co-ordination among subsections in the department began to suffer, responsibilities that had been clearly defined now seemed uncertain, and the number of customer complaints increased. The general mood also changed. People complained that nobody remembered birthdays, wedding anniversaries or career anniversaries any more. New employees felt unsupported, and often fell foul of the company's unwritten rules. It took some time for people to realize that when the company dismissed Andy, it also dismissed its 'memory': Andy had built up a detailed knowledge of the people and processes in the organization, and in the course of his 'unproductive' strolls, he made this knowledge available to everyone else.

Identity and memory

The story of Andy Miller shows that companies may suffer unexpected losses if they do not take steps to preserve knowledge in a purposeful way. Human beings are rooted in their developmental histories; they can only determine their identity by continual reference to their past experiences, and this is how each individual arrives at his or her particular capacity for learning. Many organizations now complain that they have lost part of their memory during a reorganization. This collective amnesia results from the thoughtless destruction of informal networks that support important – but often little regarded – processes. The disorder is particularly likely to affect companies that shrink rapidly; business consultants call it the 'collective Alzheimer syndrome'.

Unlearning versus preserving

The conflict in management theory between destroying and preserving old knowledge, information and skills emerges clearly in relation to the issue of unlearning. Hedberg defines unlearning as the process in which learners clear out their old knowledge (cf. Hedberg 1981, p. 18). He urges rigorous discarding of useless past experiences, in order to make way for a new beginning. Organizations must start a process of unlearning when, as a result of changes in the environment, previous patterns of interpretation and reaction – that is, the organization's theory of action – no longer meet current challenges. Unlearning means being ready to question one's own routines and to let go of the familiar. The problem is to decide whether certain knowledge assets and certain experts are no longer needed, or whether they might be important in the future.

Experience as the starting point for improvement

Should all the existing customer data be erased, because marketing was not efficient in the past, and needs to be reorganized? Should successful teams be disbanded because they have been working on the wrong problems? Should all workers over a certain age be made redundant, because they are not flexible enough to deal with future changes, and because early retirement currently attracts state subsidy? The answer to all these questions is a decided negative. It is most important that organizations should preserve valuable experience and vital data and information in a targeted fashion.

Organizational knowledge can only be developed on the basis of previous knowledge. Psychologists believe that in individuals, old experiences are not overwritten and erased by new ones. Old rules are given new markers, and are no longer used under current circumstances; however, they remain available as an option. In organizations, they increase the range of possible actions in a turbulent environment (Cohen & Levinthal 1990 make similar remarks).

Processes of knowledge preservation

Organizations wishing to manage their knowledge so that it will be accessible in the future must master at least three basic processes in knowledge management. First, they must select from the many events, persons and processes those that are worth retaining. Second, they must be able to store their experience in a suitable form. Finally, they must ensure that the organizational memory is updated (see Figure 10.1).

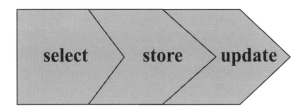

Figure 10.1 Main processes in knowledge preservation

SELECTING KNOWLEDGE WORTH SAVING

Principles of choice

In large organizations, each day brings experiences that could be useful in the future and should therefore be saved. Project reports, minutes of meetings, letters and presentations emerge in all parts of the company. Every day, customers approach members of the organization with complaints, suggestions or praise. It is simply impossible to keep track of all these events. Let us take as an example a salesman who – like his colleagues – often makes presentations about his products to business associates. He has created by himself a sales presentation that shows the customer value of the products much more effectively than previous sales aids. His colleagues know nothing about this presentation, perhaps because of poor knowledge identification in the company, or lack of communication; or perhaps the outstanding presenter has not been offered incentives to share his know-how.

Rules of selection

When deciding which knowledge to preserve, it is helpful to consider what would happen to the knowledge of any employee if he or she left suddenly. Who can find the vital documents or presentations on his or her hard disk? It may be well organized, but then again, it may not. Are the contacts and processes that are important to the job well documented?

The unexpected departure of an employee often leaves a painful gap, as a result of inadequate documentation during his or her tenure. Documentation always takes time and effort, its benefits are usually not immediate, and the person who created it rarely receives the credit. Rules for selection are therefore needed, since it makes no sense to document every little thing. The challenge is to separate valuable experiences from the rest, and to transfer the valuable data, information and skills into organizational systems where they can be useful to the whole company. Again, ARTHUR ANDERSEN provides a good example.

CASE STUDY: ARTHUR ANDERSEN

Systematic selection and preservation of knowledge using
ARTHUR ANDERSEN ONLINE

ARTHUR ANDERSEN's internal information system was
described briefly in the chapter on defining knowledge
goals. There are electronic forums on all topics which affect
the company's competence in consulting. The quality of the
contributions varies greatly; and many of them are soon
outdated and no longer useful (see Figure 10.2).
    The challenge is to analyse the divergent system of
individual pieces of information. Responsibilities for the
processes of analysis and selection are clearly assigned.
Every centre of competence in the organization (e.g. TQM)
has particular managers or teams who perform these
functions. They interact to build knowledge by condensing
individual contributions into master documents. From 12
reports on the introduction of LOTUS Notes, for example,
one master document is produced which summarizes the
main lessons learned. The synthesizing process means that
only the essentials are retained in the system in the longer
term, and the user is spared the need to go through the
individual reports. Items typically selected for retention are
best practices, best companies, presentations, process
definitions, studies, articles, and cause and effect analyses.
These are stored in a structured form in ARTHUR ANDERSEN
ONLINE, and are thus available to all members of the
organization.
    The knowledge managers in centres of competence are
also responsible for clearing out unwanted material. If this
were not done, the global data bank would grow by about
3% every day, and would soon become dysfunctional.

Parallels with human memory

The processes of selection and storage in an organization may be compared with those that take place in the human brain. Information that

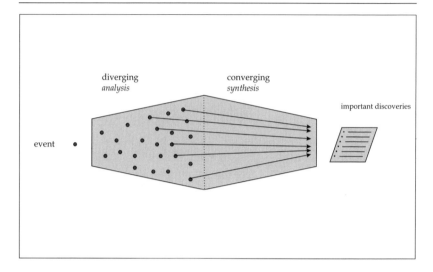

Figure 10.2   From a divergent to a convergent system

is recorded in our long-term memory must first pass through the ultra-short-term and short-term memories.[3] These are the gatekeepers of long-term memory: they separate important perceptions from irrelevant ones, thus protecting the brain from constant overstimulation. Unfortunately, the conscious part of the mind can only influence this process to a limited extent. We therefore have to use all kinds of tricks and learning techniques to outwit the gatekeepers and to filter what we want to keep from the flood of information.

Organizational routines

A similar problem exists in organizations. Selection mechanisms do not always work as systematically as planned. Organizations have routines that cause some processes – such as the filing of documents of a particular type – to proceed automatically and without question. In almost every office there are file 'cemeteries', or dusty archives, which indicate a wrong approach to preserving knowledge. The routines are firmly established, and the employees who maintain or manage these systems rarely change them without external impetus.

Knowledge documents

Organizations can never manage all the processes involved in knowledge selection. It would make no sense to try. However, in key areas, such as knowledge about customers, for example, they should strive to select meaningfully and to document efficiently. If this knowledge is recorded in documents, such as knowledge maps or lessons learned, it becomes independent of individuals and is preserved for the organization.[4] The important thing is to concentrate knowledge around certain key factors, and to relate it clearly to special problems. Only knowledge that might be useful to other people in the future is worth preserving. Anything else wastes the time of future knowledge seekers, and makes them doubt the quality of the documentation system. At the same time, we must remember that we can guess only a small part of our future information needs, so our limits should not be too narrow.

Documenting success

Another way of helping people to understand the organization's past is to preserve the main ideas in the form of management principles, vision and mission statements, stories or other kinds of symbolism. These forms of storage are useful because they provide a short cut to understanding the organization (cf. Probst & Büchel 1997, p. 21). A Swiss company, for instance, asked a consultant to document the outstandingly successful launch of a new product range. All those who had played a significant part were questioned, factors were identified that were thought to account for the success, and the story was then reconstructed. The results of the study were put together as a training case, which is now available to instructors. The story recounts a positive and meaningful event in the company's past, and can be used to motivate trainees and to impart knowledge to them.

Document management systems

Another reason for keeping knowledge documents is that they may be needed for legal reasons. In one instance, an IT worker responsible for monitoring all the larger projects in a decentralized concern complained that when he came to calculate fees owing to consultants, vital documents relating to the contract were missing. There were new projects under way, and a good deal of movement of employees, and the documents were simply not to be found. Difficulties of this kind might be avoided by using one of the new document management systems, which keep computer records of customer contracts throughout their life cycle, and store them in the firm's electronic memory.

Identifying key employees

New technologies such as work flow management and document management systems offer novel ways of preserving organizational knowledge. However, it is still people who make sensible or catastrophic choices at vital points. Employees cannot always be replaced by machines or computer systems. Their experiences are the key to organizing the company's past in a meaningful way. We have repeatedly stressed the importance of these key employees in the process of knowledge management. The surest way to avoid collective loss of memory is to identify them and retain them in the company.

STORING KNOWLEDGE

Once the knowledge worth saving has been separated from the rest, it must be stored in suitable form in the organization's knowledge base. We may distinguish three kinds of storage medium: individual employees, groups and computers. Since these operate on different principles, we shall discuss them separately.

Individual Storage: 'Who Knows About That?'

Organizations suffer permanent loss of valuable experts through dismissals, redundancies, retirement and death. In an article in *The Economist*, the expression 'unfixed assets' was used (ironically) to refer to exceptional employees. This goes to the heart of one of the main problems in the relationship between companies and their knowledge workers. Knowledge stored in the heads of employees is extremely volatile. If it is lost, the damage can only be limited by legal means, which is costly, and often has unpredictable side-effects. The simplest way to protect intellectual capital is to create an environment in which people simply do not think of moving.

Incentive systems and disincentives to leaving

If high performers are happy in their social environment, they are less susceptible to lucrative offers from outside. Expert knowledge workers, however, have a different motivational structure. Suitable incentives can only be devised by those who know this structure, and who gather more information by talking with the people involved. It is a mistake, nevertheless, to think that all experts can be kept indefinitely by an excellent working atmosphere, if pay is mediocre; some of them are bound to leave. The barriers to leaving (cf. Bonoma & Slevin 1978, p. 205) can be raised by social or material incentive systems, but the personal needs of individual employees must also be taken into account to make the barriers effective.

Flexible attachment mechanisms

It is sometimes impossible to keep valuable employees by means of incentives. It is the most able who have ideas of their own, and do not want to work for a large organization for ever. At some point, they will leave to set up an independent company, in spite of the risks. Even so, it may be possible to retain access to their knowledge after they leave by creating flexible co-operation mechanisms. These mechanisms can take many forms: the ex-employees might be invited back as teachers or consultants, for instance, or brought in for difficult discussions with customers. The main thing is to create a win–win situation. Consultancy firms, in which the yearly employee turnover rate may be up to 30%, use the exodus of home-trained employees to build up strong networks of relationships. They have 'their' people in nearly all major organizations, and thus secure access to exclusive information. There are also many ways in which retired employees could still be involved, though this is not often done. There seems to be a general feeling today that older people are no use, and they are expected to withdraw abruptly rather than gradually. However, if the company maintains a relationship with them, it retains customer contacts and access to information that would otherwise be permanently lost.

CASE STUDY: ABB CONSULTING

Retaining the experience of retired managers
Before ABB CONSULTING was created, the Swiss management of ABB faced a dilemma. On the one hand, they did not want to offer their long-serving managers early retirement, because this would have meant losing their long experience and their contacts. On the other hand, the positions were needed to give young employees the chance to rise to top jobs in reasonable time. The older managers wanted more freedom to decide when they would retire, and how quickly. The creation of ABB CONSULTING LTD offered them a way of retiring in stages. That company is now staffed entirely by former top employees of ABB SWITZERLAND, who wanted to make a new start as consultants at the age of 60. These 'elder statesmen' work mainly in subsidiaries of ABB, where they can continue to make full use of their experience and their worldwide network of contacts (see Figure 10.3).

The advisers who work for ABB CONSULTING operate in widely different fields, such as fixed-term management, public relations or co-operation with state or public bodies. There are many areas in which they can apply their knowledge. They can use their experience to act as ghost writers for present management, as competent guides in production activities (which they previously managed themselves) or as experienced process supervisors in complex projects. Normally, when an employee retires – whether willingly or not – the transfer of knowledge between the retiree and the company is at an end. ABB, however, has found a flexible alternative that benefits both sides. The company can still consult its former experts, and retired managers who want to go on working receive personal and financial recognition of the fact that they are still needed. Money that would otherwise be needed for expensive outplacement consultancy can be used more productively.

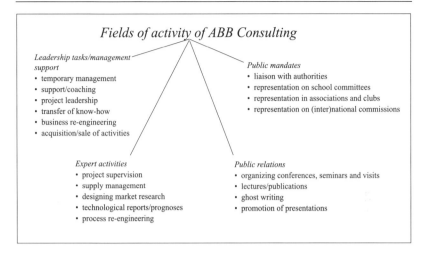

Figure 10.3   Retaining competencies through 'elder statesmen'

Systematic transfer of skills

Another way of retaining vital skills is to train successors. Long before the current holder of a position leaves, the successor should be trained step by step in the tasks he or she will have to perform, and thus acquires the skills of the 'master' over a long period. Many European organizations make heavy weather of training successors, and current employees try to hold on to their power right up to the last day by withholding important information. In Japan, there is a different tradition.

Sempai-kohai

The Japanese principle is called *sempai-kohai*. It is based on a close relationship between two men, the older *sempai*, who teaches, and the younger *kohai* who is taught (cf. *The Economist* 20.4.1996, p. 58). Every new worker is assigned to an older mentor who teaches the younger man all the tricks of the trade. The relationship is systematically strengthened by joint spare-time activities, to create an atmosphere of trust in which information of all kinds can be exchanged. The system is also excellent for the transfer of implicit knowledge. In 1993, the Japanese steel industry made a quarter of its 150 000 workers redundant. There were fears that the average level of competence would fall drastically, causing an obvious drop in quality. The fact that this did not happen was seen by external observers as corroboration of the *sempai-kohai* principle.

Selective explication

There are some relatively cheap and easy ways of reducing the damage that can be inflicted by the departure of an expert. One of the simplest methods is for trained specialists to carry out structured leaving interviews. In these interviews, knowledge which is vital to the organization – such as special documents, contacts or project involvement – are made explicit and documented. These interviews should also involve the successor. If the talks are open and positive, much valuable information is preserved, and the organization may also learn more about itself. It may learn, for example, the interviewee's reasons for leaving, and it will then be able to adjust the 'exit barriers' accordingly. At SANDIA NATIONAL LABORATORIES (Albuquerque, New Mexico), in-depth leaving interviews are recorded on audio tape and video (cf. *The Economist* 20.4.1996, p. 58). The aim is to capture something of the wisdom of the leavers, and to preserve their experience for the organization.

The Collective Memory

Human memory is fleeting and dynamic. Psychologists believe that every time we remember something, we change or rewrite our own past. The problem is that the false memories feel just like the genuine ones.[5] If we are not to be deceived by our own reconstructions of past reality,[6] we need feedback from others who were part of it, so that we can confirm or adjust our own picture. The group thus becomes a counterbalance to our own memories.

There are differences between individual remembering and the ways in which groups store shared experiences. Even now, using in-depth interviews, psychologists can draw the borders between areas that were more affected or less affected by the Thirty Years War. The horrors of that period penetrated so deeply into the collective memory that today, 350 years later, they still affect the everyday behaviour of the inhabitants of the area.[7] This phenomenon suggests that past experiences in an organization may be deeply rooted, even if they are not obvious to the casual observer.

Groups beat individuals

Collective memory is not just so much historical baggage; it can also be extremely productive. In a laboratory experiment, people were shown how to assemble a transistor radio. Some were shown in a group, and others individually.[8] A week after the training, they were invited back and asked to recall and carry out the individual steps in assembling the radio. The people who had been trained individually were put into small groups for the purpose. Those who had been trained as a group were left together and allowed to remember as a group. The result was that those who had been trained as a group remembered more details of the process and produced better radios. Detailed analysis of videos of the original training showed that they had developed a range of social and cognitive bonds; the researchers called these 'transactive memory system' (cf. Cohen & Bacdayan 1994). This group memory was superior to that of individuals.

Remembering in pairs

A further joint memory phenomenon was revealed during observations of pairs (cf. Wegner 1996, pp. 189ff.). Some individuals use another, with whom they interact closely, as an extension of their storage capacity, thus increasing their own ability to remember the past. They develop a feeling for which details of a jointly experienced situation the partner is particularly likely to note, e.g. names. This division of labour means that the partners can only remember a situation completely if they remember it together.

Documenting important processes

There are many group successes that cannot be explained by these methods of analysis. Group processes, such as problem-solving, often have a dynamic of their own, which observers and even the group members themselves have difficulty in understanding. Nevertheless, there are some steps that can be taken to preserve important processes and provide a basis for future improvements. Employees of FUJI-XEROX, a Japanese–American joint venture, documented every step and every detail in the co-operation process (cf. *The Economist* 20.4.1996, p. 58). The aim was to help future employees to learn about the company's history, and also to learn from it.

Minutes

Minutes are the traditional way of recording meetings. However, good minute-takers are rare, and the task is often regarded as irksome. Minutes tend to be either too short or too long; they are often redundant, badly structured, incomplete aggravations that are submitted too late anyway. Nevertheless, in organizations where much of the work is performed in changing project groups, minutes are the main document for preserving the development of the work to date. Japanese companies give their moderators special training in suitable documentation techniques. The aim is to ensure that facts and decisions are not forgotten, and that new group members can study the minutes of previous meetings and quickly understand the present state of group discussion.

Importance of a shared language

The spoken word is more powerful than written records. It is the best way of preserving and anchoring group experiences. Speech is closer to us than the written word. In the course of its life, a company develops its own vocabulary; new employees must learn it in order to join in the conversation. It goes far beyond the usual abbreviations, which are used for the sake of efficiency. Common words like quality, change and security are used in company-specific ways, and thus become vehicles of the company's history.

Words are often associated with strong emotions. In one industrial company, a highly paid team of consultants carried out a reorganization called 'Horizons'. It was a miserable failure. Years later, the mere mention of the word 'Horizons' was enough to put an end to any talk of a consultancy project.

Every organization has terms and expressions of this kind; they are used frequently in the course of everyday activities. Knowledge managers should therefore take trouble to anchor vital experiences or ideas in the organization's vocabulary, and to use them for their own purposes.

Group definition of terms

One way to anchor and preserve vital ideas and images is to ask groups to define terms.[9] If basic terms are explicitly analysed at the beginning of a group process, attention is drawn to any disagreements on the meaning of terms that had seemed unambiguous. A definition which is worked out by a team and suitably documented can reduce the danger of future misunderstandings. Fashionable expressions such as total quality management or process organization are especially likely to be understood in different ways. If a common basic terminology is established, people are less likely to talk past each other.

Shared experiences

In decentralized or heterogeneous companies, it is often extremely difficult to integrate different people's ideas on a particular topic. The investment needed to create a common language or to provide shared experiences can be considerable. Nevertheless, all 20 000 employees of SWISSCOM now take part in a 'Mind Change Workshop', as part of a large-scale reorganization. The participants experience change in small groups, and apply it to their particular situation. They are all shown the same video about the consequences of lack of customer orientation, and they examine the problem in groups. This gives rise to shared experiences, which can then be drawn upon at work. The 'Change SWISSCOM' programme, which embraces all the organization's structures and strategies, is turned into something that can be experienced, and is more firmly rooted in the organizational memory. It is also something that employees can relate to their own work.

The Company's Electronic Memory

Unlimited storage capacity

In recent years, the revolution in the computer industry has multiplied ways of storing material electronically. If development continues at the same rapid rate, there will soon be virtually unlimited storage space at very modest cost.

Digitization

Almost all traditional storage media can be put into digital form. Video cassettes can be replaced by DVDs, documents can be scanned, and the digital camera has been on the market for some time. In future, the ordinary computer user will be able to access the full range of storage media through a single interface. The qualitative advantages of digital storage media are that they are easy to edit, they can be used repeatedly, and they can be distributed cheaply via networks. The growth of digital media is creating the basis for a global human memory. At the same time, the Internet offers growing numbers of users access to masses of data. The Internet, and the intranets of many companies, are only the beginning of a development that even experts find difficult to evaluate. If libraries, journals, tapes, films and text archives all grow together, and if more comprehensive standards are imposed for organizing and structuring digital raw materials, then the Internet will become a meta-archive for everything.

Implications for the organizational memory

This development has major consequences for companies that operate in a knowledge-intensive environment. First, they must assume that their competitors have access to the worldwide data pool, and that they use it for their own purposes. Second, the organization of their own computerized knowledge base is an important issue. A substantial part of the know-how of knowledge-intensive companies is contained in documents that can be digitized, such as presentations, forms, building plans and reports. If these are systematically stored and reused, they constitute a competitive advantage of increasing benefit.

Loss of memory

The electronic memory can fail for many reasons. If, for example, knowledge documents from a particular workstation are not entered in the system, they are not stored in the company's electronic memory, and are not available to other employees. If a document is wrongly coded, or stored in the wrong place, it cannot be retrieved, and may be permanently lost. If a user cannot interpret the coding, or if a network or an individual computer is not connected to the central data bank, the organization can no longer remember the document.

Very few companies organize their electronic memories rigorously, so the problems just described are not uncommon. Most organizations are struggling with IT systems and data structures that have grown up with the passage of time. It can therefore be difficult to construct an efficient and user-friendly corporate memory, especially in large, international companies (see Figure 10.4).

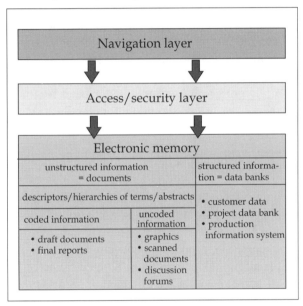

Figure 10.4 Layers in electronic memory

Data banks

The model shows that the electronic memory of an organization contains widely different classes of data. The more structured the manner of storing a computerised document, the easier it will be to find it at a later time. Least problematic are data banks that the company operates itself, using a rigid system of classification. Today, customer and product data banks are usually based on a relational data structure which labels individual records with unambiguous customer, product or project numbers. Links between the different data banks are supported by systems such SAP R3.

Unstructured information

Difficulties are more likely to arise in storing the unstructured part of the electronic memory. In many knowledge-intensive companies, an important part of the intellectual capital consists of graphics, reports, text documents of all kinds, and presentation notes. Anyone who has ever searched his or her hard disk for an important diagram knows how easily valuable information can be lost through careless storage. At organizational level, where thousands of hard disks and servers are connected, the problem is correspondingly greater. Intellectual assets can only be safely preserved in a structured manner for the company's future use if there is an agreed procedure for classification and storage.

Controlled vocabulary

Roughly speaking, there are two main trends. First, keywords can be assigned to important documents, using a controlled vocabulary that is compulsory within the organization. These 'company languages' are built up by a company process of collecting and defining relevant keywords. This allows documents to be assigned subsequently to different fields of activity within the company. The disadvantage is the effort involved in maintaining and imposing the language.

Automatic choice of keywords

The other possibility is automatic assignment of keywords by means of intelligent classification procedures. For a procedure of this kind – e.g. using case-based reasoning – the classification program needs a sufficient quantity of text, which is then checked, for example, for word frequencies. As a result of this and other analyses, each document receives descriptors. These procedures become more sophisticated and are continuously improved by feedback from active use of the system. Nevertheless, most searchers are frustrated by the low number of hits. Furthermore, these procedures can only be used on texts. Scanned documents or graphics that are stored in a system without additional textual description are extremely difficult for the organization to retrieve.

Links

Meaningful linkage of documents is one of the keys to creating an efficient electronic memory. In the same way as the brain holds whole sets of memories in systems of neuronal links, an IT system can open the way to memories that have all but disappeared. However, the chaotic system of links in the Internet and many intranets can be fatal to systematic storage of vital organizational knowledge. There is a growing tendency for hypertext links to lead nowhere, because the referenced page on the Internet no longer exists, or has been stored somewhere else. The more time the organization spends defining its vital fields of knowledge in the earlier building blocks of knowledge management, the easier it will be now to store material meaningfully in relation to these fields.

UPDATING AND REMEMBERING

Importance of updating

The process of preserving knowledge does not end with storage. It is only when the desired information can be retrieved and its quality is acceptable that the organizational memory has served its purpose. When material has been selected and suitably stored, the next step to consider is the updating process. Companies incur substantial costs when they make investment decisions on the basis of outdated and faulty knowledge. The heads of ARTHUR ANDERSEN's centres of competence are responsible for the currency of the documents in discussion forums and data banks. This institutionalizes the clearing-out process, so that the data banks, which would otherwise double their volume in about three months, maintain a relatively constant size and are – ideally – free of outdated information.

Downward spiral

If management does not update knowledge, a system can easily fall into the downward spiral shown in Figure 10.5. To manage their memories properly, companies need to solve any problems of trust and of access. If people trust the quality of the data, and if the system is easy to access, it will be used and maintained, and this in turn improves the quality of the data. However, if the current knowledge base is already faulty, the user loses confidence in it and is not ready to invest time and energy in maintaining the system. The quality of the data continues to deteriorate and the system dies. Given the present short life of knowledge, this can happen relatively quickly.

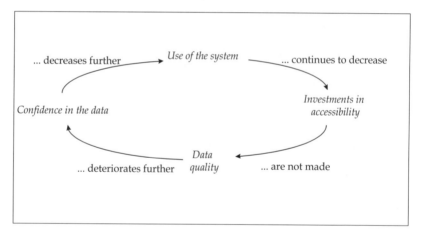

Figure 10.5 Downward spiral in an electronic knowledge base (diagram based on Manago & Auriol 1996, p. 28)

Organizational forgetting

Organizational forgetting poses another threat to the valuable memories of an organization. It is not uncommon to hear complaints like:

'We did know how to do that at one time, but we seem to have forgotten.'

There are two basic kinds of organizational forgetting. In the first kind, the memory is erased and is irretrievably lost to the organization. Employees leave, established teams break up, data are destroyed by viruses, or whole functional areas are outsourced. All these events reduce collective memory. In the second kind of forgetting, access to a memory is blocked, either for a time or permanently. At the level of the individual employee, this might happen because of temporary or permanent work overload, or unwillingness to pass knowledge on to other people. Analogous memory blocks can occur at group level and in the computerized memory (see Figure 10.6).

mode \ *form*		*individual*	*collective*	*electronic*
memory content erased		• resignation • death • forgetting • early retirement	• dispersal of established teams • re-engineering • outsourcing of functional areas	irreversible data losses through: • viruses • hardware faults • system crashes • missing back-ups • hackers • …
access not possible	*temporary*	• overload/temporary • transfers • illness/holiday • lack of training • working to rule	• taboos on old routines • collective sabotage	reversible data losses through: • overload/temporary • interface problem
	permanent	• overload/permanent • lack of awareness of importance of own knowledge • inner withdrawal	• sale of parts of company • transfer of teams • cover-up	• permanent incompatibility of systems • overload/permanent • incorrect indexing

Figure 10.6 Forms of organizational forgetting

Training

This overview shows that the retention of knowledge and skills is a permanent battle against natural forgetting. We find the same thing in other areas of life. A foreign language that we have learned but not used for a long time is gradually lost. Muscles atrophy if they are not exercised regularly. We know from the psychology of learning that repetition helps us to remember; the way in which people learn vocabulary is an example. Much of the effect of training courses may be lost if the trainees cannot immediately apply what they have learned to their work. If they try to use it at a later time, they often find that they have forgotten it, at least in part. This is the reason why organizations are increasingly moving towards on-the-job training: the material learned can be used immediately, and the organizational competency is preserved for longer.

SUMMARY

- The importance of well-established processes, and of the experience of long-serving employees, is often underestimated, especially during reorganization. This can lead to irreversible losses of know-how.
- Past experiences form a frame of reference for future learning processes. A general instruction to 'unlearn' is therefore unhelpful.
- The process of preserving knowledge can be divided into three phases: selection, storing and updating.
- The main tasks in knowledge selection are (a) identification of key employees, and (b) documentation of lessons learned as a result of major successes, or about the reasons for failures.
- Important experts and skilled employees can be bound to the organization by systems of incentives and by disincentives to leaving. The knowledge of former employees can be retained for the organization even after they have left by means of flexible attachment mechanisms.
- Collective knowledge should be embedded by means of minute-taking, group discussions, and collective development of language.
- Use of the electronic part of the organizational knowledge base is being revolutionised by progress in digitizing information and by the availability of almost unlimited storage capacity.
- The degree to which a document is structured determines how well it can be 'remembered'.
- A controlled vocabulary can be helpful in standardising the use of keywords for documents of all kinds, and thus in linking different fields of knowledge.
- Unless updating mechanisms are established, knowledge systems die sooner or later.
- Organizational forgetting is a natural process. Its causes may lie in

the individual, in groups or in the electronic part of organizational memory.

KEY QUESTIONS

- In what areas do you regularly lose valuable knowledge? What are you doing about it?
- How is the knowledge of a departing employee transferred to his or her successor?
- Do you have an electronic memory that gives you access to important events, projects and documents in the company's history?
- Once knowledge has been acquired and developed, is it carefully recorded, and made accessible and retrievable 'for ever'?

11
Measuring Knowledge

INTRODUCTION

Can you tell from your balance sheet how your company's
knowledge base has changed over the last year? Can you see
what talents and experts the company has won or lost, which
product innovations seem to be coming along well, and what
you have gained by acquiring important competencies? There
are probably only a few companies in the world that take the
trouble to measure their knowledge and draw up a balance.
These companies are pioneers; they believe that shareholders
may soon be more interested in 'knowledge accounts' than in
the traditional yearly figures. Companies can only manage
knowledge effectively if they take the trouble to identify
meaningful indices of the state of the knowledge base. Billions
are spent on training, and peanuts on evaluation. This
discrepancy must be tackled; initiatives can only be judged by
their results. Knowledge cannot be managed unless it is
measurable, or can exist at a conscious level. We shall now
describe various approaches to constructing measurement
systems, and then challenge you to develop a set of indices
tailored to your own company. You will need to use your
imagination, and be prepared to combine normative, strategic
and operational indices.

MEASURING KNOWLEDGE

What can't be measured can't be managed. (*Management saying; anonymous*)

We have naturally put a lot of money into knowledge management in recent years. It would be quite easy to calculate how much. It is true that we cannot measure the return on our investments with complete accuracy, but that is beside the point. Who can measure what we would have lost in productivity if we had NOT made the investment? (*'Knowledge manager' in an international business consultancy firm*)

In ten years' time, intellectual capital will be the most interesting factor in yearly reports. The traditional financial figures will not disappear, but they will take second place when the company's value and potential are being assessed. (*CEO of a financial services company*)

The controllers are still completely obsessed with financial indicators. We are trying to convince them that knowledge is increasingly important as an indicator of success; but it will be enormously difficult for us to put a value on something that cannot be measured by the standards of financial controlling. (*Company developer in a diversified multinational concern*)

If we are to measure the success of knowledge management, we need to be able to measure knowledge. This looks almost impossible, because the value of knowledge depends on the circumstances. To quantify knowledge, we must objectify it, and this means separating it from particular situations, times and people. We have seen that organizations can only control knowledge indirectly, by controlling the context in which it develops. Similarly, knowledge can only be recorded indirectly, and therefore not with complete precision. The idea that knowledge can be measured exactly leads us to expect objectivity where there can only be approximation. Nevertheless, raising the credibility of knowledge management in environments that are strongly measurement-oriented depends on progress in measuring and evaluating organizational knowledge.[1]

Measuring and evaluating knowledge

The process of evaluating knowledge has two phases. First, changes in the organizational knowledge base must be made visible; only then can these changes be *interpreted* in relation to knowledge goals. Many misunderstandings occur at this point. Evaluating knowledge does not mean calculating its monetary value; it means deciding whether or not knowledge goals have been met. If companies fail to measure their knowledge, and the ways in which it has changed, the cycle of knowledge management remains incomplete. This is because there is no feedback on which to base possible adjustments in the various building blocks of knowledge management.

THE PROBLEM: HOW CAN WE MEASURE KNOWLEDGE?

Limited progress

The business press carries regular reports of companies that are said to have made good progress in measuring and evaluating knowledge. ARTHUR ANDERSEN, for example, puts a fictitious rate of interest on internal company training (cf. ARTHUR ANDERSEN 1996, p. 29). At BUCKMAN LABORATORIES, efforts have been made to calculate the costs of internal knowledge management, and they are put at 3.5% of yearly profits. McKINSEY has been aiming for some time to spend 10% on intellectual capital.[2] These efforts represent necessary and welcome progress, but they also show where the main problems in knowledge management still lie.

Non-monetary dimensions

There are numerous non-financial indices that could be used to measure important dimensions of the knowledge base, but in general there is little attempt to apply them. If knowledge goals are insufficiently operationalized (see the building block 'knowledge goals'), this can also lead to difficulties in evaluating knowledge management activities.

Structured network

In consequence, it is difficult to arrange knowledge management activities along the dimensions that define company success. The evaluation of knowledge assets is hampered by the extreme difficulty of assigning causes to effects. This is shown in the structured network in Figure 11.1. Each arrow in the diagram represents a theory about a causal relationship. The diagram indicates, for example, that investment in a new IT infrastructure shortens decision times, and therefore also reduces response and delivery times; that this increases customer satisfaction, and thus makes the company more competitive. But the theory must be proved in the particular case. It happens all too often that investments in IT infrastructures do not yield the desired results. Since there are limits on the employee time and financial resources that can be made available for checking the theories, it is often difficult for knowledge managers to demonstrate that their activities are successful, and to quantify their effectiveness. Creating a structured network improves one's understanding of the interdependencies that underlie different processes, and it also helps to make hypotheses explicit

Problems of knowledge accounts

A further problem lies in the limits on drawing up knowledge accounts. The accounts of knowledge-intensive companies, when produced according to traditional accounting principles, seem less meaningful,[3] and therefore appear to lack a degree of business caution. When a company's stock market value increasingly depends on non-material assets, it becomes difficult for shareholders to judge how their capital is in fact invested. This lack of transparency is aggravated by national differences in accounting for non-material goods; there are differences, for example, in whether such goods can be entered as assets, and to what extent, or whether they qualify for tax write-offs. These differences in accounting for non-material assets can be useful from the point of view of tax liability, but they are of limited significance for strategic planning of the organizational knowledge base, because bookkeeping is always retrospective. In traditional accounting systems, knowledge can only be given a tangible financial value after it has been incorporated into saleable goods. We shall not concern

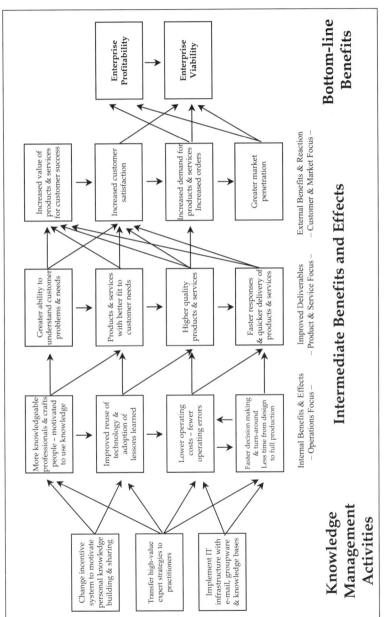

Figure 11.1 Structured network, adapted from Wiig (1996)

ourselves further with the problem of the monetary value of parts of the knowledge base. Instead, we shall focus on the measurement processes that companies need in order to pursue and attain their knowledge goals.

Resistance to measurement

The evaluation of knowledge can easily become politicized. Procedures may involve questioning the knowledge of experts, or the future significance of existing technologies. This can lead to re-evaluation of the skills portfolios of individuals, and thus to redistribution of power (cf. Peters 1993, p. 593). Measurement always prompts biased judgements.[5] It is therefore to be expected that resistance to re-evaluation of expertise will be encountered when a knowledge measurement system is put in place. Even the 'high potentials' in an organization are reluctant to undergo assessment; they often have surprisingly low tolerance for criticism, and show little sign of using feedback constructively (cf. Argyris 1987). Knowledge-oriented employee assessment criteria can also fail if they are not linked closely enough to existing incentive systems. Investing more effort in knowledge must be socially or financially rewarding for individuals, if they are to change their behaviour. Even so, many companies that claim to have implemented knowledge management are slow to adjust their incentive structures.

Measurement problems

The measurement process may be affected by a range of problems. They may be summarized as follows.

Important Aspects Are Not Measured

- It is extremely difficult to explain the gap between a company's market value and its book value. Knowledge is hardly ever entered as an asset in existing accounting systems, so it remains hidden.
- Knowledge that is critically important to the company's competitive position may be insufficiently recognized, or not recognized at

all. The company therefore fails to formulate and pursue adequate knowledge goals.

- Knowledge that is of critical competitive importance cannot be described, and therefore cannot be measured.
- There are no monitoring systems to measure changes in the individual building blocks of knowledge management (e.g. changes in transparency of knowledge, knowledge development).

The Wrong Thing is Measured

- Attention is focused on aggregated financial indicators, which do not show causal relationships. It is therefore uncertain how far these aggregated figures are affected by changes in the knowledge base.
- Only internal indices are used; there are no measures that could show how the company's knowledge resources are developing compared with those of competitors.
- The skills and abilities of individuals are measured, but collective knowledge is neglected.
- It often happens that only inputs are measured (e.g. expenditure on training), and no outputs (e.g. the success of that training).

The Wrong Measures Are Used

- Tangible and intangible assets are measured on different scales.[6]
- Quantitative measures are preferred, and qualitative ones are neglected. However, qualitative information such as customer satisfaction can be more meaningful for the future development of the company than purely quantitative information.
- The measurements have an internal frame of reference; there are no comparisons with external competitors or leading companies.

Measurements Are Made, but Nobody Knows Why

- People measure things that are easy to measure, without considering what use the results will be.
- Variables are measured that cannot be interpreted.

● Measurements are made automatically; the system of measurement and its meaning are not questioned, or not in relation to current strategy.

This list of problems shows how important it is to have a well-considered knowledge measurement system. Careful planning of the system ensures that the company knows what is being measured, and what it wants to measure.

INDICES OF KNOWLEDGE

Balanced scorecard

If knowledge management is not to be an isolated activity, it must be compatible with existing management and monitoring systems. Kaplan and Norton described a method of including knowledge in goal and assessment systems (see Kaplan & Norton 1992, 1993; Edvinsson & Malone 1997). This approach, known as the *balanced scorecard*, was developed in a study aimed at increasing the meaningfulness of traditional financial indices. The study was supported by the KPMG accountancy and business consulting company in the USA. The resulting model, shown in Figure 11.2, represents four perspectives on company activity: the company is depicted from the point of view of customers, *finance*, *internal business processes*, and learning and growth. The fourth aspect provides the connection with knowledge management. The balanced scorecard is a strategic management tool that seeks to link operational interventions in the organization's knowledge base with long-term company goals.

Flight simulator

The different perspectives on company activity are not simply juxtaposed, but are shown in their causal relationships. For each perspective, the scorecard shows strategic goals, measurement variables, operational goals and initiatives. Kaplan and Norton compare their balanced scorecard with a flight simulator, in which a large number of critical variables can be observed in their causal relationships. This

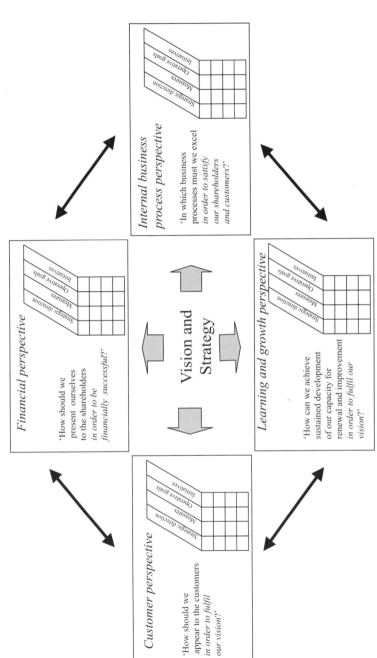

Figure 11.2 Balanced scorecard. Adapted and reprinted by permission of *Harvard Business Review*. From 'The Balanced Scorecard – Measures that Drive Performance', by R.S. Kaplan & D.P. Norton, Jan./Feb. 1992. Copyright © by the President and Fellows of Harvard College; all rights reserved

enables the company to describe the 'flight path', i.e. the strategy for reaching a particular goal.

The balanced scorecard rests on two basic convictions:

- When setting goals, organizations must ensure that they have ways of measuring them, operationalizing them and linking them to specific initiatives. These are central findings of the research into goals (see building block 'knowledge goals').
- A number of perspectives are relevant to the success of the organization. Goals should therefore be formulated and pursued in several dimensions.

The concept of the balanced scorecard does not include a method of operationalizing the knowledge dimension, nor does it offer indicators of knowledge. Each organization must work out its own set of indicators, designed to suit its own circumstances, to record and control the variables that are important to it. The balanced scorecard also supports close co-ordination between knowledge goals and knowledge measurement; ideally, this leads to rapid feedback processes. If the knowledge dimension is to complement existing systems of goals and assessment, it must define specific knowledge objectives, develop adequate indices for measuring them and integrate them into a company-wide monitoring system. The Swedish company SKANDIA is often cited as an organization that has attempted to implement knowledge measurement in this way.

CASE STUDY: SKANDIA

Indices for measuring intellectual capital
SKANDIA is a financial services company with headquarters in Sweden and operations throughout the world. It has grown rapidly during the 1990s.[7] The total volume of premiums has doubled in the space of a few years. SKANDIA AFS considers itself a pioneer in knowledge management, and relates its business success to innovations in the measurement of its own intellectual capital. The company has become a knowledge management success story, and its director of intellectual capital, Leif Edvinsson, is regarded in the knowledge community as a model manager.

According to its own account, the 'explanation gap' between SKANDIA's market value and its book value prompted the company to look at itself in a different way. SKANDIA's value on the stock exchange was several times higher than the book value of its assets. The company believed that the difference between the two lay in its intellectual capital, which cannot be shown in a balance sheet, but which nevertheless influences the estimated value. To arrive at a better understanding of its intellectual assets, and to gain more control of them, SKANDIA created a function called 'intellectual capital'. This function is responsible for all measures aimed at identifying and building intellectual assets and making them usable. Together with functions such as business development, human resources development and IT development, it has a role that extends across the company.[8]

> 'We wanted to start a framework that draws a holographic picture of the company and shows the market that we have a higher IQ than currently evaluated.' (*Member of the development team that produced the report on intellectual capital*)

Indices of five kinds track the measurement, evaluation and development of intellectual capital (SKANDIA Navigator). These are now published every six months, in the *Balanced Report on Intellectual Capital*. In addition to traditional financial measures, this report includes indices of 'customers', 'processes', 'people' and 'renewal and development' for different parts of the company (see Table 11.1).

Does this combination of indicators really measure SKANDIA's knowledge, and do changes in the variables over time reflect changes in the organizational knowledge base? From the point of view of knowledge management, all the indices are difficult to interpret. Changes in the average age of employees tells the external observer nothing about average skills levels. 'Time spent in further training' shows that training was provided, but does not tell us what skills were taught, or whether the trainees succeeded in learning them. The choice of measures is difficult for outsiders to understand. Their meaningfulness is further reduced because indices of different types – input indices, stock indices and so on – are mixed together. It seems doubtful that these indices can provide enough information internally for managing the knowledge base. If knowledge management is to be improved, the measurement system should be based on relevant objectives. It remains unclear in what areas SKANDIA wishes to change its knowledge base. For SKANDIA, intellectual capital is not a synonym for knowledge: it is the difference between market value and book value. This difference can indeed be partly explained in terms of knowledge, but is also due to expectations of profit, image factors, stock market trends and other exogenous developments.

Beware of success stories

This shows how difficult it is to define and measure indices of knowledge, and how easy it is to confuse concepts such as knowledge and intellectual capital. It would be dangerous in any case to transfer SKANDIA's set of indices to other companies. Each organization needs to develop its own set of indices, adapted to its own circumstances and problems.

MULTIDIMENSIONAL KNOWLEDGE MEASUREMENT

Shortcomings in existing measurement systems

Measurement systems like SKANDIA's Navigator or CELEMI's Intangible Assets Monitor[9] may be useful in making stakeholders more aware of the knowledge dimension. However, as tools for measuring and charting actual changes in the organization's knowledge base, they suffer from a number of shortcomings. Systems of this kind can help only to a limited extent in achieving targeted development of the knowledge base and relating it to business results.

Table 11.1 Extract from the SKANDIA Navigator (Dial area, 1996)

	1966 (6)	1995	1995 (6)	1994
Financial focus				
Volume of premiums (millions of Swedish kronor)	475	880	462	667
Volume of premiums per employee (thousands of Swedish kronor)	1955	3592	2011	3586
Customer focus				
Accessible by telephone (%)	96	93	93	90
Number of individual policies	296 206	275 231	256 766	234 741
Customer satisfaction index (max = 5)	4.36	4.32	4.33	4.15
Swedish customer barometer	No figures	69	No figures	No figures
Employee focus				
Average age	40	40	40	37
Number of employees	243	245	230	186
Training time (days/year)	7	6	5	3.5
Process focus				
IT employees/all employees (%)	7.4	7.3	7.4	8.1
Renewal and development focus				
Increase in volume of premiums (%)	2.7	31.9	47.8	28.5
Values in the damage valuation procedure	18.5	9	No figures	No figures
Number of ideas registered by the 'idea group'	90	No figures	No figures	No figures

Mixing classes of indicators

Failure to distinguish between different classes of indicators is a major problem. Indices of *content* (what does the knowledge base consist of today?) are mixed with indices of *intervention* (what knowledge interventions have been made, and what was their scope?), *transfer* (what effects did the interventions set in motion?) and classical *financial indices*. As a result, contents, inputs and outputs cannot be disentangled, and their interactions are difficult to interpret. Table 11.2

Table 11.2   Classes of indicators (North, Probst and Romhardt 1998)

Class of indicators	Definition of term	Examples
Organization knowledge base (I)	Describes the content of the organizational knowledge base at time t_x in qualitative and quantitative terms	Portfolio of employee skills according to core competencies, number and quality of external knowledge links, quality and number of internal centres of competence, patents
Interventions (II)	Describes processes and inputs (costs) for chainging organizational knowledge base	Number of 'lessons learned' workshops, producing profiles of experts, implementing action training (action training/total training %)
Intermediate results and transfer effects (III)	Measures direct results of the interventions (outputs)	Publications by employees suggestions for improvement, response times to customer queries, index of intranet use, transparency index
Business results (IV)	Measures business results at the end of the period (e.g. quarter, financial year)	Cash flow, cover, market share, image, return on investment

shows an approach that avoids mixing different indicators by separating them into four classes.[10]

Definitions of classes of indices

Class I indices reflect the constituents of the organizational knowledge base. *Class II indices* describe inputs and processes as measurable dimensions of attempts to change the knowledge base. *Class III indices* measure intermediate outcomes and transfer effects. *Type IV indices*, some of which are highly aggregated, measure business results.

This system is better suited to showing causal relationships, and to identifying and measuring change in the organizational knowledge base relative to business results.[11]

Figure 11.3 shows our multidimensional measurement system in its entirety, in the form of a structured network (see also Figure 11.1).

From intervention to change in knowledge base

To meet the organization's goals, the knowledge base (opening balance KB index t_0) is changed by targeted interventions. These might include a new system of incentives to improve transfer of knowledge, or implementation of an IT infrastructure, or particular training measures. The interventions produce intermediate results and transfer effects, for example increased transparency of knowledge, which can lead to shorter response times and thus to increased customer satisfaction. The intermediate results and transfer effects are often highly networked, and the causal links are not always clear. They influence financial and non-financial results of company activity. The company's financial results are shown in the traditional balance sheet, while the changed knowledge base is summarized in a 'closing balance' at time t_1. The change in balance is the difference between t_0 and t_1.

No standard indices

The purposes of this model are to separate indices into different classes, and to show the full context of interventions in the organizational knowledge base. Where other models mix categories, which makes it more difficult for companies to approach knowledge measurement, this one draws distinctions. However, it does not solve the basic issue of what are the 'right' indices. Defining an adequate set of indices within each class is something that every organization must do for itself, to suit its strategy, its knowledge environment and its existing monitoring systems. There is no such thing as 'the 10 most important indices of knowledge'. However, the process of choosing a set of knowledge indices to fit the organization and the context is in itself a way of examining the knowledge base, and of creating a language for talking about knowledge phenomena. It therefore offers a way of changing the knowledge culture.

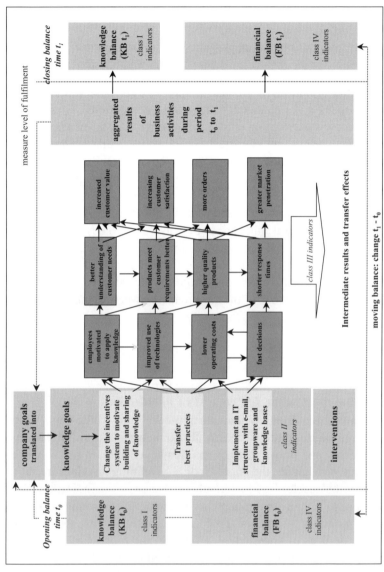

Figure 11.3 Multi-dimensional system for measuring knowledge (North, Probst & Romhardt 1998)

Alternative Measurement Methods

Alternative sources of feedback

The purpose of knowledge measurement is to provide managers with the information they need to make decisions about knowledge management. The results of the knowledge measurement process reveal areas of the company where knowledge management could be implemented. It may be helpful at this point to mention some other measurement procedures.

Phases in development of knowledge

Organizational knowledge may be evaluated by constructing an evolutionary model of competencies. Organizational competencies progress through different stages of development, starting from complete lack of understanding of the causal relationships involved in a situation, and moving towards complete knowledge, and thus to control. This approach is based on the belief that knowledge of all kinds undergoes a kind of ripening process, comprising different stages[12] (see Figure 11.4).

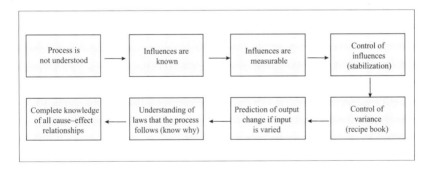

Figure 11.4 Evolutionary model of knowledge

Using this method, any knowledge problem can be examined to determine how far the company's current knowledge will suffice. Critical decisions are often made on the basis of astonishingly little knowledge. Check your own company.

Knowledge measurement and knowledge goals

Another way of evaluating knowledge is by reference to the normative, strategic and operational knowledge goals described in Chapter 4. The method involves checking whether all parts of the company have been successfully aligned with the knowledge strategy and the knowledge vision, and whether they have succeeded in implementing them at the operational level (see Figure 11.5).

	Knowledge goals	Measurement
normative	• create conditions for knowledge-oriented strategic and operational goals • aim at 'knowledge-aware' company culture • gain top-management commitment	• analyses of culture • observation of top management behaviour (e.g. agenda analyses) • analyses of credibility (gap between status quo and ideal)
strategic	• determine content of organizational 'core knowledge' • define desired portfolio of competencies • establish main levers for building competence	• multi-dimensional knowledge measurement (knowledge balance sheet/classes of indicators) • analysis of portfolio of competencies • control of the most important 'knowledge projects' • balanced scorecard
operational	• translate normative and strategic knowledge goals into concrete terms • ensure that interventions are appropriate to the level at which they are made	• control of training with clear goals for transfer of learning • measurement of use of systems (e.g. intranet) • create individual skills profiles

Figure 11.5   Measuring knowledge goals

Normative knowledge measurement

Has the company culture become more 'knowledge-aware' or 'knowledge-friendly'? Has top management changed its approach to knowledge issues? Changes of this kind can best be identified by questioning and observing employees. To discover the current status of knowledge at the normative level, we need indices of behavioural change for all groups of employees; examples are given below.

Guide to knowledge culture

● Are employees encouraged to share their knowledge?
● Is the working atmosphere open and trusting?

- Is customer value the main objective of knowledge management?
- Do employees regularly and creatively discuss their visions of the company's future?
- Does the firm provide enough information, incentives and resources to enable employees to build up the skills that they need?
- Do employees continuously improve their knowledge and skills?
- Is the quality of their work lowered by the influence of prejudices or set routines?
- Do employees believe that their mistakes will not be punished, but that they can be used as an opportunity for learning?
- Do the employees concentrate on working together to improve the products or services offered by the company?

Open line

HEWLETT PACKARD has a scheme called *open line* for carrying out regular surveys of employees. Recently, questions have been added about the atmosphere surrounding the development and sharing of knowledge. Normative knowledge measurement is directed at measures for bringing the company culture closer to an *ideal knowledge culture*, as defined by the normative knowledge goals. If corrections are needed, these will primarily affect the visions and goals of top management. The knowledge culture also involves embedding knowledge management within the company so that the knowledge aspect can be constantly emphasized in decision-making bodies.

Strategic knowledge measurement

Setting strategic knowledge goals involves determining the organization's core knowledge and finding a basis for an *ideal portfolio* of competencies. Strategic knowledge measurement must therefore be concerned with changes in vital competencies. A systematic evaluation of the most important competencies at different levels yields a more comprehensive picture of the company's general competence level. It is also helpful to check the *normative knowledge strategies,* which were defined in the building block 'knowledge goals' (see Figure 11.6).

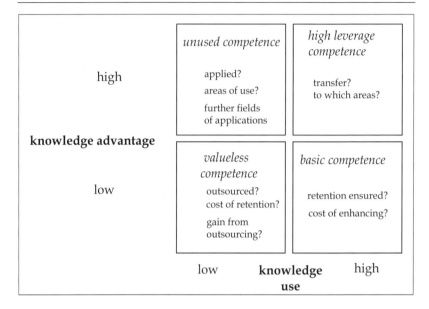

Figure 11.6 Assessing normative knowledge – implementing normative knowledge strategies

Weighting areas of competence

We have described measures for assessing separate competencies; companies must also consider the relative *weighting* of different areas of competence. Strategic knowledge measurement should ensure that the company's whole portfolio of competencies develops as desired, and that strategic priorities are observed in the process.

Strategic benchmarking

From a strategic point of view, the evaluation of knowledge must take into account changes in the competencies of competitors. Even when the company has attained its internal knowledge objectives and built up its ideal portfolio of competencies, this may still not be enough if competitors have developed even faster. The ruinous race to develop new generations of computer chips is just one example. It is therefore essential that companies carry out *strategic benchmarking*. The aim of this is to ascertain which of the company's competencies qualify as *best in the world*. The levels of competence of leading competitors must therefore be evaluated; this presents new challenges to strategic knowledge measurement.[13]

Operational knowledge measurement

Operational knowledge measurement can be carried out at the level at which the knowledge goals were formulated. For goals involving teams or project groups, the normal tools of *project tracking* are available. The knowledge objectives of individual employees can be monitored using the techniques of *management by knowledge objectives*, described above. Has Mr X, head of department Y, attained his objective, i.e. does he speak Spanish well enough to carry out business negotiations? It is important in this context that measurement should not be regarded simply as a system of goal-setting and testing; it should also create conditions which promote attainment of the objectives. The case of XMIT shows that regular surveys and evaluation of employee skills can substantially improve the use of internal potential.

CASE STUDY: XMIT

Brain pool: measuring knowledge in a telecommunications company
XMIT is a Swiss telecommunications company that specializes in installing and operating networks. The telecommunications industry is characterized by wide product variety, constantly shrinking product life cycles, new technologies and a growing need on the part of customers for integrated solutions. In spite of the introduction of standards, the technologies continue to grow in complexity. In an environment of this kind, it became increasingly important for XMIT to have the right person with the right tools and knowledge (about products and technology) available at the right time and place (with the customer or in the service department).

To achieve this goal, the following objectives were
defined:

- To build up focused knowledge of the complex
  problems surrounding networks
- To raise levels of service to provide better satisfaction of
  customer needs
- To increase the speed at which new skills are acquired
- To provide optimal support for all products in all phases
  of their life cycles
- To provide selective training (no stockpiling, training
  'just in time')
- To create transparency of knowledge (who can do
  what?)
- To ensure that know-how is shared among different
  employees (thus reducing dependency in case of illness,
  resignation, etc.)

To support these objectives, XMIT created 'Brain pool',
which holds details of the expertise of all employees who
have product know-how or *technological know-how*. Each
employee is categorized by product and type of knowledge,
using four ratings: limited, medium, high and top-level
expertise. The assessments are made by the systems
engineer and agreed with management. A trial using
self-assessment also produced good results. Gaps in the
company's knowledge are identified by comparing
knowledge on board with *optimal know-how value per
product*. These gaps form the basis for a training plan for
each product and each employee. The ratings of all
employees for all products are summarized in a matrix
(Brain pool XMIT Professional Services) (see Figure 11.7).

A similar matrix is produced for technological know-how.
Efficient management of the skills of XMIT employees must
in any case be based on regular assessments, since
expertise of this kind ages quickly. The Brain pool once
created can be used in a number of ways. It facilitates rapid
assembly of teams (picket crews) in which certain specialist
qualifications must be present. It supports a more balanced
composition of customer service teams (response centre
crews), because the use of Brain pool can ensure that there

is always a hub, a router and an NMS specialist in the team. It also permits more flexible personnel planning, and this makes the effects of absences or departures easier to manage. Finally, it supports more effective structuring of the training programme.

For the customers, Brain pool has meant better care, since the sharing of knowledge among a number of people improved the information service. This in turn led to shorter repair times, reducing the high costs of a network failure. By demonstrating the Brain pool to customers, the company was able to raise its own credibility with regard to internal skill management. This level of transparency about the working of the company created trust.

In XMIT itself, the internal transparency of products and technological know-how has been increased. Training needs and costs can now be shown more clearly, which supports the building of market-specific know-how. Internal scenario planning (illness, holidays, resignations) has been improved, which also helps with the planning and monitoring of skills.

Coaching and mentoring

Coaching and *mentoring* offer a more individual approach to examining and adjusting employees' objectives. A coach helps his or her pupil to develop confidence, to set objectives and to work out ways of implementing them. The pupil is thus helped to realize his or her potential, and to improve performance independently.[14] A mentor on the other hand provides suitable contacts and access to suitable networks. He or she introduces the protégé into the 'right circles', and watches his or her career path (cf. for example Bertoin Antal 1993). The mentor also helps to assess strengths and weaknesses which the protégé cannot see unaided.

Complementing management by knowledge objectives

When agreeing individual knowledge objectives (MBKO), indices are chosen for checking progress in a given competency. Methods of

products / employees	Router: Router A	Router B	ISDN Router	Remote Access	Hubs: Hub A	Hub B	Hub C	NMS: NMS A	NMS B	NOS: NOS A	NOS B	NOS C	...	Know-how per employee
1	L	H			M		M			L				...
2	T	L				L	M				M			
3			L				M	T	M	H				
4		H			H				M			M		
5	M			L			H		M		H			...
6		...		...		...	...							...
7					...			...						
8														
9														

Know-how
per product

Figure 11.7   The Brain pool knowledge matrix of XMIT

evaluating success may include expert judgements, opinions of superiors and tests of all kinds. These measures are aimed primarily at the hard skills of individuals, i.e. at *know-how*. By introducing coaching and mentoring, two further kinds of knowledge can be developed in a parallel and balanced fashion. These are normative knowledge about the meaning of goals and responsibility for them (*know why*), and knowledge of networks of contacts in the organization (*know who*).[15]

SUMMARY

- Knowledge measurement is an essential preliminary to assessing the efficiency of knowledge management. It shows whether knowledge objectives are appropriately formulated, and whether knowledge management activities are being carried out successfully.
- A purely quantitative approach to measuring organizational knowledge is unrealistic, and may even be counter-productive. A more promising approach is to understand causal relationships and to measure indirectly, using indicators of knowledge.
- Knowledge measurement should serve as a basis for 'knowledge accounting', which can be used in aligning the company's various activities with its knowledge vision and strategy.

KEY QUESTIONS

- Does your company have an explicitly quantitative and financial monitoring culture, or have you already tried qualitative measures of success?

- In which functions or parts of the company do you see opportunities for knowledge-based success indicators? Do you already have data that are gathered at regular intervals, or whole measurement systems, which could be used in this way, or aggregated to form a 'knowledge balance sheet'?
- What do you think are the assets and liabilities in your company's 'knowledge balance sheet'? At what level (strategic, normative or operational) are your main knowledge objectives embedded, and what methods of measurement should therefore predominate?

12

Incorporating Knowledge Management

INTRODUCTION

Can you introduce the ideas in this book into your own
company? What levers can you use to gain better control of your
knowledge? Who are the sceptics, and who are the outright
opponents of knowledge management? Many people find it
difficult to develop effective knowledge strategies based on new
information technology. Ask yourself how far you could
strengthen your knowledge base by introducing innovative
structures such as centres of competence or electronic
knowledge systems. What new management roles or positions
do you need? Who is responsible for knowledge management in
your company? Is it IT, or the research department? Who makes
knowledge visible, and builds bridges between islands of
expertise? Knowledge-based organizations now need to create
jobs for 'cross-area specialists' and 'transparency developers'. In
this chapter, we shall explain the principles behind a
knowledge-sensitive company culture. We shall also describe
innovative structural approaches and new management roles.
Our purpose is to help you to set knowledge management on a
firm basis within your company.

INTEGRATING KNOWLEDGE MANAGEMENT

Knowledge management: a fashionable topic

Knowledge management is booming, both in academic circles and in company practice. At specialist conferences – such as the annual meetings of the Strategic Management Society, or the Academy of Management – the main topic of discussion is how to manage knowledge. The business press urges companies to make better use of the 'hidden treasure' in the heads of their employees. Boards of directors are beginning to ask top management what their companies are doing about managing knowledge. The greatest threat posed by this trend is that of unfocused actionism, which tackles the symptoms rather than the problem, and results in token projects that have little chance of success. When this happens, new approaches are discredited, and are condemned to becoming short-lived fashion trends (see Figure 12.1).

Chance for new ideas

Dynamic changes that can bring new trends into an organization should not, however, be undervalued. They enable people to articulate and try out new ideas away from the restrictions imposed by set routines. The current interest in knowledge management is an opportunity to demonstrate that its concepts and approaches can benefit the organization; this can be done in a relatively short time. The first steps in introducing knowledge management can take many different forms. This chapter contains a brief overview.

FINDING THE RIGHT POINT OF ENTRY

Assessing the situation

Does your organization need to improve its competencies at all levels? If so, you should first ask yourself how satisfied you are with the

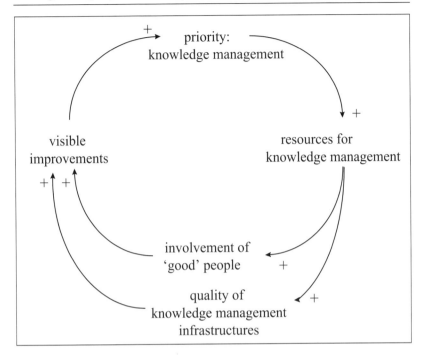

Figure 12.1 Knowledge management: 'grow or go'

results of your efforts at knowledge management up to this point. All attempts to manage knowledge must start with an honest self-assessment. The results of this assessment can be checked against a critical external appraisal – by consultants, customers or suppliers, for example – and supplemented by their perceptions.

Starting from how things are

Every organization has its own way of dealing with data, information and knowledge, and it creates its own structures, jobs and systems for the purpose. Some of the ideas that you will find in this book are probably already incorporated in your company in one form or another. Knowledge management will not transform the company; its aim is simply to sensitize management at all levels to the significance of knowledge as a resource. As we have shown, existing structures can sometimes be remodelled at low cost so as to serve the needs of knowledge. There are no standard methods for introducing knowledge management: the best way is to start with your existing structures and methods, and to apply them effectively to achieve the company's knowledge goals.

Constructing a knowledge profile

One way of doing this is to assess the company's strengths and weaknesses in terms of our building blocks of knowledge management. Figure 12.2 represents a knowledge profile of a company based on the results of a self-assessment process. Strengths and weaknesses are shown for each of the building blocks. In this case, the company's strengths – especially in research and development – are not translated into competitive products. The creativity of the knowledge developers is not steered into the right channels, discoveries are not properly preserved and the knowledge goals are not checked regularly. The company's knowledge base is therefore not being used effectively.

Levels of analysis

Plans for improving the separate knowledge processes can be derived from a knowledge profile. Profiles can be produced for the whole company, for parts of the company, for groups or teams, and for individuals. Knowledge problems of all kinds may emerge, depending on the level of analysis; they must also be tackled at the appropriate level.

Another technique for self-assessment is the Knowledge Management Assessment Tool (KMAT), developed by ARTHUR ANDERSEN in conjunction with the AMERICAN PRODUCTIVITY AND QUALITY CENTER (see Figure 12.3). This method involves asking managers to fill in a questionnaire on knowledge-related topics. The results are used to position the company along five dimensions: leadership, culture, assessment, technology and learning behaviour. There is also a benchmarking process in which the results can be compared with those of companies previously assessed.

UNDERSTANDING THE COMPANY'S OWN KNOWLEDGE CULTURE

Every company has its own culture, moulded by its history and its circumstances. The culture defines the ground rules for social behaviour and collective action. Banks, business consultancies and software

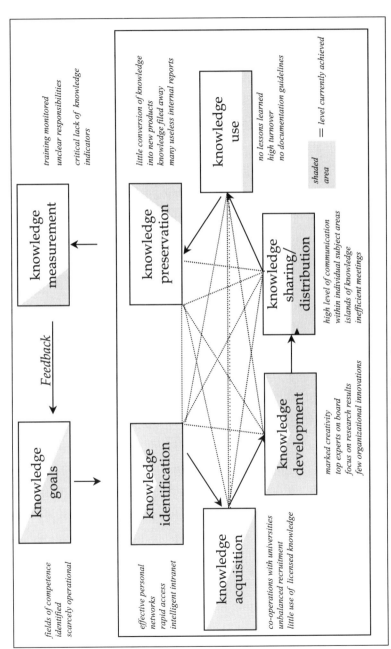

Figure 12.2 Knowledge profile of a company

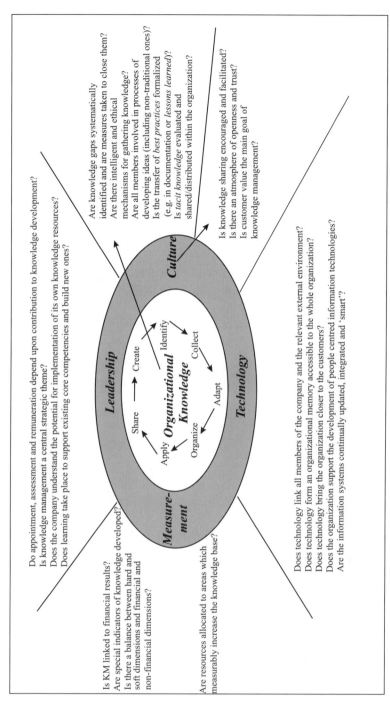

Do appointment, assessment and remuneration depend upon contribution to knowledge development?
Is knowledge management a central strategic theme?
Does the company understand the potential for implementation of its own knowledge resources?
Does learning take place to support existing core competencies and build new ones?

Are knowledge gaps systematically identified and are measures taken to close them?
Are there intelligent and ethical mechanisms for gathering knowledge?
Are all members involved in processes of developing ideas (including non-traditional ones)?
Is the transfer of *best practices* formalized (e.g. in documentation or *lessons learned*)?
Is *tacit knowledge* evaluated and shared/distributed within the organization?

Is knowledge sharing encouraged and facilitated?
Is there an atmosphere of openness and trust?
Is customer value the main goal of knowledge management?

Is KM linked to financial results?
Are special indicators of knowledge developed?
Is there a balance between hard and soft dimensions and financial and non-financial dimensions?

Are resources allocated to areas which measurably increase the knowledge base?

Does technology link all members of the company and the relevant external environment?
Does technology form an organizational memory accessible to the whole organization?
Does technology bring the organization closer to the customers?
Does the organization support the development of people centred information technologies?
Are the information systems continually updated, integrated and 'smart'?

Leadership

Organizational Knowledge

Create

Share ← Identify

Apply → Collect

Organize ← Adapt

Culture

Technology

Measure-ment

Figure 12.3 The ARTHUR ANDERSEN Knowledge Management Assessment Tool

houses all have different ways of dealing with internal information. Companies differ in the extent to which knowledge is internally politicized and used as a power base. There may also be marked discrepancies between reality, i.e. the actual culture, and the desired or ideal culture. Glossy brochures tell shareholders and employees that the company is a learning organization: tolerant of mistakes, open, experimental and creative. However, companies that are self-styled champions of learning often look quite different to the impartial observer (see Figure 12.4).

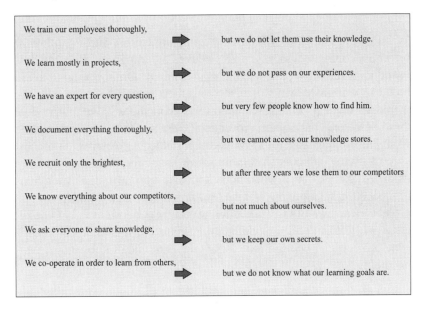

We train our employees thoroughly,

but we do not let them use their knowledge.

We learn mostly in projects,

but we do not pass on our experiences.

We have an expert for every question,

but very few people know how to find him.

We document everything thoroughly,

but we cannot access our knowledge stores.

We recruit only the brightest,

but after three years we lose them to our competitors

We know everything about our competitors,

but not much about ourselves.

We ask everyone to share knowledge,

but we keep our own secrets.

We co-operate in order to learn from others,

but we do not know what our learning goals are.

Figure 12.4   Paradoxes in dealing with knowledge (cf. Roehl & Romhardt 1997 and Romhardt, 1998)

Loss of reality

The paradoxes shown in Figure 12.4 account for the discrepancies between the company's self-image and the perceptions of outsiders, and between its stated objectives and its actual condition. They express a disturbed relationship with the reality of the organization, and with the culture that moulds it. A letter that we received from the chairman of the board of a large industrial company will serve as an illustration.

After we had introduced the basic ideas of knowledge management to him, he wrote that the issues we raised were already covered in the statement of principles of total quality management, and that the significance of organizational learning was affirmed in the company's vision and mission statement. Further initiatives were therefore considered unnecessary. This shows the extent to which problems can be repressed.

Sensitization

Making people aware of their own company culture and its influence on knowledge processes is, we believe, an important step towards introducing effective knowledge management. Organizations have a broad repertoire of ways of protecting their established routines. We therefore suggest holding 'sensitization workshops'. The purpose of these is to help participants to understand their own ways of dealing with knowledge, and to show them possible alternatives.[1] The best way of giving impetus to this initiative is for the management team itself to take part in a workshop. It is also helpful if the workshops are preceded by a review of internal knowledge-related initiatives and projects. Reviews of this kind often reveal links between failed knowledge projects and cultural defensive mechanisms. Successful knowledge projects can be used to illustrate the potential of knowledge management.

TRYING OUT NEW KNOWLEDGE STRUCTURES AND KNOWLEDGE SYSTEMS

Ambivalence of structures

Organizational structures are aids to attaining the company's objectives. They reduce complexity and support the actions of members of the organization. However, there is no such thing as the ideal structure. Structures and systems are always a compromise between conflicting objectives. Decentralization, for instance, creates freedom of enterprise and may have positive effects on internal knowledge development. At the same time, the autonomy of parts of the company reduces the transparency of globally distributed knowledge assets, and therefore restricts their use. Decisions on structure can thus be ambivalent in their effects on our building blocks of knowledge management.

Do not imitate, think

Companies that are leaders in knowledge management, such as ARTHUR ANDERSEN, MCKINSEY, SKANDIA and PHONAK, know how to cope with these conflicting tendencies, and how to allow for them when creating new structures. Their solutions should not simply be copied, however, because every company must start from its current culture and the structures it has inherited. It is nevertheless useful to examine the approaches adopted by successful knowledge-oriented companies.

CASE STUDY: BUCKMAN LABORATORIES

Principles of knowledge-friendly structures
Bob Buckman is chairman of a company that produces special chemicals in Memphis, Tennessee. Buckman believes that knowledge is acquired at the front line, moves upwards through the organization, is examined, processed and reorganized, and then given back to the front line. In his opinion, this process requires new organizational structures with the following features:

- It should reduce the number of transmissions of knowledge between individuals to one, to achieve the least distortion of that knowledge.
- Everyone should have access to the knowledge base of the company.
- Each individual should be able to enter knowledge into the database of the system.
- The system should function across time and space with the knowledge base available 24 hours a day, seven days a week, since the company never closes.
- It should be easy to use for people who are not computer experts – be searchable on every word in the knowledge base.

- It should communicate in whatever language is best for the understanding of the user (BUCKMAN competes in over 60 countries).
- As questions are asked of the knowledge base by the users, and answers given, it should be updated automatically – the accumulation of technical questions and answers would generate our knowledge bases for the future.[2]

An internal department called 'Knowledge Transfer' was created to implement these requirements. The department has the following responsibilities:

- Accelerate the accumulation and dissemination of knowledge by all BUCKMAN LABORATORIES associates worldwide.
- Provide easy and rapid access to BUCKMAN LABORATORIES' global knowledge bases.
- Eliminate time and space constraints in communications.
- Stimulate associates to experience the value of enterprise knowledge sharing in servicing customers.
- Respect the dignity of each individual by cultivating an environment which enhances his or her professional development, and recognizes each as a valued member of a service-oriented team.'[2]

The result is a completely non-bureaucratic organizational structure, because the traditional information pathways and filtering systems are eliminated. In a structure of this kind, power goes to those individuals who are best at transferring knowledge to others.

The role of staff groups

Traditional staff groups have now fallen into disrepute. In the past, they were created by management to be the respected guardians of specialist knowledge. Today, they tend to be much reduced in size and authority. Quality circles, task forces and project teams now carry a large share of the company's expert knowledge. There are two main reasons for this. The first is that concepts developed by staff groups are often unusable from the point of view of line management. The second is that many supposed experts are more concerned with cultivating their own power and position than with developing productive ideas.

Pressure groups

A central pressure group can be an effective means of supporting knowledge management. GENERAL MOTORS, for example, is now establishing a unit called Corporate Strategy and Knowledge Development. Its role is to improve the company's ability to formulate knowledge-oriented strategies. When setting up groups of this kind, companies should take care not to lose contact with the front line. Knowledge management requires company-wide standards or rules of play, and enablers who can develop and establish them in collaboration with line management. The recruitment of experienced line managers for central functions increases acceptance of these structures, and ensures that they do not result in fanciful theories that would simply be an annoyance to a line manager returning to his normal functions.

Structuring around centres of competence

Companies are usually organized on a functional, regional or product basis. Our description of MCKINSEY showed how internal centres of competence can be used to focus skills selectively and develop them further. In addition to the regional office structure, which performs basic administrative functions, and the powerful project form of organization – mastered by the consultancy business – there is a third type of structure, which we might call the knowledge structure of the company. Many large companies still lack a knowledge structure. Experts, ideas and projects on related topics are not linked, but remain isolated.

Hypertext organization

Ikujiro Nonaka, the well-known Japanese management researcher, suggests that knowledge structures can be incorporated by means of hypertext forms of organization (Nonaka & Takeuchi 1995, p. 169) (see Figure 12.5). The special feature of this model is that three structural levels coexist in one organization: the business system level, the project team level and the knowledge base level. The employees of such organizations must be able to navigate easily through all three levels, like the links in a hypertext file. In other words, they must carry out their agreed functions within the business system, and think and make decisions in a process-oriented manner, as members of changing project teams. They must also be able to reflect on their discoveries and enter the lessons learned in a suitable form in the knowledge base, thus feeding them back to the business system and the project teams.

Other approaches to incorporating knowledge management may be found in Tom Peters' suggestions for creating effective structures (Peters 1992, p. 398). According to Peters, the main elements in an effective knowledge management structure are:

- Core volunteer leadership group
- Volunteer expert network
- 'School' for would-be volunteer experts (on-the-job)
- Small number of super-experts with towering competence
- Network management structure to:
  – pick the brains of busy people
  – package information attractively
  – attend to the psychology of network management (providers, users)
  – distribute information swiftly, carefully
  – provide clients with swift access (guaranteed) to experts
  – establish publication strategy (informal to formal)
  – measure use/effectiveness
- Lots of get-togethers (physical)
- Culture that 'demands' (and rewards) network contributions with formal and informal incentives.

Nuclei of knowledge management

Existing organizational structures need not always be completely transformed for the sake of knowledge management. The German chemicals giant BASF, for example, set up a knowledge management group in its research division. The task – set by EVP research and development – was to evaluate the potential benefits to the company

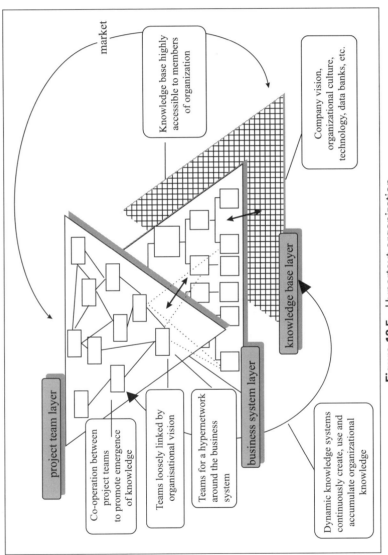

market

Knowledge base highly accessible to members of organization

Company vision, organizational culture, technology, data banks, etc.

project team layer

Co-operation between project teams to promote emergence of knowledge

Teams loosely linked by organisational vision

Teams for a hypernetwork around the business system

business system layer

knowledge base layer

Dynamic knowledge systems continuously create, use and accumulate organizational knowledge

Figure 12.5 Hypertext organization

of knowledge management, and to identify specific starting points for strategy development. The group consisted of 14 employees from all areas of research. They looked through the relevant literature after work, developed a common language for talking about knowledge, and identified fields of action, which were then presented to management. Initiatives of this kind should be supported. Employees who are interested in the subject must find each other and work together to show the potential benefits of better knowledge management.

WANTED: KNOWLEDGE MANAGERS

New professions

Knowledge management needs knowledge managers (Davenport 1996). New staff and line jobs are needed to support the necessary processes. If knowledge management is introduced in a one-sided fashion into personnel or IT, it will not last. It affects all functions and all levels in the hierarchy to a greater or lesser extent. Because of its interdisciplinary nature, companies need to create new management positions, and adjust existing job descriptions and applicant profiles. In the longer term, new positions in knowledge management will develop. We shall now describe four new management roles, which in our judgement will soon become important.

Management position: chief knowledge officer

Main duties: to structure the organizational knowledge base and guide its development

The task of the chief knowledge officer (CKO) is to make the whole organization aware of the importance of knowledge as a resource, and to mobilize efforts accordingly. He or she represents the knowledge angle to the top management team, of which, ideally, the CKO is a member. The CKO is responsible for knowledge infrastructures such as centres of competence and information systems. He or she helps all managers to translate general company goals into feasible knowledge objectives. The CKO endeavours to identify islands of knowledge and to make them productive within the knowledge management process.

In his or her daily activities, the CKO should set an example of the desired knowledge culture.

Management position: competence area specialist

Main duties: to structure an area of competence and guide its development

The most important areas of knowledge should be embedded in the organizational structure. We suggest building up areas of competence, under the leadership of competence area specialists (CASs). The task of the CAS is to network company experts in a particular field, e.g. project management, and to gather and condense the available internal and external knowledge on the subject. The CAS brings knowledge of the competence area into company decisions, and is responsible for setting up and running the infrastructure of the competence area (news groups, conferences, best practice workshops, etc.).

Management position: cross-area specialist

Main duties: to network areas of competence, set up contacts and identify new business opportunities

The job of cross-area specialists is to 'sniff out' unused knowledge assets and make them known to the appropriate areas of competence. To this end, they take part in the main events organized by competence areas. They then assess and quantify opportunities for creating synergies, and organize networking workshops between areas. In this way they help to create an interfunctional and interdisciplinary network of relationships within the organization, and are intermediaries for internal and external contacts.

Management position: transparency specialist

Main duties: to create sufficient transparency in the organizational knowledge base

The internal transparency specialist takes stock of all the accessible parts of the organizational knowledge base and assesses how much effort it would take to identify additional types of knowledge. In collaboration with the employees involved, he or she decides on a desired level of transparency, taking into account data protection and the need to keep company secrets. The transparency specialist checks that existing intranets, internal publications and memo systems are user-friendly. It is his or her job to integrate the internal information systems into an efficient electronic knowledge base that permits flexible and user-friendly links between competence areas and bearers of knowledge. To this end, the transparency specialist must standardize input formats, keywords and feedback systems as necessary, and implement the results through the company leadership.

Only a few companies have so far created positions such as chief knowledge officer, cross-area specialist, transparency specialist or competence area specialist. However, we are now seeing a rapid growth in the number of management positions with the stated objective of improving understanding and management of knowledge assets. The old job descriptions and applicant profiles can no longer meet the challenges of the knowledge society.

SUMMARY

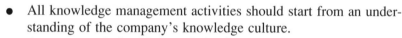

- All knowledge management activities should start from an understanding of the company's knowledge culture.
- Attempts to deal with knowledge issues embroil companies in a range of paradoxical situations. These situations should be regarded as a basis for discussing knowledge management in the future.
- Establishing learning arenas or centres of competence can be an effective catalyst for further knowledge management measures.
- The appointment of knowledge managers such as chief knowledge officer, competence area specialist or transparency specialist is a signal that knowledge management is now important to the company. However, without the support of top management, the knowledge managers have no hope of succeeding.

KEY QUESTIONS

- Where do you see nuclei of knowledge management in your organization?
- What structural opportunities do you see?

- Who are the promoters of knowledge management, and how might their positions be enhanced?
- Who are the enemies of a new approach to knowledge? Why do they reject it, and how might they be won over or involved?

13
Getting Started

INTRODUCTION

If by now you know what you do not know, and if you have
given honest answers to the questions at the end of each
chapter, you have taken the first steps towards effective
knowledge management. The field has seen early successes, the
techniques are constantly being improved, and the subject is
high on the management agenda. The various examples that we
have described give you some idea of how other companies are
already managing their knowledge, and deriving sustainable
competitive advantages from their efforts. Now it is up to you to
make your first move, and to examine the treatment of
knowledge in your working environment. In this chapter, we
offer some hints on getting started. You will not be able to do
everything, but successful knowledge management grows from
small beginnings. We wish you plenty of energy and
enthusiasm!

GETTING STARTED

1. Check your organization, your department or yourself against our building blocks of knowledge management.

Our building blocks of knowledge management offer you a series of suggestions, frameworks for analysis and instruments which you can use to test the treatment of knowledge in your working environment, and your own knowledge-related behaviour. Take stock of your knowledge honestly, and identify points where improvements might be made. Which kinds of knowledge are critical for you? In what ways are they treated incorrectly – or correctly? How might things be improved, or how might you apply solutions that have been tried elsewhere?

2. Knowledge is the raw material of the future. Try to understand it better and use it to serve your purposes.

Recognize the differences between implicit and explicit knowledge; between individual and group competencies; and between data, information and knowledge. You can use these distinctions in your own work if you examine the knowledge-intensive processes and ask yourself which elements are particularly important in them.

3. Look at things from the knowledge angle, and see your organization through different eyes.

Knowledge management will bring direct benefits if it helps you to analyse problems from a new perspective. Consider typical financial, organizational or sales problems from the knowledge angle, and explore the knowledge processes that influence them. Financial problems are always knowledge problems too. Conversely, knowledge problems always include financial problems.

4. Reorient yourself in your personal knowledge environment.

Try to rethink your own ways of dealing with knowledge. Which sources of knowledge do you use? With which internal and external experts do you have contact? What skills do you possess that can help to build the company's competence in the long term?

5. Maintain your own portfolio of competencies.

Your own individual skills date with increasing speed. Review them, and ask yourself which of them are currently in demand on the market. What contribution do your skills make to achieving your company's most important goals? Educate yourself selectively by basing your training objectives on the insights you have gained. Nobody else can take responsibility for your competencies.

6. Find like-minded people inside and outside your company.

If you want to introduce knowledge management throughout your company, you need allies in other areas, to help you to attract the necessary attention and gain widespread support for your knowledge strategy. External experience groups on the topic can be most helpful, because they will give you access to knowledge management projects that have already been carried out successfully.

7. Make use of existing knowledge systems and information infra-structures.

Do you know about all the knowledge systems and information infra-structures that are available to you? If not, try to find out about them, and evaluate their potential benefits for your own work. Ask people who use the systems and are enthusiastic about them to tell you their experiences, and let them show you how to use them.

8. Develop a language for talking about knowledge.

Try to use a more differentiated knowledge vocabulary in your every-day speech. Make a conscious effort to use terms from this book in presentations, meetings and documents. Explain their meaning clearly to others. Draw up a glossary of the most important terms.

9. Knowledge management needs knowledge managers. Appoint or assign some.

Set up a task force to deal with especially urgent knowledge problems. Consider how best to anchor knowledge management in your organization, and create the necessary positions. Knowledge management is a cross-divisional task, and it is complicated by the different functional principles that apply today in different areas, such as personnel, IT, research and development or business planning. To increase its impact, knowledge management must be incorporated in the medium term in the structure of the organization.

10. Make sure you have the support of top management for knowledge projects. You will soon find out that knowledge management can be a highly political issue.

Knowledge management involves re-evaluating existing portfolios of competencies within the company, and it necessitates some changes in priorities. As a result, people who were previously regarded as experts often lose their special status. Transparency of knowledge reduces informational advantages, which are often important in political games, and thus weakens the power base of those who were previously better informed. Knowledge management therefore has natural enemies, and many of the necessary measures can only be carried out with the full support of top management.

11. Anchor knowledge management in the structures of the organization.

Knowledge management is a cross-divisional and cross-functional task which is made more difficult by the existence of different principles in different areas (see point 9 above). Plans to make better use of knowledge as a resource must be built into the structure and culture of the organization in the medium term. 'Knowledge goals' must be integrated into company strategy and project planning. Infrastructures are needed to support employees in coping with the flood of information.

12. Make use of the revolution in communications technology. It is the driving force behind the global knowledge society.

Technological advances in communication are one reason why proponents of knowledge management attract an audience at this particular time. Completely new forms of organization are possible because the knowledge base can be shared by electronic means. The trend towards worldwide networking of all workplaces has led to the appearance of communication structures that cannot be described in terms of traditional organizational models. Modern information technologies, such as groupware applications and intranets, do indeed seem to be revolutionizing the ways in which organizations use their knowledge bases. The linking of these technologies with the unique skills and experience of individual workers seems to be the source of the energy that drives knowledge management forward.

Good luck!

14

First Experiences of Implementation or: If We Didn't Call It Knowledge Management . . .

Since this book first appeared, 'knowledge management projects' have been launched in many companies. The results have often been extremely satisfying. Some projects, however, have been unsuccessful, or have only produced results after surmounting considerable diffi-culties. We have put together some 'lessons learned' from our experi-ence of implementation. We hope that they will be useful to you in designing your own knowledge management projects.

The following key questions and guidelines are based mainly on the experiences of the companies which form the Geneva Forum for Organizational Learning and Knowledge Management. They are: DAIMLERCHRYSLER, DEUTSCHE BANK, HOLDERBANK, HEWLETT PACK-ARD, INSELSPITAL, MOTOROLA, NOVARTIS, ROCHE DIAGNOSTICS, SIEMENS, SWISSCOM, UBS and WINTERTHUR INSURANCES. We have taken the insights and experiences of project managers and others who are responsible for managing knowledge in those companies and con-densed them into a series of key questions. If the questions are answered before a knowledge management project is launched, it should be possible to avoid at least some of the commoner difficulties in implementation.

KEY QUESTION 1: WHAT KINDS OF KNOWLEDGE ARE RELEVANT TO OUR NEEDS?

Knowledge management has become a fashionable activity, and there is often an element of 'me too' about it. Some companies rush into knowledge management projects so as not to fall behind their competitors. In their hurry, they may overlook vital questions such as which of the company's knowledge assets are the most important, and what the aims of any intervention should be. Companies are often too ready to accept that knowledge is a 'major competitive factor', while the people working on the project may lack a clear working definition of what knowledge is, or a clear understanding of the goals.

Certain questions should therefore be asked before a project is defined. They are: What knowledge is vitally important to us from a strategic point of view? What knowledge is relevant and valuable, and thus likely to affect our business results? In relation to which intellectual assets could we take measures to improve the acquisition, sharing, preservation or utilization of knowledge? The answers to these questions will help companies to avoid knowledge management projects that are tool-driven, or that address only the specific needs of a particular function. Knowledge management projects do not necessarily affect the company's IT infrastructure or its organizational structure, and they are not automatically the responsibility of IT or the personnel department. Careful answers to the questions listed above can be helpful in deciding where the emphasis of the project should lie, and who should be chiefly responsible for its implementation.

KEY QUESTION 2: IS THE LABEL 'KNOWLEDGE MANAGEMENT' HELPFUL?

We have already said that 'knowledge management' is a fashionable term, but that does not make it a motivating or a serviceable one. A project should not be a response to short-lived fashion trends, nor should it be undertaken out of feelings of rivalry. On the contrary: it should be named and defined in such a way that it addresses a real need. This promotes acceptance and avoids the danger that the project will be dismissed as a crackpot idea from head office, or the 'flavour of the month'.

There are many terms which could replace the label 'knowledge management', and which offer a better definition of a project, without denying the fact that it is knowledge-related. The terms 'lessons learned', 'learning organization', 'best in class', 'best practice transfer', 'service level performance', 'network of relationships', 'yellow pages', 'expert network', 'customer focus' and 'competitive intelligence' all include in their meaning the transfer, utilization or acquisition of knowledge. In any case, it is not helpful to offer 'knowledge management' as the overall project goal if it is possible to give a more precise definition of the topic and its specific relationship to knowledge. Another possibility is to build a knowledge dimension on to existing projects. A project on improving co-operation between research departments, for instance, might benefit from the addition of a knowledge perspective, or a customer focus project might be approached from the point of view of knowledge acquisition.

KEY QUESTION 3: CAN THE PROJECT GENERATE MEASURABLE RESULTS?

Knowledge management projects have something in common with building sites. When the project is defined, it is often given a fundamentally strategic direction, e.g. in relation to 'knowledge products', new markets or safeguarding core competencies. However, a project of this kind often involves comprehensive changes to processes and structures, e.g. new technological platforms, or a process-oriented reorganization. The main danger springs from the fact that a project which is broadly defined will also be of a long-term nature. The absence of results in the short and medium term leads to frustration, and often to the death of the project.

Setting goals that can be realized in the short term – or 'quick wins' – can offer a way out of this dilemma, while leaving the general long-term concept intact. The 'quick wins' must be carefully chosen. The schema shown in Figure 14.1 has proved useful in this respect; it classifies projects and sub-projects according to their contribution to the value of the company, their knowledge dimension, and their time frame.

The project portfolio allows projects to be placed in one of four quadrants according to their potential contribution to company value and the extent to which they are knowledge-related. The time frame is represented by the size of the circles. Projects that can be completed

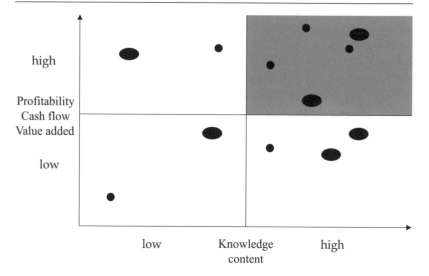

Profitability
Cash flow
Value added

low

low   Knowledge   high
                content

Figure 14.1 Knowledge management project portfolio

in the short term and can give quick results are represented by small circles, while larger ones indicate projects with a long-term focus. From the knowledge management point of view, the most interesting projects are without doubt those in the upper right quadrant (shaded grey). To achieve quick wins, it is advisable to choose the projects in this quadrant that can be realized in the short term.

In drawing attention to the importance of quick wins, we do not mean to point the way to blind actionism and isolated projects. It is important for the company to develop an overall framework for knowledge-related issues. Nevertheless, it is both feasible and useful to define short-term (sub-) projects which have a marked knowledge dimension and which – if successfully implemented – have an effect on cash flow, profitability or the value of the company. Successful initiatives of this kind have an encouraging and motivating effect both on the organization's decision-making bodies and on the employees involved in the project work. Results need not be measurable in a financial sense; they can also be defined in terms of stakeholder benefits, from the point of view of representatives of different interest groups. However, it should always be remembered that knowledge must have some kind of value. Table 14.1 provides a summary of different measurement areas and approaches.

Table 14.1   Measuring knowledge management projects

Stakeholder and Approach to measurement	
Employees	Market value of employees, employability, employee satisfaction, productivity/quality, creativity
Customers	Customer loyalty, winning new customers, response (time) to customer queries, key accounts, lost customers
Investors	Existence/communication of a knowledge management system, transparency, project portfolio, reporting
Society	Image improvement through knowledge management, 'risk of knowledge loss'

KEY QUESTION 4: HAS SUFFICIENT ATTENTION BEEN PAID TO BUY-IN PROCESSES?

Buy-in processes are often neglected in the run-up to knowledge management projects. These projects must have broad support and be seen as (urgently) necessary and meaningful if they are to bring about real changes in the organization. If there is no buy-in process to persuade people that the project is necessary, there is a danger that it will be rejected, or that it will meet with active or passive resistance. 'We already have re-engineering, TQM, customer focus and MBO. Why do we need knowledge management as well?'

The target groups of buy-in processes are the decision-makers and those affected by the project. Decision-makers often feel the need for change as a result of benchmarking processes that reveal strategic gaps. A similar readiness to accept change must be encouraged in those who will be affected by it. The more concrete the project, and the closer to the particular employee, the greater will be his or her involvement in implementation.

During the buy-in process, it can be critical to create win–win situations, i.e. to demonstrate links between the value of the project to the person affected and its benefit to the company. Vision, goals, procedural stages, instruments and incentives should be suitably aligned. The following questions should be asked when planning a buy-in process: Is there discernible pressure for change, and is it sufficient to support the introduction of the project work? Does the project bring discernible personal advantages? Can adequate communication be guaranteed between the decision-makers and those affected by the project?

KEY QUESTION 5: IS ENOUGH ATTENTION BEING PAID TO COMMUNICATION?

Many of the projects that we have followed have shown that systematic communication is an essential precondition for launching knowledge management projects and carrying them through. One reason is that in most cases, knowledge management involves personal communication within networks of relationships, or interaction between people and machines. Communication between the decision-makers and those affected by the project is critically important. It is not always realized how easily knowledge management can become divorced from knowledge utilization. Many knowledge management projects are delegated to technological experts, who may overemphasize technical solutions; these may then be implemented without any real understanding of the purposes they are intended to serve. Blind faith in technology does not solve problems, and does not guarantee genuine implementation of solutions.

Successful communication reduces present and future resistance, lowers barriers to implementation and recruits possible supporters. Valuable pointers may be found in the answers to the following questions: Are we taking enough time to think about possible obstacles to implementation? Are we examining critically our own thought and behaviour patterns, which are often the greatest barriers? Is the purpose of the project formulated clearly enough to be easily communicable? Which employees should be targets of communication, since they are affected by the project and might resist it? Who can take over the role of sponsor and communicator for knowledge management, and act as 'cheerleader'? Which are the most suitable channels of communication?

KEY QUESTION 6: DO WE HAVE KNOWLEDGE FLOWS OR KNOWLEDGE ASSETS?

Many knowledge management projects are in danger of focusing too quickly on documenting and preserving intellectual assets. An exercise of this kind promises to be successful, and access to the relevant intellectual assets is often already assured. Knowledge management thus becomes a matter of perspiration rather than inspiration. Furthermore, the documentation of knowledge assets only covers explicit knowledge, which can be put into written form and stored in patent summaries, directories of experts, and other similar systems. Knowledge, however, is always action-oriented. It is continuously re-created, changed and used. Implicit knowledge, experience, creativity and innovation are much more difficult to record than explicit knowledge. The processes of interpreting, transferring, examining and recombining knowledge assets create organizational knowledge flows, and these are the real challenge to knowledge management.

KEY QUESTION 7: ARE WE PAYING ENOUGH ATTENTION TO THE NEED FOR A KNOWLEDGE-ORIENTED CULTURE, AND TO THE ULTIMATE UTILIZATION OF KNOWLEDGE?

The mere availability of instruments does not guarantee that they will be used. Peter Rothstein of LOTUS NOTES says that if people do not want to share their knowledge, giving them an electronic tool will not make them. The knowledge-related aspects of the company culture have a much greater influence on the success or failure of knowledge utilization. A knowledge-oriented culture means trust and open discussion of problems. The introduction of electronic tools ('high tech') should therefore always be combined with openness, personal interaction and communication ('high touch'). It is unrealistic to expect employees to make active efforts to share their knowledge when the company's organization and culture do not promote trust.

Structures and incentive systems create the framework for a knowledge-oriented culture. Managers should also support it in their own actions, commitment, dialogue and meaningful statements. Requirements should thus be combined with leadership by example. Clear statements from top management have often worked wonders for the implementation of knowledge management projects.

Daniel Vasella, CEO of NOVARTIS, summarizes the importance of knowledge to his company as follows: 'Our success in building a high performance organization will be substantially based on the capability of sharing and exploiting our professional knowledge better and faster than our competitors.' Thomas Schmidheiny of HOLDERBANK, the world's leading cement manufacturer, makes an equally clear statement: 'At HOLDERBANK we are clearly committed to our decentralized structure to maintain entrepreneurial spirit. To cope with the coming challenge we have to learn continuously, exchange best practices and master the learning process.'

In SIEMENS, Heinrich von Pierer has expressly included knowledge and skills in the company vision. Under 'Employees and Performance Measures', the vision statement says:

> The knowledge and skills of our managers and employees are the real basis of our success. We help our employees to develop their enormous potential to the full. We improve our knowledge and skills continuously, transforming them effectively into customer value and hence into business success. We learn from the best: from our most demanding customers, our strongest competitors, and the leading companies in other branches of industry. We share knowledge and experience within our company, and work together unreservedly, across all departmental and divisional boundaries. We claim world class performance. We set the benchmarks for others.'

Knowledge management projects need the support of top management. The statements just quoted show how top managers can promote a knowledge-aware organizational culture, and support the development of competence in knowledge management.

APPENDIX 1: CASE STUDY
MAKING EXPERT KNOWLEDGE USABLE:
EXPERIENCES WITH THE NOVARTIS
'KNOWLEDGE MARKETPLACE'

INTRODUCTION

NOVARTIS was formed in December 1996 as the result of a merger between CIBA-GEIGY and SANDOZ, both of which were chemical and pharmaceutical companies with headquarters in Basle. NOVARTIS has 275 subsidiaries and operates in 142 countries. It employs 87 000 people, and in 1997 it had a turnover of 31 billion Swiss francs; this makes it one of the leading global competitors in the 'life sciences' industry (see Exhibit 1 at the end of this appendix). The company's organizational structure is strongly decentralized. There are three divisions: Health Care, Agribusiness and Nutrition. These divisions are subdivided into 10 operationally and legally autonomous sectors (see Exhibit 2).

Knowledge is an important issue for NOVARTIS. In 1997, the company's spending on research and development exceeded 3.6 billion Swiss francs. The company was granted 16 000 patents worldwide; 12 000 further applications are currently being processed. The leadership of NOVARTIS aims to make the company a high-performance organization, and believes that knowledge management will play a major part in this. Dan Vasella, the CEO, has said that the company's success in building a high-performance organization will be based primarily on its ability to share and utilize its professional knowledge better and faster than its competitors.

SIGNIFICANCE OF KNOWLEDGE MANAGEMENT IN NOVARTIS

Since the merger, NOVARTIS has been faced with the task of net-working the knowledge of the two original companies, i.e. CIBA-GEIGY and SANDOZ. In the life sciences industry, research and development are exceptionally important, so it is vital that NOVARTIS should be able to create and utilise knowledge. However, the company's present organizational structure is such that knowledge is largely stockpiled within the independent business areas. Furthermore, the global nature of the company's operations means that important holders of knowledge cannot always meet. For these reasons, the company needs techniques for managing internal knowledge systematically. NOVARTIS has therefore introduced a knowledge management programme aimed at facilitating the development and use of knowledge across boundaries.

The following example will illustrate the potential benefits to NOV-ARTIS of a programme of this kind. In 1998, Frank Lasarasina of NOV-ARTIS PHARMACEUTICAL in New Jersey wished to introduce the 'bal-anced scorecard' method, developed by Kaplan and Norton of the Harvard Business School. Lasarasina felt that he needed more detailed knowledge of the balanced scorecard method, and of possible imple-mentation problems. He turned to the 'NOVARTIS Virtual Forum' for help. Bernard Wasen, who worked for NOVARTIS SEEDS in the Netherlands, and David Chu, of the Consumer Health division in Nyon, indicated their interest and opened a discussion with Lasarasina. Within a few days, the group found a suitable technique for imple-menting the scorecard method.

VISION AND MISSION

One of the main challenges in the life sciences industry is to reduce the time to market. The ability to use knowledge already present in the company can be a great help. At present, the average time from the beginning of research to the introduction of a new product is 11.3 years. The cost is about $US500 million. Each day's delay in bringing the product to market represents lost turnover of about a $US1 million. These figures underline the importance of promoting and systematiz-ing internal knowledge sharing.

The basic setting for knowledge sharing in NOVARTIS had been the 'champion communities'. This term denotes more or less informal meetings – over a cup of coffee, or a beer in the evening – during which employees would talk about work and share information. Scientists usually exchange knowledge readily, to satisfy their professional curiosity. In an international company, however, the opportunities to meet are limited. NOVARTIS therefore decided to create virtual links for knowledge sharing.

The aim of the NOVARTIS knowledge management programme is to convert accumulated knowledge into a company asset. The following measures are intended to ensure that knowledge is used across organizational barriers:

- Provision of quick and easy access to a global knowledge base
- Elimination of temporal and spatial constraints on communication
- Encouraging employees to share their knowledge more

To promote systematic use of knowledge, NOVARTIS formed a committee of leading scientists, known as the 'Science Board'. This committee has four main tasks:

- To facilitate the transfer of knowledge
- To observe emerging technologies and sponsor new projects
- To maintain and promote networks of like-minded people
- To maintain external contacts with universities, consultancy firms and other institutions

The Science Board has an extensive budget for carrying out these tasks. At present, the budget is used primarily to finance new technology projects.

KNOWLEDGE MARKETPLACE

The introduction of the 'Knowledge MarketPlace' was an important step in the implementation of knowledge management in NOVARTIS. The MarketPlace consists of three linked elements: a directory of internal experts (the Yellow Pages); a directory of external experts (the Blue Pages); and a discussion forum that works like a news group (the Virtual Forum). The platform for these instruments is the company-wide intranet, together with a LOTUS Notes system introduced by SANDOZ before the merger.

Paul Sartori, a NOVARTIS manager, has defined the Knowledge MarketPlace as a medium through which employees can contribute to the company's activities, participate in them and influence them while at the same time shaping their own future. He believes that knowledge sharing is part of every job, and that the real assets of NOVARTIS are the intellectual competencies of its employees. According to Sartori, NOVARTIS differentiates itself from other companies by the way in which it taps these competencies and enables them to develop.

The three components of the Knowledge MarketPlace are interlinked. Group discussions on specific topics are held through the Virtual Forum: one person opens the discussion, and others who are interested in the topic can then offer their views. These discussions give rise to an international library of information on a wide variety of subjects. Members wishing to pursue a topic further can also contact each other directly, by e-mail or telephone. According to Hannon, a NOVARTIS executive, the Forum has enormous potential. It will transform the ways in which information is exchanged and knowledge is shared in NOVARTIS, and will provide quicker access to expertise than was formerly possible. New knowledge is then transmitted via the Virtual Forum to others who have similar problems.

The Blue Pages and the Yellow Pages have complementary functions in creating transparency of knowledge. The Blue Pages are a directory of external experts. The persons and institutions listed there have served NOVARTIS particularly well in the past, and are therefore recommended for future projects. The profiles of the external experts are entered by NOVARTIS employees who participate in the Knowledge MarketPlace.

The Yellow Pages are a directory of internal experts, listed according to name and personal expertise. All NOVARTIS employees are invited to enter a personal profile in a structured format on their computers. This information is then available to other members. The Yellow Pages aim to create a 'virtual champion community'. Entries cover the following points:

- Location in NOVARTIS (telephone number, place)
- Professional background
- Special fields of activity
- Practical experience
- Training

Any employee who needs information on a special field or topic can search the Yellow Pages for keywords or phrases. As soon as the right person is identified, contact can be made and knowledge shared. The major difference between the Yellow Pages and an ordinary company directory is that the former is not produced centrally. Dr Staeheli, who is the Officer of the Science Board and is also responsible for the Knowledge MarketPlace, is the only employee who spends time maintaining the Yellow Pages. This illustrates the principle of personal responsibility, which is an important part of the leadership concept in NOVARTIS. With regard to the Yellow Pages, this means that

- Each employee decides whether or not he or she wishes to provide a personal profile and appear in the Yellow Pages
- Each employee decides what information he or she wishes to give

This principle offers a simple solution to the problem of protecting personal data, since each employee is responsible for his or her own details as they appear in the system. Dr Staeheli stresses that the knowledge resources are the responsibility of each individual, and are under his or her control.

PROBLEMS AND OBSTACLES

A system of this kind can only be functional if the number of entries made reaches a certain critical mass. If there are not enough entries, the probability of finding experts who can help with a particular topic is too low. Use of the system declines, which in turn reduces the incentive to make an entry, and this can lead to a downward spiral. The Yellow Pages are only attractive as a way of finding contacts and crossing the functional and geographical barriers to knowledge sharing if they contain enough entries.

Initially, the project was not as successful as had been hoped. The next step was therefore to try to increase the number of employees who used the system. An analysis was made of the reasons why the systems was underutilized, and many individual, cultural and organizational obstacles were identified.

INDIVIDUAL FACTORS

Lack of time

Many potential users complained that they were far too busy to search for information on the intranet or Internet. Potential 'experts' were afraid that they would be flooded with enquiries as soon as their names appeared in the Yellow Pages.

Information overload

The icons for the Virtual Forum, the Blue Pages and the Yellow Pages are just three out of almost two hundred which appear on the screen of the average NOVARTIS employee. The Knowledge Management Team has succeeded in having its icons placed in the top left-hand area of the screen, but this arrangement can be changed by the individual user. Meanwhile, more and more managers are complaining of growing informational overload. They take a defensive position, and make only the most selective use of new sources of information.

Lack of familiarity with technology

The Yellow Pages often seem too impersonal, particularly to employees who are not especially familiar with the new information and communications technologies. Many employees prefer personal communication, and are reluctant to accept virtual substitutes. An intranet cannot fully replace the informal exchange of information during a coffee break.

The pressure of expectations

Many employees feel shy about putting themselves forward as experts. The act of volunteering one's name also incurs an implicit obligation, since an expert ought to be able to give reliable answers to specific questions. The fear of being asked a question and not knowing the answer prevents many employees from putting their details into the system.

CULTURAL FACTORS

Doubts about quality of information

There is no official check on the quality of the information offered by these self-styled experts. Potential users therefore tend to doubt the reliability of the information, and this reduces the likelihood that they will in fact use the Yellow Pages.

After-effects of the Merger

Many employees are unsure about whether NOVARTIS is really trying to promote a general culture of knowledge sharing and knowledge management. The fact that the company is an amalgamation of two former rivals strengthens their suspicions, and leads them to doubt whether the 'knowledge culture' of the new organization is genuine. Moreover, there are widespread fears of job losses in the wake of the merger. An atmosphere of this kind is not usually conducive to knowledge sharing. Many employees believe that knowledge is power, and tend to hoard their knowledge so as to avoid weakening their own positions.

ORGANIZATIONAL FACTORS

Pay systems

The pay systems in NOVARTIS operate on a sector basis. There are consequently very few incentives to sharing knowledge between sectors. Each new user of the system did receive a small present, but incentives of this kind cannot guarantee that people will continue to use the system regularly and effectively.

User Orientation

The project has suffered because its launch was not preceded by any formal market research. It is therefore unknown whether the instruments meet employees' needs. Moreover, there was no clear definition of the target groups who were to make use of the new instruments.

Lack of support from top management

The project was approved by top management, but this support was not successfully communicated to the employees. There was also a failure to budget for the personnel resources needed to implement the project successfully, so the senior managers who lead the project are burdened with many non-essential tasks.

POSSIBLE SOLUTIONS

Decentralization

One has the general impression that the central co-ordination of knowledge management is reaching its limits. Decentralization, for example by nominating an honorary 'knowledge officer' in each department, might be one way to attract wider support for knowledge management tasks. A knowledge officer of this kind could personally attract colleagues' attention to knowledge-related issues. This would not, of course, make training and co-ordinating activities superfluous: the members of Dr Staeheli's team could continue to perform these tasks on a central basis. Another way of supporting the implementation of knowledge management would be to hold regional meetings with specialists at middle and upper levels.

Incentives and rewards

The prospect of improving one's performance by sharing knowledge should in itself act as incentive. The potential benefits of the system to individual employees should therefore be made clear (see below).

The company might also create a system of financial and non-financial incentives. Honorary involvement – e.g. as a departmental knowledge officer – must be included in the performance assessment system, and should lead to appropriate compensation.

Communication

With the help of the internal marketing and communication departments, it should be possible to introduce a targeted campaign to promote knowledge management activities. The Virtual Forum might be a selling point, because it is interactive, and therefore satisfies people's pleasure in communicating better than the 'unresponsive' Yellow Pages. Many employees fear informational overload and increasing demands on their time. Communications should be aimed at showing that the instruments described above are especially well suited to simplifying the process of knowledge acquisition by individuals. If employees can make contacts and obtain information through an internal system, this makes their task easier. The methods described above place the onus of seeking information on the user; informational overload is thus largely avoided.

Exhibit 1: Financial Highlights
Key Figures 1997
CHF millions

Sales	31,180
Health Care	*18,742*
Agribusiness	*8,327*
Nutrition	*4,111*
Industry	*–*
Operating income	6,783
Net financial income/expense	120
Exceptional income/expense	–
Net income	5,211
Cash flow from operation activities	4,679
Free cash flow	1,309
Change in net liquidity	1,224
Investment in tangible fixed assets	1,554
Depreciation and amortization	1,292
Group research and development	3,693
Pharmaceuticals research and development	2,629
Dividend of NOVARTIS AG	1,736

Exhibit 2:   The Group Structure

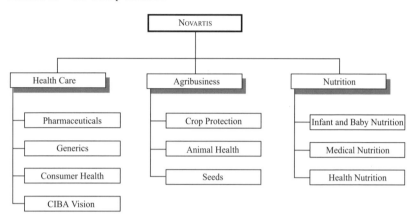

Exhibit 3:   Entry form for Yellow Pages
General Data

First Name(s): ———————————   Street: ———————————
Last Name: ———————————   ZIP: ———————————
Company: ———————————   City: ———————————
Department: ———————————   Country: ———————————
Phone: ———————————   Fax: ———————————
E-mail: ———————————

1.   Expertise and skills in technology and methods
Please describe your education and professional training. Users of the Yellow Pages
will search by keywords, so please include the keywords you would like to be found
in a 'Search'.
Please avoid acronyms and abbreviations unless previously defined.

2. Goals of current and most recent assignments

Current and most recent assignments are another indicator of your professional skills. The goals of your assignments and what you achieved in them will tell a prospective discussion partner more than a list of project names.
Please avoid acronyms and abbreviations unless previously defined.

3. Area of knowledge and level of expertise

Please indicate your main areas of expertise by selecting the most appropriate keywords:

- Analytical Science ☐
- Biological Science ☐
- Chemical Science ☐
- Facility Development & Engineering ☐
- Health, Safety & Environment ☐
- Information, computational technology ☐
- Management & Business Administration ☐
- Markets ☐
- Material Science ☐
- Medical Science ☐
- Processing Technologies ☐
- Product Application & Trials ☐
- Registration & Certification ☐
- Sourcing & Supply ☐

and please give details below:

Please indicate your level of expertise in those areas:

	Area 1	Area 2	Area 3
● Recognized expert	☐	☐	☐
● Significant experience	☐	☐	☐
● Moderate experience	☐	☐	☐
● Limited experience	☐	☐	☐
● Not yet categorized	☐	☐	☐

The terms listed at the beginning of this question refer to areas of expertise and not to organizational departments, e.g. one person in R&D might indicate that he or she has expertise in Chemical Science, while a second might have expertise in Information/Computational Technology, and a third in Management & Business Administration.

4. Unique or specialized equipment or tools
If you have access to unique or specialized laboratory or plant equipment, or if you are using unique instruments or software tools, etc. please describe their characteristics and specifications.
Please avoid acronyms and abbreviations unless previously defined.

5. Optional information on certificates, qualifications, membership of professional organizations, etc.
These details can provide further information on your expertise. Please feel free to provide them if you are happy to do so.
Please avoid acronyms and abbreviations unless previously defined

Reminder
To keep the data on this form up to date, you will be asked to revise it periodically.
Please specify the intervals at which you would like a reminder:
Remind me to update this form every 90 ☐ 180 ☐ 360 ☐ days
Send reminder to: _____
Date: _____

Exhibit 4: Example of a Yellow Page
First Name(s): Joerg **Street:** R-1001.4.28
Last Name: Staeheli **ZIP:** CH-4002
Company: NOVARTIS International AG **City:** CH-4002 Basel
Department: Corporate Knowledge Mgmt **Country:** Switzerland
Phone: +41–61–697–0428 **Fax:** +41–61–697–4027
E-mail: *joerg.staeheli@group.novartis.com*

> **Expertise in skills in technology and methods**
> Consulting in
> - Technology Portfolio Management
> - Supply Chain Management, Lead-time Management
> - Benchmarking Best Practices
> - Value Chain Analysis
> - Technology Transfer
> - Doing Business on the Internet

Goals of current and most recent assignments
Senior Officer Corporate Knowledge, Secretary of the Technology Advisory Board
- Host of 'The Knowledge Market Place'
- Directs knowledge networking initiatives in order to facilitate full use of knowledge across sector boundaries
- Organizes and conducts knowledge fairs on a scientific/technological topic of group-wide interest
- Initiates and administers Technology Advisory Board (TAB) meetings and monitors progress of funded projects
- Facilitates new and current relations with technology-oriented institutions
- Acts as gatekeeper to the 'Industrial Liaison Program' at the 'Massachusetts Institute of Technology' MIT
- Monitors trends of science/technology applied to productivity, processes and systems, evaluates opportunities, promotes relevant subjects
- Represents Novatis in science/technology-oriented organizations

Domain	Sub-domain	Area (optional)	Expertise Level
Management & Business Administration	Technology Management	Technology Transfer	Recognized Expert
Management & Business Administration	Organizational Design/ Organizational Behaviour	Knowledge Management	Recognized Expert

Unique or specialized equipment or tools

Optional information on certificates, qualifications, membership of professional organizations, etc.

Remind me every 180 days to update this form.
Send reminder to: Joerg Staeheli/INTERNATIONAL/CHBS/SANDOZ

APPENDIX 2: CASE STUDY
KNOWLEDGE IN USE IN HOLDERBANK

HOLDERBANK: THE BACKGROUND

HOLDERBANK is a Swiss cement producing company, founded in 1912 in the Swiss village of the same name. It grew from humble beginnings to become a global network, and is now the world's largest producer of cement. The HOLDERBANK group operates in more than 60 countries, and has over 100 cement factories. In 1997, the group's net turnover was SF11 265 million, with net profits of SF618 million. Its products include cement, clinker and related compounds. The company also offers consulting and engineering services for the whole cement production process. Thanks to a well-balanced portfolio, HOLDERBANK holds a strong market position not only in the major industrial countries, but also in the growing markets of Latin America, Africa and Asia. The group has a decentralized structure, combined with a clearly defined group strategy; this gives the individual companies high levels of autonomy and operational flexibility. Decisions are made by companies acting as local enterprises, so all actions must satisfy customer and market requirements. The group endeavours to make global use of its globally acquired know-how. HOLDERBANK MANAGEMENT AND CONSULTING (HMC) acts as a service centre and an interface in supporting the exchange of information throughout the holding.

THE HOLDERBANK HOLDING

HOLDERBANK has a global presence, so there are many different interests to be co-ordinated. Drawing on its long experience, the group has adopted a structure based on function and geography. HOLDERBANK is represented by local companies which operate under different names in each country. These local companies co-ordinate all the centres of production in their region and are run by local managers. Because of the group's decentralized structure, companies are monitored largely by financial results, so local management enjoys a high level of autonomy.

The global nature of HOLDERBANK's activities and acquisitions policy results in enormous variety: different markets, different company cultures, different national cultures. This variety has always been regarded as an advantage because, in the words of one manager, it offers opportunities 'to discern the specific taste of each market and accumulate huge reserves of expertise in different environments'.

At the same time, HOLDERBANK is engaged in a continual search for a 'glue' that will hold the diversity together and make it productive. With this end in view, and to increase the expertise of its employees, HOLDERBANK has developed a large-scale training programme covering all functions, countries and hierarchical levels. The aims of this programme are to improve the competencies of employees and to create some common working patterns to serve as a 'common language'. Participants exchange experiences during the training, and an international network of relationships is formed.

HOLDERBANK MANAGEMENT AND CONSULTING LTD

HOLDERBANK Management and Consulting Ltd. (HMC) plays a central role in this new development strategy. Exchange of knowledge within the group is a major concern of HMC and its 320 highly skilled employees; they are supported in this by the leadership of the group. HMC also plays an important part in developing and implementing training programmes, workshops and management seminars. According to management statements, HMC wishes to become a 'know-how broker' for the whole group. To this end it uses modern technology, such as virtual conferences, Yellow Pages and data banks of practical information to support exchanges amongst managers in different countries. The company is aware that tools of this kind are not in themselves sufficient to build relationships, so it also organizes management meetings, or personal meetings at international seminars. The informal learning atmosphere cultivated at these events strengthens a feeling of trust, which is an essential precondition for creating a knowledge network within the group.

THE FASTER LEARNING ORGANIZATION

Faced with increasing competition, and the growing complexity and dynamism of the cement industry, HOLDERBANK must address a number of specific problems:

- *Environmental opportunities and dangers* A growing body of environmental regulations compels companies to reduce emissions of dangerous gases; the cost of doing so cuts into profits. By developing a new technology to reduce emissions, a company could gain an important competitive advantage over the rest of industry.
- *Saturated markets versus growth markets* It is increasingly important to identify growth markets and to build up a strong presence in them, to ensure future success. A dominant position in saturated markets is no longer sufficient.
- *Global and regional 'shooting stars'* Many local competitors act faster than HOLDERBANK and are becoming important competitors on the world market.

HOLDERBANK's goal is lasting success, i.e. its aim is to continue to be the most efficient group of manufacturers of building materials in the world. This can only be achieved if the group has well-motivated employees with better than average skills. HOLDERBANK therefore regards its employees as an important competitive advantage, and knowledge is categorized as a company asset. Constant learning must take place if the group is to retain its competitive advantage. A learning organization focuses on

- Systematic problem-solving
- Experimenting with new approaches
- Transfer of knowledge throughout the whole organization
- Learning from its own experiences and history
- Learning from the experiences and best practices of other companies

In the past, access to technology and capital were the critical success factors in the cement industry. In the future, speed of innovation and reaction to market changes will be decisive. HOLDERBANK realized that faster learning was essential to support a decentralized organization. Local companies were sometimes slow to implement decisions; this could no longer be tolerated. Mr Baumgartner, HMC's head of corporate training, asks: 'Why should we continue to reinvent the wheel, and keep on making the same mistakes, when the knowledge is already present in the company and only needs to be shared?' For management, the question was: 'How can we accelerate changes in the behaviour of employees, so that they share their knowledge with each other?' In order to address these questions, a new training concept was introduced at the meeting of the HOLDERBANK Group in Davos, Switzerland, in 1995. The concept was called: 'HOLDERBANK – a faster learning organization'.

HMC was given the difficult task of implementing this concept. To create a faster learning organization, learning was needed at three levels:

- *Learning at company and group levels* Knowledge should be exchanged between individuals in the subsidiary companies, and between the subsidiaries themselves. This was to be achieved by replication of best practices and creating a supportive environment.
- *Team learning* Within each subsidiary, knowledge should be exchanged within and between teams.
- *Individual learning* Each employee should learn from his or her own experiences, communicate them to colleagues, and learn in turn from their experiences.

It is hoped that interactions among these three levels of learning will lead to a stronger learning culture and hence to a faster learning organization. At the heart of the process lies the identification of best practices. So what are they?

BEST PRACTICES

Best practices fall into two groups: (1) practices relating to technology or management, and (2) practices relating to the behaviour of people. Here we are concerned not so much with practices in themselves, but with methods and structured approaches which can be used to identify knowledge at individual, local and company levels. The aim is to identify especially successful practices or methods that have been developed and applied in one subsidiary, and make them accessible to the rest of the group. The reinvention of the wheel will thus be avoided.

HMC has launched a new initiative aimed at faster replication of best practice. It is a structured programme consisting of four steps:

Step 1	Step 2	Step 3	Step 4
Find best practice (BP)	Describe BP	Transfer BP	Institutionalize BP
Locate area with above-average performance, to define focus and potential for improvement	Describe and document BP adequately	Determine a suitable transfer model	Repeat process at other locations

HMC uses two basic tools to identify best practices (Step 1) and to describe them (Step 2):

- *Field research* Employees of HMC go to the individual companies in the holding and apply various research methods, such as interviews and the learning matrix.
- *Workshops* Employees from different subsidiaries and different levels in the hierarchy come together to seek solutions to specific problems.

HMC uses two techniques for this: identification of unwritten rules, and the learning matrix.

Identification of Unwritten Rules

In every company, there are unwritten rules which influence people's behaviour. They exist alongside the official, written rules issued by management. Since the unwritten rules are concerned with informal knowledge about 'how this outfit really works', they are difficult to identify. They develop through the interaction of employees, their experiences and the actions of superiors. They are culturally determined, and some are scarcely discernible. The distinction between written and unwritten rules is paralleled by one which is sometimes made between official reality and hidden reality.

Unwritten rules are considered neither good nor bad in themselves. They are identified in order to reveal hidden but powerful realities which may impede change in general, and learning in particular. Figure A.1 contains examples of unwritten rules in the companies of the HOLDERBANK GROUP:

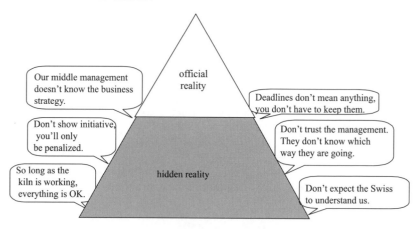

Figure A.1

It is not always clear whose behaviour needs to change for these barriers to learning to be overcome. To find out whether the barriers exist only within individual companies or throughout the whole group, interviews are carried out by a third party. Once the unwritten rules are identified, the next step is to look for the reasons behind them. This leads to discussion of how the unwritten rules influence the actions of the group, the subsidiaries, teams and individuals.

The Learning Matrix

The learning matrix is used to classify learning needs and activities. The desired state of affairs is compared with current reality, and this reveals potential gaps in learning. Learning needs are then analysed, arranged in order of importance and grouped in clusters. Finally, specific learning and development activities are implemented in order to meet the learning needs.

Learning unit	Individual	Team	Company	Whole group
Vision				
Business strategy				
Business procedure				
Procedures				

HOLDERBANK uses various methods and instruments for transferring knowledge (Step 3) and institutionalizing it (Step 4). The company makes a distinction between face-to-face methods and methods based on technological means of communication.

Face-to-face methods	Technology-based methods
Centre of competence: consists of groups of experts who support the transfer and institutionalization of best practices. The aim is to help others to implement successful processes and procedures	Virtual classroom: learning network for distance discussions and interaction with colleagues and course leaders. Experts interact in virtual conferences
Migrating knowledge, or international transfer of employees: expatriates act as carriers and integrators of knowledge	Computer tools: Simulators, computer-based training, and CD-ROMs support transfer of core knowledge throughout the group
International seminars: networking and personal transfer of knowledge are HOLDERBANK's main methods of transferring practices and expertise	Data bank of helpful practices: Who has done what, and when, and where, and how?
Mutual visits: systematic procedure for identifying and communicating strategic and operational information	Audiovisual aids: Description and transfer of helpful practices

According to one employee, 'Information technology creates the infrastructure for transferring knowledge, but it is the people who put life into group learning.' This expresses HOLDERBANK's view of the relationship between technology and personal contacts. At a time when many companies are using electronic communications to save on travel costs, HOLDERBANK is investing a great deal of money to bring its employees together to share their experiences.

In spite of its policy of identifying best practices, the company faces three major obstacles which slow down the learning process: its culture, its management style and its organizational structure. These obstacles can only be overcome by establishing a new company culture in which the sharing of knowledge is accepted and encouraged.

Initially, HOLDERBANK had asked all its subsidiaries to supply three best practices each, and to enter them in a global system. Unfortunately, the best practices offered were mostly superficially described, and were rarely used or expanded by the other subsidiaries. HOLDERBANK has therefore adopted a different approach to creating a system of global best practices.

In the first stage, best practices are exchanged only at national level, since personal contacts are stronger at that level and employees are readier to exchange knowledge. In selecting best practices, great attention is paid to quality. In the next stage, best practices are exchanged on a regional basis, to build up readiness for exchange at a global level.

LEARNING IN HOLDERBANK COMPANIES AND IN THE HOLDERBANK GROUP

The following three examples show how HOLDERBANK is turning the concept of the faster learning organization into reality. The first is an example of a learning situation within a HOLDERBANK subsidiary; the other two concern interorganizational learning between different subsidiaries within the group.

Learning within a company

HISALBA

HISALBA, the Spanish subsidiary of HOLDERBANK, consists of three cement factories and several terminals in southern Spain. The factory in Jerez was chosen because of its strategic position. However, it had relatively high production costs and problematic union relations.

The cluster formation of the factories in southern Spain offered enormous potential for synergies in market share, maintenance costs, management structures and personnel. A team from HMC was sent to Spain to try to realize these potential synergies; the Jerez factory was to serve as a prototype. The team's mission was to improve performance, to develop a learning programme designed specifically for the company, and to make systematic use of the potential synergies. The first essential was to change the attitudes and behaviour of the workforce. Personal interviews and informal conversations between the team from HMC and HISALBA employees had revealed factors which were deeply rooted in HISALBA's company culture, and which would hinder progress in learning. These 'unwritten rules' exerted a strong influence on the behaviour of employees and blocked lasting improvement.

Making faster learning a reality at HISALBA

One of the unwritten rules at HISALBA was: 'Don't pile work on to the people on your shift.'

Others were: 'Shifts are families', and 'Workers have a duty to their shift, not to the company.' Different shifts did not share information and knowledge with each other, so at shift changes, information on the state of the equipment was incomplete. This resulted in fire practices, high maintenance costs and unnecessary breakdown time.

At the beginning of the learning programme, scepticism was rife, and the process was long and arduous. Mistrust was expressed in anonymous comments like: 'What they really want is to brainwash us into doing things that will make our work harder.' The works committee initially urged the workers to refuse to take part in the 'faster learning' project.

The team from HMC assembled the results of informal conversations and of interviews and discussed them in meetings with management and the workers' committee. In the course of several meetings, a significant number of obstacles were identified and prioritized.

Based on the analysis of learning needs, four projects were started as Hisalba. They were concerned with improving management style, strengthening the company identity, increasing customer focus and introducing systematic training at all levels (see Figure A.2).

After a year, the first changes in behaviour were noticeable. The project initiatives were creating trust between management and employees. Co-operation between workers' committees and factory management was growing. The workers were beginning to analyse problems voluntarily and independently, and to suggest solutions. The whole process was supported by both top management and unions.

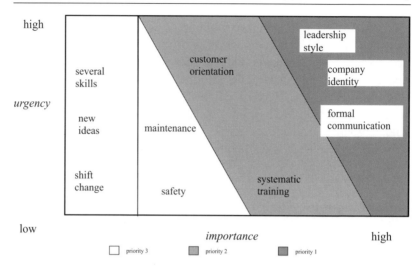

Figure A.2

The 'lessons learned' in the first project were:

- The greatest challenge is to make the unwritten rules explicit and to overcome them.
- Clear and intelligible communication is essential.
- Top management must lead by example.
- Management must first familiarize itself with the real needs of employees.

Interorganizational learning in the HOLDERBANK GROUP

The two following examples illustrate inter-company learning between HOLDERBANK subsidiaries. They are success stories which the company now presents on video, to give impetus to knowledge replication processes and to promote further transfer of knowledge.

Knowledge sharing between Mexico and Germany

At Lägendorf in Germany in 1990, HOLDERBANK had only one kiln for producing clinker. Its capacity was no longer sufficient to meet demand, so clinker had to be imported from Denmark and eastern Europe. The production team at Lägendorf therefore planned to build an additional kiln. The estimate for the whole project was DM 150 million, and the idea was returned for revision by headquarters as being too costly. After some discussion, the project leaders Joachim Patzke and Marian Uwa concluded: 'We must find a way of making a significant reduction in cost. Many people believe that this is impossible, so we need a convincing example to help us to bring everyone on board.'

The German team heard that a kiln was being built in Mexico using a completely new approach. This was the 'stripped-down' concept, according to which one builds only that which is absolutely necessary to start production. Silos and other storage facilities, which were needed in the past for safety reasons, are not built at all, because modern technology and controlled processes make them superfluous. The Mexicans were a long way ahead with this concept; they had many years' experience, and had developed knowledge that could now be replicated.

In 1993, the German project team visited the Mexican factory, Apasco, for the first time. Marian Uwa recalls: 'We wanted to duplicate what Apasco were doing in Ramos. Their success converted us to the stripped-down concept. But there were still some sceptics in our team. We kept on hearing how environmental regulations were much easier to meet in Mexico than in Europe, so the stripped-down concept would never work in Germany.'

Vicente Galdeano Bazano, the head of Apasco, declared: 'We probably have one of the most profitable factories in the world: we were the first to use a neutron analyser, which safeguards the quality of production. At the same time we saved millions of dollars by reducing storage capacity and not putting walls and roads around the building.'

Marian Uwa concluded: 'We were impressed by the high quality of the technical equipment at Apasco. They had not tried to make do with cheaper equipment. On the contrary: they had bought the best quality at the best price. Obviously, we wanted to do the same.' The team finally became convinced that a kiln could be built at Lägendorf for DM 115 million.

The Lägendorf team built a functional factory, omitting all unnecessary building. As in Mexico, there was no compromise on the technical quality of the equipment. They were able to save DM 33 million, and the factory was ready three months earlier than planned. Apasco thus became a best practice for many other companies in the HOLDERBANK GROUP.

A similar exchange of knowledge about the stripped-down concept took place between Mexico and the USA, as described below.

Transfer of knowledge to Devil Slide, Utah, USA

The American company HOLNAM was planning a new production centre at Devil Slide in Utah.

> Vicente Galdeano and I met for the first time in 1990, when Apasco was in the process of building the Ramos Arizpe factory in Mexico and I was working at the Midlothian plant. Vicente and some of his colleagues visited our factory in the USA to discuss organization and operations. In return, they invited us to visit their construction site. Since then we have continued to exchange information. When we began process planning for a new factory at Devil Slide, we naturally contacted Vicente for more information on the stripped-down concept. The details that Vicente gave us helped us to decide on equipment. Thanks to his knowledge, we saved a lot of money on our new factory. He was more credible than anyone else because he was already involved in building and running a factory of the same kind. His interest and his contribution were greatly appreciated. (*Barry Lower, project leader, Devil Slide*)

Vicente Galdeano made the following remarks on the exchange of knowledge and experience between Mexico and the USA:

> We were invited to co-operate over Devil Slide, and we are doing our best to help with another HOLDERBANK success. At our two last meetings on the stripped-down concept, we shared our experiences of cost reduction. In the first week, we exchanged concepts and ideas. Later we concentrated on details such as technical and operational experiences at Apasco.

Barry Lower believes in retrospect that the support of top management was a critical factor. Relations with the Mexicans were based on trust and openness, and there was an atmosphere of give-and-take. As a result, significant savings were made by using the stripped-down concept.

These examples of knowledge sharing are still only individual cases, but they form part of a planned process. It was the task of HMC to present the concept, to inspire employees and management with enthusiasm for it, and to put the subsidiary companies in touch with each other. HOLDERBANK now wishes to extend these activities and to exchange and transfer knowledge on a professional basis.

Notes

CHAPTER 1: THE CHALLENGE OF KNOWLEDGE MANAGEMENT

1. This began in the financial year 1993 as a pioneering attempt by a few committed employees in Assurance and Financial Services (AFS). Since then, it has developed into a 25-page professional supplement (SKANDIA 1994). Today, SKANDIA is trying to make hidden intellectual capital visible in the various business areas, and to trace its development.
2. Cf. Davis & Botkin (1994). They distinguish 'knowledge-based products' from 'knowledge-based services'.

CHAPTER 2: THE COMPANY'S KNOWLEDGE BASE

1. In the past, discussion in business management circles has focused mainly on 'information'. Now, the term 'knowledge' is essential in business studies, and is used with the same meaning as in everyday speech (see Wiegand 1996, p. 166). A clear definition of the term is therefore needed. For examples of the wide range of definitions to be found in the business management literature, see Kogut & Zander (1992), Weick & Roberts (1993), Nevis et al. (1995), Machlup (1962), Nonaka (1991), Sackmann (1992), von Krogh, Roos & Slocum (1994) and Romhardt (1996).
2. Cf. Glazer (1991): 'Data is what comes directly from sensors, reporting on the measurement level of some variable. Information is data that has been organized or given structure – that is, placed in context – and thus endowed with meaning.'
3. Cf. Bohn (1993): 'Information tells the current or past status of some part of the production system. Knowledge goes further; it allows the making of predictions, causal associations, or prescriptive decisions about what to do.'
4. On SAATCHI & SAATCHI, see the account in *The Economist* (27.5.1995).
5. For an overview of the theory and concepts of organizational learning, see Probst & Büchel (1997).
6. See Barney (1986, 1989, 1991) on the term 'strategic factor markets' and the dependency of company success on two further factors: 'expectations about the future value of strategic resources, and luck'.
7. Dierickx and Cool (1989) call this phenomenon 'causal ambiguity'.

CHAPTER 3: BUILDING BLOCKS OF KNOWLEDGE MANAGEMENT

1. 'Action research' is an approach which aims to unite theoretical discovery with practical problem-solving in social scientific research. This approach was first described by Lewin (1946), and has been developed considerably since then. Cf. Argyris & Schön (1989), Whyte, Greenwood & Lazes (1989), Pasmore & Friedlander (1982), Peters & Robinson (1984), Stebbins & Snow (1982), Susman & Evered (1978). For an overview of literature and concepts, see Probst & Raub (1995).
2. For a short introduction to the building blocks of knowledge management see Probst & Raub (1996), Probst & Romhardt (1997a, b), and Romhardt (1998).
3. The Forum for Organizational Learning and Knowledge Management has existed since 1995. Its members include major companies such as AT&T INTERNATIONAL, SWISSCOM, UBS, WINTERTHUR INSURANCES, HOLDERBANK, DEUTSCHE BANK and HEWLETT PACKARD EUROPE. It holds workshops at regular intervals on issues relating to learning and knowledge in organizations. Scientific support is provided by the GENEVA KNOWLEDGE GROUP, a research and consulting company which specializes in learning and knowledge. The partners are Michel Binggeli, Dr Bettina Büchel, Professor Gilbert Probst, Dr Steffen Raub and Dr Kai Romhardt. The contact address of the Geneva Knowledge Group is: Geneva Knowledge Group, Avenue Dumas 7, PO box 62, CH-1211 Geneva 25.
4. Cf. for example the 'innovation quotient inventory', in which questions are organized into the following categories: strategy, structure, systems, style, staff, shared values, and skills.
5. An example of this is the 'Knowledge Management Assessment Tool' of ARTHUR ANDERSEN/APQC (1995). This also takes into account processes of knowledge management, at least in the model. For a discussion of the opportunities offered by knowledge management and of its limits, see Roehl & Romhardt (1997).

CHAPTER 4: DEFINING KNOWLEDGE GOALS

1. This view is expressed, for example, by Bea & Haas (1995).
2. Bleicher (1992, p. 265) remarks that goals, as an element in the strategic guidance of company development, determine the practical course of events and, from the human point of view, steer the behaviour of the employees into an agreed and desired path. (This statement is emphasized in the original.)
3. This description is based upon *The Economist* (18.11.1995); Uhl (1993); and the Internet home pages of 3M (http://www.3m.com) and IMATION (http://www.imation.com).
4. We have included typical knowledge issues in the St. Gall Management Concept. Cf. Bleicher (1992).

5. Cf. ARTHUR ANDERSEN/APQC (1995, p.2). One of the first items in the leadership area of the Knowledge Management Assessment Tool is: 'The organization believes there is a strong correlation between knowledge management and improved business performance.'
6. Garvin, for example, writes that the 'not invented here' syndrome (NIH) has an opposite, namely the SIS principle: this stands for 'steal ideas shamelessly' (Garvin, 1993, p. 86).
7. On interpreting a vision as a 'method for thinking', see Hinterhuber (1989, p. 27), quoted in Bleicher (1992).
8. Itami (1987, p. 16) remarks: 'invisible assets created by business operations may have negative effects on the existing stock of invisible assets'.
9. For a summary of the literature on diversification strategies and diversification success see Ramanujam & Varadarajan (1989).
10. This account is based on Stewart (1995).
11. On the rise of NEC, see the account in Prahalad & Hamel (1990, pp. 79–80).
12. For more detail, see the now famous article by Prahalad & Hamel in the *Harvard Business Review* (1990), and Hamel & Prahalad (1994).
13. Cf. most importantly the contributions of Stalk, Evans & Shulman (1992), Mahoney (1995) and Leonard-Barton (1992, 1995).
14. Leonard-Barton (1992, 1995) addresses this problem when she indicates that every 'core capability' carries within it potential 'core rigidity'.
15. A 'tool kit' for competence-oriented analysis of competition and for strategy development is described by Klein & Hiscocks (1994). Cf. also Klein, Edge & Kass (1991).
16. This system follows that of Collis & Montgomery (1995, pp. 124ff.) They distinguish between investing in resources, upgrading resources and leveraging resources.
17. Instruments for dealing in a more concrete fashion with knowledge goals, including goals at individual level, are currently discussed primarily under the general heading of skill-based management.
18. On the function of goals cf. also Staehle (1991a, pp. 405–419). Hauschildt (1977, p. 9) describes goals as statements of a normative nature describing a real state of affairs that is desired by a decision-maker, that he or others should try to achieve, and that always lies in the future.
19. Cf. the system described in Bea & Haas (1995, pp. 67ff.).
20. Nagel (1992, p. 2626) remarks that goal formulations represent evaluation standards which can be used, for example, to compare and judge solutions of different kinds.
21. On the co-ordinating function, Nagel (1992, p. 2626) states that formulating goals can serve as an aid to communication and a basis for joint understanding and action.

CHAPTER 5: IDENTIFYING KNOWLEDGE

1. An earlier version of this chapter formed a contribution to the graduate students' forum 'Innovation, but how?' of the German National Scholarship

Foundation. We thank GABLER for permission to publish extracts in Romhardt (1997).

2. 'Benchmarking is the search for those best practices that will lead to superior performance of a company. Establishing operating targets based on the best possible industry practices is a critical component in the success of every business.' Cf. Camp (1989, XI).

3. Problems in best practice transfer and suitable techniques are discussed in detail in Chapter 8, 'Sharing and distributing knowledge'.

4. In the German car industry, consultants had to force some of their clients to visit companies in Japan, to prove to them that the revolution in car production there was real, and not an invention of the press. See Clark & Fujimoto (1992) for a graphic account.

5. The classification of knowledge maps is based on the account in Eppler (1995). See also Eppler (1997).

6. A description of other major knowledge categories may be found in Romhardt (1996, pp. 11ff.).

7. Other kinds of knowledge maps include systems design techniques, which support systematic modelling of dependencies, and maps of knowledge structures. These show in graphic form to which field of knowledge an item of information belongs, and what its significance is within that field. Space does not permit a fuller discussion of these techniques here.

8. This unconscious knowledge has been acquired by experts as a result of a complex process which takes place during their daily activities in a specific context. The knowledge is of great value to the organization, but even the experts themselves find it very difficult to describe. The concept of tacit knowledge was developed by Polanyi (1967). For Nonaka, the Japanese management researcher, the utilization of tacit knowledge is the starting point of all attempts at knowledge management. Cf. Nonaka (1991, 1994) and Nonaka & Takeuchi (1995).

9. Weick criticizes this neglect of collective components of knowledge: 'The preoccupation with individual cognition has left organization theorists ill-equipped to do much more with the so-called cognitive revolution than apply it to organizational concerns one brain at a time.' See Weick & Roberts (1993, p. 358).

10. On the problems of transferring context, cf. Müller-Stewens & Osterloh (1996).

11. Three full-time employees in HOFMANN-LAROCHE gathered the necessary information over a period of two years. Input was needed from about 300 experts. Cf. Preissler, Roehl & Seemann (1997).

12. In the original, Weick & Roberts use the term 'heedful interrelating'. See Weick & Roberts (1993).

13. On the difficulties of drawing the boundary between inside and outside the organization, cf. Wiegand (1996).

14. A collective blind spot exists when the content of the organization's external knowledge is unknown, and the organization is also unaware of the general availability of that knowledge in the world. Cf. Schüppel (1996).

15. Examples include the RAND CORPORATION, the SYSTEM DEVELOPMENT

CORPORATION (SDC) and the STANFORD INSTITUTE (SRI), all in California. These companies have made names for themselves as think-tanks for the state sector. Cf. Kreibich (1986, pp. 340–346).

16. Examples of this trend include: Rommel *et al.* (1993)/McKINSEY; Scott-Morgan (1994)/ARTHUR D. LITTLE; and Winslow & Bramer (1994)/ ANDERSEN CONSULTING.

17. All user figures are estimates; they are out of date almost immediately, because of extremely rapid growth (50–100% per year). Our figures are based on the Microsoft Encarta96 Encyclopedia. It is estimated that by the year 2000, there will be 100 million computers in the network.

18. Yahoo! (http://www.yahoo.com/). Other search engines are: Alta Vista (http:// www.altavista.digital.com/); Hotbot (http://www.search.hotbot.com); Lycos (http://www.lycos.com/); Magellan (http://www.mckinley.com/); Excite (http:/ www.excite.com/); Infoseek (http://www.infoseek.com/); Webcrawler (http:// www.webcrawler.com/). These details are not guaranteed, because the Internet service market is a dynamic one with a very high 'mortality rate'.

19. HEWLETT-PACKARD is one of the largest intranet users worldwide; cf. Hinnen (1996).

20. The uses to which such home pages can be put is demonstrated by MICROSOFT on http://www.microsoft.com. From this page, one can access the MICROSOFT Knowledge Base (KB), which is the primary source of product information for software developers and MICROSOFT customers. The comprehensive collection of articles, which is updated daily, contains detailed information on procedures, answers to technical questions, lists of program errors, and lists of ways of removing errors. These can be accessed by means of text and keyword enquiries.

CHAPTER 6: ACQUIRING KNOWLEDGE

1. Most organizations are both buyers and sellers on these knowledge markets. The brain gain of one organization is often the brain drain of another. Here we consider the markets from the point of view of the buyer. The company's use of its own knowledge assets and their capitalization on knowledge markets are treated in the chapter on knowledge sharing and distribution. Measures to avoid a brain drain are discussed in the chapter on preserving knowledge.

2. Katz & Allen (1982) observed that project teams which work on a common research project for more than five years reduce their communication with the outside world and produce inferior research results.

3. Cf. the remarkably self-assured prefaces to modern management classics such as Peters & Waterman (1982), Senge (1990) and Hammer & Champy (1993).

4. Simon (1991, p. 130) goes a step further: he asserts that in all research laboratories, more information is derived from evaluating and incorporating the content of scientific articles than from the laboratory's own research activities.

5. The decrease in logistics between producers and suppliers continues to accelerate because of the requirements of the 'just-in-time' concept. Industries

with high logistics costs are increasingly transferring the know-how behind efficient and reliable logistics management to suppliers and haulage contractors. Cf. Lieb, Millen & Wassenhove (1993) and Laarhoven (1994).

6. Popular attributes: flexible, dynamic, mobile, professionally competent, persevering, committed, able to communicate, natural.

7. Our thanks to Gert Stürzebecher for his support.

8. For Badaracco, product links are the answer to the challenge of migratory knowledge. Knowledge in the areas of finance, marketing, production, culture and strategy migrates very quickly, so companies must ensure their access to sources of knowledge by entering flexible co-operations. Cf. Badaracco (1991, pp. 53ff.). For other forms of co-operation, see Büchel et al. (1998).

9. For Badaracco (1991, p.107), knowledge links are ' . . . alliances that give (companies) access to the skills and capabilities of other organizations and sometimes enable them to work with other organizations to create new capabilities'. They therefore go further than forms of co-operation based on product links, because they also permit the transfer of more deeply embedded knowledge.

10. Closely modelled on Badaracco (1991, pp. 131ff.).

11. According to Schafer (1981), the two additional activities are analysing or observing (a) the competition (i.e. supply) and (b) sales channels (i.e. the distribution system).

12. Von Hippel (1988, pp. 11ff.) goes further: he calls for a new customer-active paradigm, in which he assigns the key role in the search for new product ideas to the customer. Cf. also von Hippel (1978).

13. This case is taken from Davenport (1996, pp. 36f.).

14. Companies often find themselves in a dilemma. On the one hand, technical standards for the development of programs and hardware components and the introduction of powerful software packages (e.g. SAP) increase compatibility between previously separate system groups and facilitates many procedures. On the other hand, companies lose much of their ability to present a differentiated appearance to customers and competitors. Many outputs are interchangeable.

15. 'Some economists have described this kind of knowledge as a "book of blueprints". It is unitized, organized in packages labeled all you need to know about X.' See Badaracco (1991, p. 36).

16. On obtaining knowledge via technical storage media, see Schüppel (1996, p. 224).

CHAPTER 7: DEVELOPING KNOWLEDGE

1. Further examples may be found in Saad, Roussel & Tiby (1991, pp. 123ff.).

2. For further classification of types of innovation, see Hauschildt (1993).

3. On self-organization, cf. Probst (1987).

4. Some suggestions on creating a positive context for learning may be found in Probst (1987, p. 132).

5. Cf. Romhardt (1994). The failed launch of the MERCEDES-BENZ S-class is an example.

6. 'Organizational slack' and 'necessary redundancy' are topics of discussion in the field of organization theory. Their treatment suffers from various deficiencies, most notably the failure to integrate a sufficiently transparent criterion of efficiency. Cf. Probst (1987) and Staehle (1991b).

7. On the need for faster learning in the product area, cf. Wildemann (1996).

8. The classification of problems into these three types follows Gomez & Probst (1995, pp. 13–22), as do the remarks which follow.

9. For a description of these methods see Kreibich (1986, pp. 394ff.).

10. The space management approach may be mentioned in this context. This approach is concerned with spatial organization, i.e. who sits close to whom at work. New 'neighbourhoods' can be created, removing structural inefficiencies in communication due to functional boundaries. Cf. Lullies, Bollinger & Weltz (1993, pp. 187–198).

11. The machine bureaucracy is a co-ordinating mechanism which underlies the standardization of work processes. An efficient technostructure plays the key role in this. Cf. Mintzberg (1983, p. 42).

12. On distinguishing different types of group, cf. Katzenbach & Smith (1994, pp. 118ff.).

13. The paradox of the creative team may be stated as follows: 'Contribute your personal, creative and thought-provoking views and knowledge, but don't endanger the unity of the group!' For a full analysis of these paradoxical social situations, see Watzlawick, Weakland & Fisch (1992, pp. 84ff.). On the need for a balance between consensus and diversity in the process of organizational learning, see Fiol (1994).

14. Pautzke distinguishes three forms of information pathology: structural, doctrinal and psychological. See Pautzke (1989). Information pathologies generally lead to decisions being made on the basis of too little information, and thus constitute a significant barrier to learning. Cf. Probst & Büchel (1997, pp. 78f.).

15 We do not wish to imply that 'more communication' necessarily leads to better work. On the contrary: in many organizations, managers spend a large part of their time in unproductive meetings. It is therefore vital to consider when and at what intervals team meetings should be held.

16. For the concept of 'languaging', see von Krogh, Roos & Slocum (1994).

17. This description is based on Tichy (1989) and Schertler (1995). We should also like to thank Tobias Radel, who reconstructed the 'work-out' process from the knowledge angle in his working paper for the graduate students' symposium of the German National Scholarship Foundation in Schauinsland, 1995.

18. Leonard-Barton (1994) illustrates her concept by reference to the success story of the American steel producer CHAPARRAL STEEL. She develops her ideas further in Leonard-Barton (1995).

19. For a more detailed presentation of the learning arena concept, and a differentiation of three kinds of learning arena, see Romhardt (1995).

20. This description is based on that by Brook Manville, the Knowledge Director

of McKINSEY. It has been supplemented by reference to Peters (1992) and Katzenbach & Smith (1994).

21. High-reliability organizations are companies whose activities are such that the damage is enormous if things go wrong, but it is most unlikely that they will. The term 'high-reliability organization' was introduced by LaPorte & Consolini (1991). We are grateful to Willke (1996) for making the connection with knowledge management.

22. For the preparation of this case study we are indebted to the DAIMLER-BENZ 'Research, Society and Technology' initiative. We are especially indebted to Heiko Roehl for organizing the scenario experiences from the point of view of knowledge management. Further reading: Minx & Mattrisch (1995), Geus (1988) and Gomez & Probst (1995, pp. 126ff.).

23. The first stage was to establish the key question for the investigation. It was: 'How will global air traffic develop by the year 2015?'. In the second stage, more than 120 factors which influence air traffic were identified. These were then reduced to 26 factors, or 'descriptors', which were used to generate scenarios. The descriptors include factors such as viability of airlines, flight schedules and acceptance of air travel. The third stage was to estimate future developments in the descriptors. This led in the fourth stage to the development of different pictures of the future. The descriptors and projections were networked during computer conferences, and aggregated to yield internally consistent scenarios. In the fifth stage, the scenarios were interpreted. The different future worlds were illustrated by hypothetical situations, and present structures were compared with future scenarios to show how they would have to change.

CHAPTER 8: SHARING AND DISTRIBUTING KNOWLEDGE

1. On the limited transferability of 'implicit knowledge', see Nonaka & Takeuchi (1995) and Spender (1996).

2. The VERIFONE study is based on information in Ogilvie (1994). For an additional account, see also von Krogh & Venzin (1995).

3. On the definition of a virtual company, cf. Brütsch (1996) and Davidow & Malone (1993).

4. The concept of the 'production impresario' is described by North & Aukamm (1996).

5. These interchange relationships go beyond the simple exchange of data within an inter-company information-sharing group. Examples of the simpler form of data transfer, which is often based on electronic data interchange systems (EDI), include bank clearing systems and reservation centres in the tourist industry. Cf. Kubicek (1992).

6. Cf. with interventional approaches based on systematic thinking (Gomez & Probst 1995; Senge 1990; Ulrich & Probst 1988).

7. For an examination of different forms of individual knowledge and an

illustration of organizational access to individual knowledge, see Pautzke (1989).

8. See Nonaka (1991) or Nonaka & Takeuchi (1995) on the 'implicit knowledge' aspect.

9. Cf. this assessment with Lyles & Schwenk (1992), Bourgeois (1980), and Fiol (1994).

10. On the scientific aspects of socialization within companies, see Wiswede (1992).

11. Cf. ARTHUR ANDERSEN (1996, p. 25). These training activities cost about 6% of yearly turnover, i.e. about $US400 million.

12. For a more comprehensive account of the learning arena concept, see Romhardt (1995).

13. This view of international assignments first appears in Edström & Galbraith (1997). For a more detailed discussion of the subject and further literature, see Harzing (1995).

14. The information for this example comes from Katzenbach & Smith (1994) and Peters (1992).

15. Wagner (1995, p. 71) describes computer-supported co-operative work (CSCW) as 'the academic precursor of groupware systems'. In practice, the two terms are used more or less synonymously. 'Workgroup computing' is another alternative.

16. E-mail is often placed in the extended category of groupware, but Wagner (1995, p. 78) is against this, for the reasons given in the text.

17. Cf. the following short account of different groupware categories with Wagner (1995, pp. 79–99).

18. ARTHUR ANDERSEN (1996, p. 18) also regards technology as a 'bridge' which can span barriers to the sharing and distribution of knowledge in the interplay of personnel, structure and processes (ARTHUR ANDERSEN, 1996, p. 18).

19. Cf. the UCLA/ARTHUR ANDERSEN report, quoted in ARTHUR ANDERSEN (1996, p. 19).

20. Goodman & Darr (1996, p. 14) refer to a relevant study by the INTERNATIONAL DATA CORPORATION.

21. For a more detailed discussion of these factors see Goodman & Darr (1996).

22. The term 'hybrid solutions' was coined by Davenport (1996, p. 35).

23. HUGHES uses the graphic expression 'pointers to people' for this technique of indexing experts. Cf. Davenport (1996, p. 35).

24. For further categories of 'information pathologies' in organizations, see Scholl (1992).

25. Goodman & Darr (1996, pp. 8–9) also name 'organizational legitimization' as an essential precondition for the sharing of best practices.

26. For more information, see Chapter 5, 'Identifying knowledge'.

27. For a scientific presentation of the results, see Szulanski (1996). For an executive summary, see Szulanski (1994).

CHAPTER 9: USING KNOWLEDGE

1. The difficulties in this area are compounded by the theoretically questionable

concept of 'unlearning', which we prefer to avoid here. Despite its undisputed attraction in practical contexts, learning theorists tend to avoid the term, because learning processes are not thought to be immediately reversible. From a theoretical point of view, 'unlearning' can be better described as a learning process in which an old knowledge component is replaced by a new one which is more up to date or more relevant.

2. On the concept of 'action learning', see also Revans (1983), Vince & Martin (1993) and Wallace (1990).

3. Davenport (1996, p. 39) describes the successful use of war games in POLAROID.

4. For many examples of successful reorganization of office space see Ogilvie's article (1994).

CHAPTER 10: PRESERVING KNOWLEDGE

1. Based on Oberschulte (1996). Oberschulte makes further links between organizational learning and organizational memory.

2. In particular, redimensioning simply for the sake of reducing costs has led in many companies to enormous losses of competencies. Cf. Mitroff (1995, p. 27).

3. For a detailed account of the different forms of memory, see Vester (1978, pp. 43ff.). On the role of immediate memory, see Wessells (1994, pp. 107ff.).

4. On the need to record knowledge in knowledge documents see Schüppel (1996, pp. 256f.).

5. The brain involuntarily mixes experiences with narrated events. Cf. Kotre (1996).

6. We shall not elaborate any further on the many approaches to constructing reality, such as the positions of radical constructivism, the sociology of knowledge, and psychiatry. The following publications are recommended to the interested reader by way of introduction: Watzlawick (1986, 1988); Berger & Luckmann (1996) and Sacks (1995).

7. These observations are compatible with the Freudian concept of a collective superego. For modern approaches to research on collective memory, see Hejl (1991).

8. A detailed account of the experiment may be found in Liang, Moreland & Argote (1992).

9. Schüppel (1996) includes this method in the process of managing implicit knowledge potentials. See Schüppel (1996, pp. 264f.)

CHAPTER 11: MEASURING KNOWLEDGE

1. This chapter was reworked for the present edition, making particular use of material in North, Probst & Romhardt (1998), Romhardt (1998) and Roehl & Romhardt (1997).

2. These examples are given by Davenport (1996, pp. 34–35).

3. 'The components of cost in a product today are largely R&D, intellectual assets, and services. The old accounting system, which tells us the cost of material and labor, isn't applicable.' (ARTHUR ANDERSEN consultant). See Stewart (1994).

4. On the role of non-material assets in accounting processes, and international legal differences, see Krucker (1996).

5. Cf. Weick (1995, p. 88). The same is true of every attempt at research that has a social aspect. According to Weick, every piece of social science that is somehow related to current values will invariably attract judgements such as 'interesting', 'irrelevant', 'trivial' or 'absurd', depending on the values with which it is linked and the extent to which they are supported (see Weick 1994, p. 88).

6. For detailed criticism see Sveiby (1997).

7. SKANDIA is perhaps the best documented 'case' of knowledge management. Our analysis started with the special supplements on intellectual capital that SKANDIA has been including in its yearly and half-yearly financial reports since 1992. We then examined the IMD case 'SKANDIA Assurance and Financial Services: Measuring and Visualizing Intellectual Capital' by Oliver *et al.* (1996). Our understanding of SKANDIA's efforts to evaluate intellectual capital was then refined on the basis of several lectures given by its Director of Intellectual Capital, Leif Edvinsson, in Basle, Zürich and Utrecht.

8. According to the company's own statements, these measures quickly received the support of top management, as is shown in the following remark made by SKANDIA's CEO at that time: 'In ten years, measurement of intellectual capital will become the most closely watched numbers in the annual report and financial figures will become the supplements.'

9. In the Intangible Assets Monitor, the intangible assets 'external structure', 'internal structure' and 'competence of employees' are assessed from the points of view of 'growth/renewal', 'efficiency' and 'stability'. Sveiby (1997) used this approach to categorize and evaluate the customer base of the Swedish company CELEMI. Customers were assigned to the categories *image-promoting, organization-promoting* and *competence-promoting*. This led to a deeper understanding of why companies have special customers, and what they expect of them.

10. Classes of indicators are further differentiated in North, Probst & Romhardt (1998).

11. Neither the SKANDIA Navigator nor the Intangible Assets Monitor offers this level of differentiation. In SKANDIA, the following were all carried out at the same level of abstraction: (a) describing of parts of the knowledge base, e.g. average age of employees; (b) quantifying inputs for changing the organizational knowledge base, e.g. training costs; (c) measuring intermediate results and transfer effects from organizational processes, e.g. whether people could be reached by telephone; and (d) listing financial indicators, e.g. volume of premiums. Similarly, in the implementation of Sveiby's Intangible Assets Monitor in CELEMI, results, e.g. value creation per employee, are mixed with purely descriptive elements, e.g. average age of employees.

12. The eight-phase scheme described here was developed by Bohn (1993), mainly with regard to technological knowledge. Cf. also Bohn (1994).
13. Ways of measuring the competencies of competitors are discussed for example by Klavans (1994).
14. For a detailed description of the coaching concept, see Whitmore (1994).
15. Defillippi & Arthur (1994) distinguish these three categories of knowledge.

CHAPTER 12: INCORPORATING KNOWLEDGE MANAGEMENT

1. Sensitization workshops on knowledge management are offered for example by the GENEVA KNOWLEDGE GROUP. Information can be obtained from the GENEVA KNOWLEDGE GROUP, Geneva Knowledge Group, Avenue Dumas 7, PO box 62, CH-1211 Geneva 25.
2. Following Peters' account (1993, pp. 572f.).

Bibliography

Argyris, C. (1987) Skilled Incompetence, *Harvard Business Review*, **5**, 74–79.
Argyris, C. (1990) *Overcoming Organizational Defenses – Facilitating Organizational Learning*, Boston: Allyn and Bacon.
Argyris, C. and Schön, D.A. (1989) Participatory Action Research and Action Science Compared: A Commentary. *American Behavioral Scientist*, **32**(5): 612–623.
Arthur Andersen (1996): *Improving Knowledge Sharing in International Businesses*, Andersen Worldwide, SC, April.
Arthur Andersen and APQC (1995) The Knowledge-Management Assessment Tool, Prototype Version, released at the Knowledge Imperative Symposium, Houston, Texas, September 1995, developed jointly by Arthur Andersen and the American Productivity and Quality Center.
Badaracco, J.L. (1991) *Knowledge Link: How Firms Compete Through Strategic Alliances*, Boston, MA: Harvard Business School Press.
Balzer, A. and Wilhelm, W. (1995) Die Firma, *manager magazin*, April, 42–57.
Barney, J.B. (1986) Types of Competition and the Theory of Strategy: Toward an Integrative Framework, *Academy of Management Review*, **11**(4): 791–800.
Barney, J.B. (1989) Asset Stocks and Sustained Competitive Advantage: A Comment, *Management Science*, **35**(12): 1511–1513.
Barney, J. (1991) Firm Resources and Sustained Competitive Advantage, *Journal of Management*, **17**(1): 99–120.
Bea, F.X. and Haas, J. (1995) *Strategisches Management*, Stuttgart, Jena: UTB/ Gustav Fischer Verlag.
Berger, P.L. and Luckmann, T. (1996) *The Social Construction of Reality: A Treatise in the Sociology of Knowledge*, Garden City: Doubleday.
Bertoin Antal, A. (1993) Odysseus' Legacy to Management Development: Mentoring, *European Management Journal*, **11**(4): 448–454.
Binnig, G. (1992) *Aus dem Nichts – Über die Kreativität von Natur und Mensch*, 4th edn, Munich/Zürich: Piper.
Bleicher, K. (1992) *Das Konzept Integriertes Management*, 2nd edn, Frankfurt/New York: Campus.
Bohn, R. (1993) *Technological Knowledge – How to Measure, How to Manage*, Research Report No. 93–07, University of California, San Diego, Graduate School of International Relations and Pacific Studies, La Jolla, CA.
Bohn, R.E. (1994) Measuring and Managing Technological Knowledge, *Sloan Management Review*, **36**(1): 61–73.
Bonoma, T.V. and Slevin, D.P. (1978) Management and Type II Error, *Business Horizons*, **4**, 61ff.

Boos, F., Exner, A. and Heitger, B. (1994) Soziale Netzwerke sind anders, in: Heitger, B. and Boos, F. (eds) *Organisation als Erfolgsfaktor*, Vienna: Service-Fachverlag.

Boudreau, J.W. (1991). Utility Analysis for Decisions in Human Resource Management, in: Dunnette, M.D. and Hough, L.M. (eds) *Handbook of Industrial and Organizational Psychology*, 621–745, Palo Alto, CA: Consulting Psychologists Press.

Bourgeois III, L.J. (1980) Performance and Consensus, *Strategic Management Journal*, **1**(3): 227–248.

Brockhoff, K. (1992) *Forschung und Entwicklung – Planung und Kontrolle*, Munich/Vienna: Oldenbourg.

Brütsch, D. (1996) Virtuelles Unternehmen: Herausforderung oder Fiktion? in: *io Management Zeitschrift*, **65**(1/2): 6–7.

Büchel, B., Prange, C., Probst, G. and Rüling, C. (1998) *International Joint Venture Management*, Singapore: Wiley.

Camp, R.C. (1989) *Benchmarking – The Search for Industry Best Practices that Lead to Superior Performance*, Milwaukee: ASQC Quality Press.

Clark, K.B. and Fujimoto, T. (1992) *Automobilentwicklung mit System – Strategie, Organisation und Management in Europa, Japan und USA*, Frankfurt/New York: Campus.

Cohen, M.D. and Bacdayan, P. (1994) Organizational Routines Are Stored as Procedural Memory: Evidence from a Laboratory Study, *Organization Science*, **5**(4): 554–568.

Cohen, W.M. and Levinthal, D.A. (1990) Absorptive Capacity: A New Perspective on Learning and Innovation, *Administrative Science Quarterly*, **35**(1): 128–152.

Collis, D.J. and Montgomery, C.A. (1995) Competing on resources: Strategy in the 1990s, *Harvard Business Review*, **73**(4): 118–128.

Davenport, T.H. (1996): Some Principles of Knowledge Management, *Strategy & Business*, **1**(2): 34–40.

Davenport, T.H. and Prusak, L. (1998) *Working Knowledge*, Boston: Harvard Business School Press.

Davidow, W.H. and Malone, M.S. (1993) *Das virtuelle Unternehmen*, Frankfurt (Main): Campus.

Davis, S. and Botkin, J. (1994) The Coming of Knowledge-based Business, *Harvard Business Review*, **72**(5): 165–170.

Defillippi, R.J. and Arthur, M.B. (1994) The boundaryless career: A competency-based perspective, *Journal of Organizational Behavior*, **15**(4): 307–324.

Dierickx, I. and Cool, K. (1989) Asset Stock Accumulation and Sustainability of Competitive Advantage, *Management Science*, **35**(12): 1504–1511.

Dörner, D. (1996) *Die Logik des Misslingens – Strategisches Denken in komplexen Situationen*, Hamburg: Rowohlt.

Drucker, P.F. (1988) The Coming of the New Organization, *Harvard Business Review*, **66**(1): 45–53.

Drucker, P.F. (1992) The New Society of Organizations, *Harvard Business Review*, **70**(5): 95–104.

Economist (27.05.1995) It's people, stupid, 67–68.

Economist (11.11.1995) The Knowledge, 55.

Economist (18.11.1995) And then there were two, 82–83.

Economist (20.04.1996) Fire and forget?, 57–58.

Edström, A. and Galbraith J. (1977) Transfer of Managers as a Coordination and Control Strategy in Multinational Organizations, *Administrative Science Quarterly*, **22**(2): 248–263.

Edvinsson, L. and Malone, M.S. (1997) *Intellectual Capital, New York: Harper Business*.

Eichenberger, P. (1992) *Betriebliche Bildungsarbeit: Return on Investment und Erfolgscontrolling*, Wiesbaden: Deutscher Universitäts-Verlag.

Eppler, M.J. (1995) Persönliche Informations-Portfolios – Ein integriertes Konzept für die individuelle Informationsbewirtschaftung. Diplomarbeit, Hochschule St Gallen.

Eppler, M. (1996) Wissensmanagement und Informationslogistik. *Technische Rundschau*, N. 31/32, 12–15.

Eppler, M. (1997) Praktische Instrumente des Wissensmanagements – Wissenskarten: Führer durch den 'Wissensdschungel', *Gablers Magazin* No. 8: 10–13.

Eppler, M. (1998) Informative Action, Dissertation, Universität Genf.

Fiol, C.M. (1994) Consensus, Diversity, and Learning in Organizations, *Organization Science*, **5**(3): 403–420.

Fitz-enz, J. (1995) *How to Measure Human Resource Management*, New York: McGraw-Hill.

Garvin, D.A. (1993) Building a Learning Organization, in *Harvard Business Review*, **71**(4): 78–91.

Geus, A.P. de (1988) Planning as Learning, *Harvard Business Manager*, **2**: 70–74.

Glazer, R. (1991) Marketing in an Information-Intensive Environment: Strategic Implications of Knowledge as an Asset, *Journal of Marketing*, **55**(4): 1–19.

Gomez, P. and Probst, G.J.B. (1995) *Die Praxis des ganzheitlichen Problemlösens – Vernetzt denken – Unternehmerisch handeln – Persönlich überzeugen*, Berne/Stuttgart/Vienna: Haupt.

Goodman, P.S. and Darr, E.D. (1996) Exchanging Best Practices through Computer-aided Systems, *Academy of Management Executive*, **10**(2): 7–18.

Hamel, G. and Prahalad, C.K. (1994) *Competing for the Future: Breakthrough Strategies for Seizing Control of Your Industry and Creating the Markets of Tomorrow*, Boston: Harvard Business School Press.

Hammer, M. and Champy, J. (1993) *Reengineering the Corporation*, New York: Harper Business.

Handy, C. (1990) *The Age of Unreason*, Boston, MA: Harvard Business School Press.

Harrigan, K.R. and Dalmia, G. (1991) Knowledge Workers: The Last Bastion of Competitive Advantage, *Planning Review*, **19**(6): 4–9.

Harzing, A. (1995) Organizational Bumble-Bees: International Transfers as a Control Mechanism in Multinational Companies, Paper to be presented to the 10th Anniversary Workshop on the 'State of the Art of Strategic HRM and its future', EIASM, Brussels, March.

Hauschildt, J. (1977) *Entscheidungsziele. Zielbildung in innovativen*

Entscheidungsprozessen: theoretische Ansätze und empirische Prüfung, Tübingen.

Hauschildt, J. (1993) *Innovationsmanagement*, Munich: Vahlen.

Hedberg, B. (1981) How Organizations Learn and Unlearn, in: Nystrom P.C. and Starbuck, W. (eds) *Handbook of Organizational Design*, 3–27, New York: Oxford University Press.

Hejl, P.M. (1991) Wie Gesellschaften Erfahrungen machen oder: Was Gesellschaftstheorie zum Verständnis des Gedächtnisproblems beitragen kann, in: Schmidt, S.J. (ed.) *Gedächtnis – Probleme und Perspektiven der interdisziplinären Gedächtnisforschung*, 2nd edn, 293–336, Frankfurt (Main): Suhrkamp.

Hinnen, M. (1996) Nur mit kompetenten Partnern ins Internet – Das Unternehmensinternetzwerk von Hewlett Packard, *TR Transfer*, **14**: 16–18.

Hinterhuber, H.H. (1989) *Strategische Unternehmensführung*. Vol. I: *Strategisches Denken*, 4th edn, Berlin/New York: de Gruyter.

Itami, H. (1987) *Mobilizing Invisible Assets*, Cambridge (MA): Harvard University Press.

Kaplan, R.S. and Norton, D.P. (1992) The Balanced Scorecard – Measures That Drive Performance, *Harvard Business Review*, **70**(1): 71–79.

Kaplan, R.S. and Norton, D.P. (1993): Putting the Balanced Scorecard to Work, *Harvard Business Review*, **71**(5): 134–142.

Katz, R. and Allen, T.J. (1982) Investigating the Not Invented Here (NIH) Syndrome: A Look at the Performance, Tenure, and Communication Patterns of 50 R&D Project Groups, *R&D Management*, **1**: 7–19.

Katzenbach. J.R. and Smith, D.K. (1994) *The Wisdom of Teams: Creating the High-Performance Organization*, New York: HarperBusiness.

Kirkpatrick, D. (1996) Why Microsoft Can't Stop Lotus Notes, *Fortune*, December 12, 1994, 61–71.

Kirsch, W. (1992) *Kommunikatives Handeln, Autopoiese, Rationalität. Sondierungen zu einer evolutionären Führungslehre*, Munich: Kirsch

Klavans, R. (1994) The Measurement of a Competitor's Core Competence, in: Hamel, G. and Heene, A. (eds) *Competence-based Competition*, 171–182, Chichester: John Wiley & Sons.

Klein, J.A., Edge, G.M. and Kass, T. (1991) Skill-based Competition, *Journal of General Management*, **16**(4): 1–15.

Klein, J.A. and Hiscocks, P.G. (1994) Competence-based Competition: A Practical Toolkit, in: Hamel, G. and Heene, A. (eds) *Competence-based Competition*, 183–212, Chichester: John Wiley & Sons.

Klimecki, R., Lassleben, H. and Riexinger-Li, B. (1994) Zur empirischen Analyse organisationeller Lernprozesse im öffentlichen Sektor: Modellbildung und Methodik, in: Bussmann, W. (ed.): *Lernen in Verwaltungen und Policy-Netzwerken*, 9–38, Berne: NFP 27.

Klimecki, R., Probst, G.J.B. and Eberl, P. (1994) *Entwicklungsorientiertes Management*, Stuttgart: Schäffer-Poeschel.

Kogut, B. and Zander, U. (1992) Knowledge of the Firm, Combinative Capabilities, and the Replication of Technology, *Organization Science*, **3**(3): 383–397.

Kotre, J. (1996) *Weiße Handschuhe. Wie das Gedächtnis Lebensgeschichten schreibt*, Munich: Carl Hanser.

Krackhardt, D. and Hanson, J.R. (1994) Informelle Netze – die heimlichen Kraftquellen, *Harvard Business Manager*, 1: 16–24.

Kreibich, R. (1986) *Die Wissenschaftsgesellschaft*, Frankfurt (Main): Suhrkamp.

Krucker M. (1996), Bedeutung und Behandlung immaterieller Werte in der Rechnungslegung von Unternehmen der Mode- und Kosmetikbranche (eine international ausgerichtete empirische Studie), thesis at the University of St. Gall.

Kubicek, H. (1992) Informationsverbund, überbetrieblicher, in: Frese, E. (ed.): *Handwörterbuch der Organization*, 3rd edn, 994–1009, Stuttgärt: Schäffer-Poeschel.

Kupfer, A. (1996) Alone Together: Will Being Wired Set Us Free? *Fortune*, March 20, 1995, 56–62.

Kurbjuweit, D. (1996) Die Propheten der Effizienz, *Die Zeit*, 12 January, 9–11.

Laarhoven, P.v. (1994). Logistics Alliances: The European Experience. An Early Report on the Development to Date of One Key Building Block of the 'Network Economy', *McKinsey Quarterly*, 1: 39–49.

LaPorte, T. and Consolini, P. (1991) Working in Practice But Not in Theory: Theoretical Challenges of 'High-Reliability Organizations', *Journal of Public Administration Research and Theory*, 1(1): 19–47.

Leonard-Barton, D. (1992) Core Capabilities and Core Rigidities: A Paradox in Managing New Product Development, *Strategic Management Journal*, 13(Special Issue): 111–125.

Leonard-Barton, D. (1994) Die Fabrik als Ort der Forschung, *Harvard Business Manager*, 1: 87–99.

Leonard-Barton, D. (1995) *Wellsprings of Knowledge: Building and Sustaining the Sources of Innovation*, Boston: Harvard Business School Press.

Lester, T. (1996) The know-How of Knowledge, in: *Information Strategy*, November 1996, 13–15.

Lewin, K. (1946) Action Research and Minority Problems, *Journal of Social Issues*, 2(4): 34–46.

Liang, D.W., Moreland, R. and Argote, L. (1992) Group versus Individual Training and Group Performance: The Mediating Role of Transactive Memory. Paper presented at the 1992 meetings of the Operational Research Society of America/The Institute of Management Science in San Francisco and at Carnegie Mellon University.

Lieb, R.C., Millen, R.A. and Wassenhove, L.N.v. (1993) Third-party Logistics Services – A Comparison of Experienced American and European Manufacturers, *International Journal of Physical Distribution & Logistics Management*, 23(6): 35–44.

Lullies, V., Bollinger, H. and Weltz, F. (1993) *Wissenslogistik: Über den betrieblichen Umgang mit Wissen bei Innovationsvorhaben*, Frankfurt (Main): Campus.

Lyles, M.A. and Schwenk, C.R. (1992) Top Management, Strategy and Organizational Knowledge Structures, *Journal of Management Studies*, 29(2): 155–174.

Machlup, F. (1962) *The Production and Distribution of Knowledge in the United States*, Princeton.

Mahoney, J.T. (1995) The Management of Resources and the Resource of Management, *Journal of Business Research*, **33**(2): 191–101.

Manago, M. and Auriol, E. (1996) Mining for Or, *OR/MS Today*, February, 28–32.

Mintzberg, H. (1983) Structure in Fives: designing Effective Organizations, Englewood Cliffs: Prentice Hall.

Minx, E. and Mattrisch, G. (1995) Szenarien als Hilfsmittel bei der Produkt- und Organisationsentwicklung, in: Gausemeier, J. (ed.) *Die Szenario-Technik – Werkzeug für den Umgang mit einer multiplen Zukunft*, Paderborn: HNI-Verlagsschriftenreihe Vol. 4.

Mitroff, I.I. (1995) Warum schaffen wir es nicht? *io Management Zeitschrift*, **3**: 27–31.

Morgan, G. (1986) *Images of Organization*, Newsbury Park, CA/New Delhi/London: SAGE Publications.

Müller-Stewens, G. and Gocke, A. (1995) *Kooperation und Konzentration in der Automobilindustrie – Strategien für Zulieferer und Hersteller*, Chur/Basle: Fakultas.

Müller-Stewens, G. and Osterloh, M. (1996) Kooperationsinvestitionen besser nutzen: Interorganisationales Lernen als Know-how-Transfer oder Kontext-Transfer, in *Zeitschrift für Organisation*, **1**: 18–24.

Müller-Stewens, G. and Pautzke, G. (1992) Führungskräfteentwicklung, Organisatorisches Lernen und Individualisierung, in: Geissler, H. (ed.) *Neue Qualitäten des betrieblichen Lernens*, 137–147, Frankfurt (Main): Lang.

Nagel, P. (1992) Zielformulierung, Techniken der, in: Frese, E. (ed.) *Handwörterbuch der Organisation*, 3rd edn, 2626–2634, Stuttgart: Schäffer-Poeschel.

Nevis, E.C., DiBella, A.J and Gould, J.M. (1995) Understanding Organizations as Learning Systems, *Sloan Management Review*, Winter, 73–85.

Nonaka. I. (1991) The Knowledge-Creating Company. *Harvard Business Review*, **69**(6): 96–104.

Nonaka, I. (1994) A Dynamic Theory of Organizational Knowledge Creation, *Organization Science*, **5**(1): 14–37.

Nonaka, I. and Takeuchi, H. (1995) *The Knowledge-Creating Company: How Japanese Companies Create the Dynamics of Innovation*, New York/Oxford: Oxford University Press.

North, K. and Aukamm, T. (1996) 'Think global – Act local': Neuansätze zur Planung von Auslandsproduktionsstätten der Automobilindustrie, *REFA-Nachrichten*, **49**(2): 15–21.

North, K., Probst, G. and Romhardt, K. (1998) Wissen messen: Ansätze, Erfahrungen und Kritische Fragen, *ZfO* 3/98: 158–166.

Oberschulte, H. (1996) Organisatorische Intelligenz – ein Vorschlag zur Konzeptdifferenzierung, in: Schreyögg, G. and Conrad, P (eds) *Managementforschung 6: Wissensmanagement*, 41–81, Berlin/New York: de Gruyter.

O'Dell, C. and Grayson, C.J. (1998) If Only We Knew What We Know, *California Management Review*, **40**(3): 154–174.

Odiorne, G.S. (1965) *Management by Objectives: a System of Managerial Leadership*, New York: Pitman Publishing Corporation.

Ogilvie, H. (1994) This Old Office, *Journal of Business Strategy*, **15**(5): 26–34.

Oliver D., Marchand, D.A. and Roos, J. (1996) Skandia Assurance and Financial Services: Measuring and Visualizing Intellectural Capital. *IMD-Case*: 1–23.

Pasmore, W. and Friedlander, F. (1982) An Action-Research Program for Increasing Employee Involvement in Problem Solving, *Administrative Science Quarterly*, **27**(9): 343–362.

Pautzke, G. (1989) *Die Evolution der organisatorischea Wissensbasis: Bausteine zu einer Theorie des organisatorischen Lernens*, Herrsching: Barbara Kirsch.

Peters, M. and Robinson, V. (1984) The Origins and Status of Action Research, *Journal of Applied Behavioral Science*, **20**(2): 113–124.

Peters, T.J. (1992) *Liberation Management – Necessary Disorganization for the Nanosecond Nineties*, London: Macmillan.

Peters, T.J. (1993) *Jenseits der Hierarchien – Liberation Management*, Düsseldorf/ Vienna/New York/Moskow: Econ.

Peters, T.J. and Waterman, R.H. (1982) In Search of Excellence – Lessons from America's Best-Run Companies, New York: Harper & Row.

Phillips, J.J. (1991) *Handbook of Training Evaluation and Measurement Methods*, Houston, TX: Gulf Publishing Company.

Picot, A. and Reichwald, R. (1994) Auflösung der Unternehmung? *Zeitschrift für Betriebswirtschaft*, **64**(5): 547–570.

Polanyi, M. (1967) *The Tacit Dimension*, New York: Doubleday Anchor.

Prahalad, C.K. and Hamel, G. (1990) The Core Competence of the Corporation, *Harvard Business Review*, **68**(3): 79–91.

Preissler, H., Roehl, H. and Seemann, P. (1997) Haken, Helm und Seil – Erfahrungen mit Instrumenten des Wissensmanagements, *Organisationsentwicklung*, 2/97: 5–16.

Probst, G., Raub S. and Romhardt, K. (1996) *Interkulturelles Lernen und Kulturmanagement in internationalen Unternehmen*, Berne: Schweizerischer Nationalfonds zur Förderung der wissenschaftlichen Forschung/ Abschlußbericht.

Probst, G.J.B. (1987) *Selbst-Organisation: Ordnungsprozesse in sozialen Systemen aus ganzheitlicher Sicht*, Berlin, Hamburg: Parey.

Probst, G.J.B. (1993) *Organisation: Strukturen, Lenkungsinstrumente, Entwicklungsperspektiven*, Landsberg: Moderne Industrie.

Probst, G.J.B. and Büchel, B.S.T. (1997) *Organisational Learning – The competitive advantage of the future*, Hertfordshire: Prentice Hall Europe.

Probst, G.J.B and Gomez, P. (1991) *Vernetztes Denken: Ganzheitliches Führen in der Praxis*, Wiesbaden. Gabler.

Probst, G.J.B and Raub, S.P. (1995) Action Research: Ein Konzept angewandter Managementforschung, *Die Unternehmung*, **49**(1): 3–19.

Probst, G.J.B. and Raub, S. (1996) Wissensmanagement in der Praxis, *io Management*, **65**(10): 33–36.

Probst, G.J.B. and Romhardt, K. (1997a) Bausteine des Wissensmanagements – ein praxisorientierter Ansatz, in: *Lernende Organisation*, edited by Dr Wieselhuber & Partner Unternehmensberatung, 129–143, Wiesbaden: Gabler.

Probst, G.J.B. and Romhardt, K. (1997b) Faktor Wissen, *Manager Bilanz* No. 2: 6–10.

Quinn, J.B. (1992) *Intelligent Enterprise: A Knowledge and Service Based Paradigm for Industry*, New York Free Press.

Quinn, J.B. (1993) *Managing the Intelligent Enterprise: Knowledge & Service-based Stategies, Planning Review*, 21(5): 13–16.

Ramanujam, V. and Varadarajan, P. (1989) Research on Corporate Diversification: A Synthesis, *Strategic Management Journal*, 10(6): 523–551.

Raub, S. (1996) Performance Measurement im Personalbereich, in: Benz, P. (ed.): *Personalhandbuch der SGP*, Zürich: Huber.

Rehäuser, J, and Kremar, H. (1996) Wissensmanagement im Unternehmen, in: Schreyögg, G./Conrad, P. (eds) *Managementforschung 6: Wissensmanagement*, 1–140, Berlin/New York: de Gruyter.

Revans, R. (1983) *The ABC of Action Learning*, Bromley: Chartwell-Bratt.

Rieker, J. (1995) Prinzip Schneeball, in: *manager magazin*, October 1995, 152–155.

Risch, S. and Sommer, C. (1996) . . . und raus bist du! *manager magazin*, **5**, 220–229.

Roehl, H. and Romhardt, K. (1997) Möglichkeiten und Grenzen des Wissensmanagements: Auf der Suche nach einem neuen Umgang mit der Ressource Wissen in der Organisation, *Gablers Magazin*, Nos 6/7, 42–45.

Romhardt, K. (1994) Zur Evolution der organisatorischen Lernfähigkeit einer Branche am Beispiel der Automobilindustrie, Diplomarbeit der Hochschule St. Gallen.

Romhardt, K. (1995) Das Lernarenakonzept: Ein Ansatz zum Management organisatorischer Lernprozesse in der Unternehmenspraxis. Cahier de recherche, Université de Genève/HEC.

Romhardt, K. (1996) Interventionen in die organisatorische Wissensbasis zwischen Theorie und Praxis – Welchen Beitrag kann die Systemtheorie leisten? Cahier de recherche, Université de Genève/HEC.

Romhardt, K. (1997) Interne und externe Wissenstransparenz als Ausgangspunkt fur organisatorische Innovation, in: *Organisation von Innovation – Strukturen, Prozesse, Interventionen*, edited by Heideloff, F. und Radel, T., München/ Mering: Hampp, 75–103.

Romhardt, K. (1998) Die Organisation aus wissensorientierter Perspektive – Möglichkeiten und Grenzen von Intervention in die organisatorische Wissensbasis. Dissertation, Université de Genève. Wiesbaden, Gabler.

Rommel, G., Bruck, F., Diederichs, R., Kempis, R. and Kluge, J. (1993) *Einfach Überlegen – Das Unternehmenskonzept, das die Schlanken schlank und die Schnellen schnell macht*, Stuttgart: Schäffer-Poeschel.

Saad, K.N., Roussel, P.A and Tiby, C. (1991) *Management der F&E-Strategie*, Wiesbaden: Gabler.

Sackmann, S.A. (1992) Möglichkeiten der Gestaltung von Unternehmenskultur, in: Lattmann, C. (ed.) *Die Unternehmenskultur*, 153–187, Heidelberg: Physica.

Sacks, O. (1995) *An Anthropologist on Mars*, London: Picador.

Sandelands, L.E. and Stablein, R.E. (1987) The Concept of Organization Mind, *Research in the Sociology of Organizations*, **5**: 135–162.

Schafer, E. (1981) *Absatzwirtschaft*, 3rd ed., Stuttgart: Schäffer-Poeschel.

Schein, E.H. (1992) *Organizational Culture and Leadership*, 2nd edn, San Francisco: Jossey-Bass.

Schertler, W. (1995) Strategie organisationalen Wandels von General Electric GE, in: Kasper, H. (ed.): *Postgraduate Management Wissen*, 225–257, Vienna: Ueberreuther/*manager magazin*.

Schmitz, C. and Zucker, B. (1996) *Wissen gewinnt – Knowledge Flow Management*, Düsseldorf/Munich. Metropolitan.

Schneider, S. and Barsoux, J.-L. (1997) *Managing across Cultures*, Prentice-Hall, London.

Scholl, W. (1992) Informationspathologien, in: Frese, E. (ed.). *Handwörterbuch der Organisation*, 900–911, Stuttgart: Schäffer-Poeschel.

Schülin, P. (1995) Strategisches Innovationsmanagement: Ein konzeptioneller Ansatz zur strategischen Steuerung der betrieblichen Innovationstätigkeit – dargestellt am Beispiel pharmazeutischer Unternehmen. Dissertation der Hochschule St Gallen.

Schüppel, J. (1996) Wissensmanagement-Organisatorisches Lernen im Spannungsfeld von Wissens- und Lernbarrieren. Dissertation, Hochschule St. Gallen.

Scott-Morgan, P. (1994) *The Unwritten Rules of the Game*, New York: McGraw Hill.

Seemann, P. and Stucky, S. (1996) Practical Management of Knowledge. Workshop-Unterlagen zur Tagung 'Know-how flott machen' des Gottlieb-Duttweiler-Instituts on 9/10 February 1995, Rüschlikon.

Senge, P. and Scharmer, C.O. (1996) Infrastrukturen des Lernens: Über den Aufbau eines Konsortiums lernender Unternehmen am MIT, *Zeitschrift für Organisation*, **1**: 32–36.

Senge, P.M. (1990) *The Fifth Discipline: The Art & Practice of the Learning Organization*, New York: Doubleday.

Simon, H.A. (1991) Bounded Rationality and Organizational Learning, *Organization Science*, **2**(1): 125–140.

SKANDIA (1994) Annual Report.

Sommer, C. (1996) Denken mit Netz, *manager magazin*, March, 94–98.

Spender, J.-C. (1996) Competitive Advantage from Tacit Knowledge? Unpacking the Concept and its Strategic Implications, in: Moingeon, B. and Edmondson, A. (eds): *Organizational Learning and Competitive Advantage*, 56–73, London: Sage.

Staehle, W.H. (1991a) *Management*, Munich: Vahlen.

Staehle, W.H. (1991b) Redundanz, Slack und lose Koppelung in Organisationen: Eine Verschwendung von Ressourcen? in: Staehle, W.H. and Sydow, J. (eds): *Managementforschung 1*, 313–345, Berlin/New York: de Gruyter.

Stalk, G., Evans, P. and Shulman, L.E. (1992) Competing on Capabilities: The New Rules of Corporate Strategy, *Harvard Business Review*, **70**(2): 57–69.

Stebbins, M.W. and Snow, C.C. (1982) Processes and Payoffs of Programmatic Action Research, *Journal of Applied Behavioral Science*, **18**(1): 69–86.

Stewart, T.A. (1995) The Information Wars: What You Don't Know Will Hurt You, *Fortune*, June 12, 75–77.

Stewart, T.A. (1994): Your Company's Most Valuable Asset: Intellectual Capital, in: *Fortune*, 20, 3 October 1994: 28–33.

Stewart, T.A. (1997) *Intellectual Capital*, New York: Currency-Doubleday.

Susman, G.I. and Evered, R.D. (1978) An Assessment of the Scientific Merits of Action Research, *Administrative Science Quarterly*, December, 582–601.

Sveiby, K.E. (1997) *The New Organizational Wealth*, San Francisco: Berrett-Koehler.

Szulanski, G. (1994) *Intra-firm Transfer of Best Practices Project – Executive Summary of the Findings*, Houston: APQC.

Szulanski, G. (1996) Exploring Internal Stickiness: Impediments to the Transfer of Best Practice within the Firm, *Strategic Management Journal*, **17**: Winter Special Issue, 27–43.

Tapscott (1996) *The Digital Economy: Promise and Peril in the Age of Networked Intelligence*, McGraw-Hill, New York.

Tichy, N.M. (1989) GE's Crotonvill: A Staging Ground for Corporate Revolution, *Academy of Management Executive*, **3**(2): 99–106.

Uhl, O.W. (1993) Innovations-Management bei 3M, *Zeitschrift Führung und Organisation*, **62**(4): 221–223.

Ulrich, H. and Probst, G.J.B. (1988) *Anleitung zum ganzheitlichen Denken und Handeln: Ein Brevier für Führungskräfte*, Berne: Haupt.

Vester, F. (1978) *Denken – Lernen – Vergessen: Was geht in unserem Kopf vor, wie lernt das Gehirn, und wann läßt es uns im Stich?* Munich: dtv.

Vince, R. and Martin, L. (1993) Inside Action Learning: An Exploration of the Psychology andl Politics of the Action Learning Model, *Management Education and Development*, **24**(3): 205–215.

Von Hippel, E. (1978) Successful Industrial Products from Customer Ideas – Presentation of a New Customer-Active Paradigm with Evidence and Implications, *Journal of Marketing*, **42**(1): 39–49.

Von Hippel, E. (1988) *The Sources of Innovation*, New York/Oxford: Oxford/ University Press.

Von Krogh, G., Roos, J. and Slocum, K. (1994) An Essay on Corporate Epistemology, *Strategic Management Journal*, **15**, Summer, 53–71.

Von Krogh, G. and Venzin, M. (1995) Anhaltende Wettbewerbsvorteile durch Wissensmanagement, *Die Unternehmung*, **49**(6): 417–436.

Wagner, M.P. (1995) *Groupware und neues Management: Einsatz geeigneter Softwaresysteme für flexiblere Organisationen*, Braunschweig/Wiesbaden: Vieweg.

Waldenfels, B. (1991) *Der Stachel des Fremden*, 2nd edn, Frankfurt (Main): Suhrkamp.

Wallace, M. (1990) Can Action Learning Live Up to its Reputation? *Management Education and Development*, **21**(2): 89–103

Watzlawick, P. (1986) Wie wirklich ist die Wirklichkeit? 14th edn, Munich/Zürich: Piper.

Watzlawick, P. (1988) *Die erfundene Wirklichkeit – Wie wissen wir, was wir zu wissen glauben? Beiträge zum Konstruktivismus*, Munich/Zürich: Piper.

Watzlawick, P., Beavin, J.H. and Jackson, D.D. (1993) *Menschliche Kommunikation – Formen, Störungen, Paradoxien*, Berne/Stuttgart/Toronto: Hans Huber.

Watzlawick, P. Weakland, J.H. and Fisch, R. (1992) *Lösungen – Zur Theorie und Praxis menschlichen Wandels*, 5th edn, Berne/Göttingen/Toronto: Hans Huber.

Wegner, D.M. (1996) Transactive Memory, in: Mullen, B. and Goethals, G.R. (eds): *Theories of Group Behavior*, 185–208, New York: Springer.

Weick K.E. (1994) *Der Prozess des Organisierens*, Frankfurt (Main): Suhrkamp.

Weick, K.E. and Roberts, K.H. (1993) Collective Mind in Organizations: Heedful Interrelating on Flight Decks, *Administrative Science Quarterly*, **38**(3): 357–381.

Wessells, M.G. (1994) *Kognitive Psychologie*, Munchen/Basel: UTB.

Whitmore, J. (1994) *Coaching für die Praxis: Eine klare, prägnante und praktische Anleitung für Manager*, Frankfurt (Main): Campus.

Whyte, W.F., Greenwood, D.J. and Lazes, P. (1989) Participatory Action Research: Through Practice to Science in Social Research, *American Behavioral Scientist*, **32**(5): 513–551.

Wiegand, M. (1996) *Prozesse Organisationalen Lernens*, Wiesbaden: Gabler.

Wiig, K. (1996) Knowledge Management is No Illusion, in: *Proceedings of the First International Conference on Practical Aspects of Knowledge Management*, 30/31 October, Basle.

Wildemann, H. (1996) Die Produktklinik – eine Keimzelle für Lernprozesse, *Harvard Business Manager*, **1**: 39–49.

Willke, H. (1996) Dimensionen des Wissensmanagements – Zum Zusammenhang von gesellschaftlicher und organisationaler Wissensbasierung, in: Schreyögg, G. and Conrad, P. (eds) *Managementforschung 6 – Wissensmanagement*, 263–304, Berlin/New York: de Gruyter.

Winslow, C.D. and Bramer, W.L. (1994) *FutureWork – Putting Knowledge to Work in the Knowledge Economy*, New York: Free Press.

Wiswede, G. (1992) Sozialisation, in: Frese, E. (ed.) *Handwörterbuch der Organisation*, 3rd edn, 2269–2274, Stuttgart: Schäffer-Poeschel.

Wöhe, G. (1990) *Einführung in die Allgemeine Betriebswirtschaftslehre*, 17th edn, Munich: Vahlen.

Index

Index complied by Terry Halliday, Indexing Specialists, Hove, UK